Integrating Corporate Communications

The Cost-Effective Use of Message and Medium

James L. Horton

QUORUM BOOKS
Westport, Connecticut • London

Library of Congress Cataloging-in-Publication Data

Horton, James L.
    Integrating corporate communications : the cost-effective use of
message and medium / James L. Horton.
        p.   cm.
    Includes index.
    ISBN 0–89930–895–3 (alk. paper)
    1. Communication in management—Cost effectiveness.
2. Communication in organizations. 3. Corporations—Communication
systems.   I. Title.
HD30.3.H67   1995
658.4'5—dc20   95–3778

British Library Cataloguing in Publication Data is available.

Library of Congress Catalog Card Number: 95–3778
ISBN: 0–89930–895–3

First published in 1995

Quorum Books, 88 Post Road West, Westport, CT 06881
An imprint of Greenwood Publishing Group, Inc.

Printed in the United States of America

The paper used in this book complies with the
Permanent Paper Standard issued by the National
Information Standards Organization (Z39.48–1984).

10 9 8 7 6 5 4 3 2 1

timedia, telecommunications or information technology. Communication is submerged because it is omnipresent. Academics and consultants often assume a manager knows how to communicate and believe their job is to tell the manager what to communicate. Their assumption is often wrong. Communication is a difficult craft with an endless stream of messages and media.

A second challenge to managers is that each specialty focuses on part of a manager's task, but rarely on the whole. Moreover, within the parts are schools of thought, some of which overlap but use different languages and metaphors. For example, engineering discusses information technology, computer integration, work design and ergonomics.[2] Quality management, which has multiple masters with differing views, bases some of its assumptions on industrial engineering, but not all.[3] Both engineering and quality management have much to say about communication, but they often say it in different ways. Submerging communication into various disciplines obscures its role and confuses managers. After years of counseling executives, it has become clear to me that few know what effective corporate communication is. Moreover, their communications efforts often end in disappointment, despite good planning and implementation.

What managers often do is to learn languages, messages and media that are deemed or perceived to be essential to their organizations. They become skilled in accounting or finance, for example. Over time, they tend to identify with financial languages and fail to understand that operating a company takes more than a balance sheet, income statement and periodic internal financial reports.

Information technologists who establish databases and telecommunications systems often lose sight of the distancing effect of these media on the hurly-burly of making products and serving customers. They also forget that computerization can create clutter. (For example, managers complain that they often receive a hundred messages a day on E-mail, few of which they read or answer.)

This book is built on the premise that managers need a way in which to assess messages and media in business independent of the various business disciplines. It provides a way for defining corporate communication in terms of individuals whose actions support or jeopardize the survival and success of an organization. This provides a method to measure messages and media and to decide what is essential.

Most organizations still churn out reports and send them to executives who barely look at them. Many have newsletters and magazines that are throwaways among their intended readers. Message sending with a low probability of success depletes time, talent and money and diverts the focus away from what a company should do to survive and succeed.

This book discusses communications from a holistic point of view and ties together business disciplines treated as separate topics. It starts at the roots of communication and economic transactions to show how they re-

Introduction

A manager's job is to get results to ensure the survival and success of a business. Managers rarely have the luxury of parsing business disciplines into finer points of view. They are practitioners who use tools to get a job done. They use whatever specialized languages, concepts and disciplines they need to complete tasks at hand.

Managers use judgment to construct a total picture of a business environment. They use reason and intuition to formulate messages and media skills to direct action to profitable ends. Complicating their tasks is a constantly changing business environment with opportunities and threats. Managers are guides, enablers and balancers, who work in a realm between concept and implementation in business. They simplify actions for employees and customers and provide the clarity needed to accomplish economic transactions. Like most leaders, they find that management is as much persuasion as it is driven by personal power.

We have long lists of the leader's requisites—determination, focus, a clear goal, a sense of priorities, and so on. We easily forget the first and all-encompassing need—followers. Without them, the best ideas, the strongest will, the most wonderful smile have no effect. . . . It is not the noblest call that gets answered but the answerable call.[1]

One challenge managers face with business communication is that few business disciplines focus on communication alone. The academic and consulting communities often treat communication as a subtopic of other management crafts, such as marketing, accounting, organizational behavior, public relations, public affairs, human factors, advertising, direct mail, mul-

Acknowledgments

If this book clearly states a message about corporate communication, it is due to the efforts of several people. Foremost among them is my wife, Karen, who generously supported my efforts and served as the first reader of my work. The most important editor was Edward J. Horton, my father, who put 30 years of management experience and years as a teacher at my service through his sharp eye and relentless questions. Irv Schenkler, associate professor of Management Communication at the Leonard N. Stern School of Business of New York University, provided valuable advice about how to format the work. John Maher, a former colleague and long-time worker in the field of communications at its highest levels, provided common sense missing from the first drafts. Similar thanks go to Ann Horton, who provided valuable editing advice; to Peter Shinbach; and to Joe Roy, a former client and corporate speech writer. To all these assistants, I extend my appreciation.

Finally, my thanks go to Eric Valentine, publisher at Quorum Books, whose patience has been admirable. I hope it is rewarded. Any errors in this work are mine alone, and readers' comments and criticism are welcome.

Contents

For Karen

late. It defines economic transactions as a subset of communication. It shows that few communications or economic transactions are done in isolation. It demonstrates that all corporate activities are dependent on communication for completion, from raw resources to the economic transaction. Finally, it describes corporate messages and media as tools to achieve economic transactions and build wealth, and it shows how the sender, message, media and receiver interact.

Communication is a fundamental part of the managerial craft and stands alongside other skills that a manager practices to ensure the survival and success of a business. One need not know communication theory to practice communication at a basic level, but to achieve great skill requires a pragmatic understanding of communication concepts.

In order to describe communication in a holistic fashion, I define corporate communication and integrate it around eight principles that managers can use in their daily activities. These principles are built on assumptions about communication and the economic enterprise. They are tied to the basics of any ongoing business—namely, survival and success.

Survival is the first rule for managers, employees, customers, interested individuals and the other parties that are essential to a company's existence and success. Survival is rarely a function of one element, such as money, jobs or power, but depends on several, including one's view of oneself, of others and of the world. However, having said this, it is important to note that corporate communication does not have an intrinsic moral or ethical dimension. A manager may persuade one to do right or wrong. Message senders and message receivers also can be second-guessed against changed societal or ethical standards. What was perceived as ethical in one decade may be judged immoral in another. (For example, cigarette advertising.)

I hope that by the time you have finished this volume, you will understand the role of communication in the firm and how to apply principles of effective corporate communication. To help in understanding, the book provides a chapter-by-chapter view of the elements of corporate communication.

Corporate communications are tools used by managerial craftspeople much as carpenters use saws, planes and hammers. Managers should know which tools to use and how to use them to achieve productive and profitable results. Careful integration of tools will help you build a house faster than a random choice. Similarly, careful integration of corporate communications will build an organization better than haphazard messages and media.

NOTES

1. Garry Wills, "What Makes a Good Leader?" *The Atlantic Monthly* 273, no. 4 (April 1994): 64.

2. Gavriel Salvendy, ed., *Handbook of Industrial Engineering,* 2d ed. (New York: John Wiley & Sons, Inc.), p. 2780.

3. Richard Tabor Greene, *Global Quality: A Synthesis of the World's Best Management Methods* (Milwaukee, WI: ASQC Quality Press, 1993), p. 886.

1

A Prelude to Corporate Communication

For the Emperor is a secretive man; he does not let anyone know what plans he has, and he does not seek advice. However, as he begins to carry out his plans, those in his court get to know about them, and then advise him to act differently. And since he is not of firm character, he allows himself to be dissuaded. This is why what he orders one day is countermanded the next, why it is never known what he wants or proposes to do, and why nobody can rely upon his decisions.
—Niccolò Machiavelli, *The Prince*[1]

Business is a subset of communication. One may communicate and never conduct an economic transaction, but one cannot conduct an economic transaction and not communicate (Figure 1.1).

To understand corporate communication, look at communication. Every living thing communicates, whether it is a microbe, plant, lower-order invertebrate, higher-order mammal or human. Humans, like other social animals, depend on communication to organize society. Every human has a unique intellect, behavior, capacity for growth and change and ability to articulate thoughts and feelings and choose courses of action. Every human is limited by his or her environment, as well as by the state of knowledge and of society before and during the time the person is alive.

How individuals view one another has a fundamental effect on corporate communication. Some persons believe humans are perfectible or perfect. Therefore, they communicate to persons as ideal creatures. Others see humans as improvable. Therefore, they communicate with the expectation that, over time, humans come to act in better ways. Still others believe

Figure 1.1
Business: A Subset of Communication

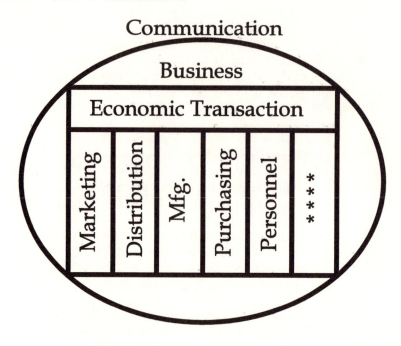

Communication

Business

Economic Transaction

Marketing | Distribution | Mfg. | Purchasing | Personnel | ****

humans are fundamentally flawed. No matter how well one communicates to them, each one is damaged goods who will receive messages poorly. Yet other individuals see humans as *leaning* toward self-interest or even as *always* self-interested and acting without regard for others. Some persons believe humans are controlled by outside forces, such as the environment, genetics, gods, furies, stars, fate or third parties. One communicates to them as individuals blessed or cursed by circumstances. Finally, there are those who see humans as free-willed and capable of making choices based on both self-interest and the interests of others. In corporate communication, all beliefs coexist side by side with message development, transmission and reception.

Time also is a factor. Humans cannot know the future. If they could, there would be no risk, no hunger or thirst, no stock market and no gaming industry. Humans make and communicate judgments about the present and future based on their limited capacities to detect what is occurring in the environment. Some are better judges than others, but none have 20–20 foresight. An optimist expects predominantly good to come from events, while a pessimist expects predominantly harm. A balanced person may expect either good or harm, depending on the shape and evolution of events. Each person chooses messages and media reflecting personal expectations. At any given time, all three persons may be right or wrong. The outcome of events and one's expectations feed back into experience and behavior as a basis for future communication. If one tries to be objective, over time the collision of events, expectations and communication will breed caution about the business environment and its openness to change.

Communication starts with the senses—sight, sound, taste, touch and smell (Figure 1.2).[2] The biological structures of the senses are complex, but from these natural media and the human brain, humans have developed signs and signaling which are studied in semiotics (Figure 1.3).[3] Humans use established procedures to transfer messages and meaning, but their perception is selective: what one observes is not always what another sees. While the five senses are the primary receptors of events and messages, not all are primary media. Primary, or natural, media are voice, body movement and expression, tactile sensation, taste and smell. Secondary media include signs, writing, clothing, environmental change such as room decoration, building siting and landscaping, cooking and much more. Virtually every human activity can be interpreted as some kind of communication, whether eating or sleeping, healing others, bearing children or burying the dead.

Communication occurs between at least two parties but is not always bidirectional. Every message has a purposeful sender—someone who sends it—but it may not necessarily have a designated receiver. A message may be sent to no one in particular. Communication also is either informational or effective. Informational communication occurs when a person sends a message without intending a specific result, whereas effective communication intends a specific outcome.

Most communication is informational, and it often transmits data from which effective messages are built. With effective communication, there is not only a message and intended receiver, but also an intended result. Effective communication is bidirectional by definition because the message sender must verify that the intended result occurred. Business uses both informational and effective communication to complete economic transactions and to ensure its survival and success.

Communication is a craft (Figure 1.4). Those who communicate well are distinguishable from those who do not. Niccolò Machiavelli's description of the emperor, quoted at the start of this chapter, has as much validity today as when it was written. A craft is an art, skill or dexterity. Much communication craft is intuitive. We learn some grammar, or rules of communication, as we grow so that we can transmit messages efficiently and effectively. We then study other points of grammar as we need them. Most humans become proficient in one or two systems of verbal or nonverbal communication, and some excel in one or two, but few excel in all.

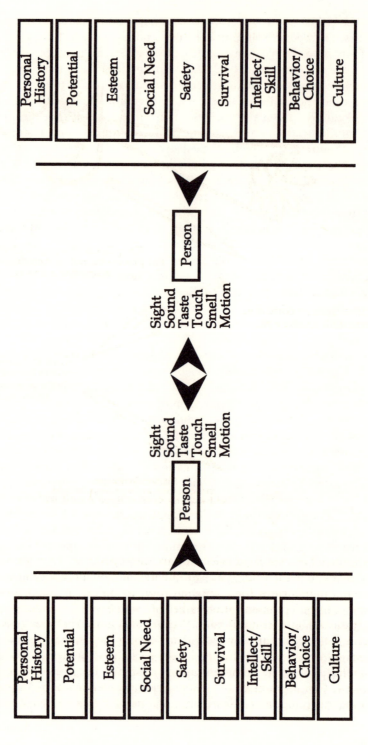

Figure 1.2
Communication

Figure 1.3
Communication Is Biological and Physical

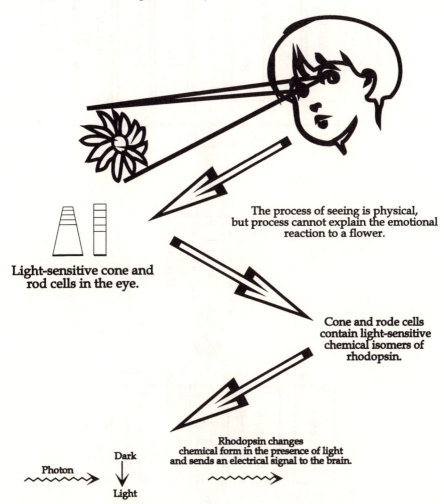

The process of seeing is physical, but process cannot explain the emotional reaction to a flower.

Light-sensitive cone and rod cells in the eye.

Cone and rode cells contain light-sensitive chemical isomers of rhodopsin.

Rhodopsin changes chemical form in the presence of light and sends an electrical signal to the brain.

Photon

Dark

Light

Grammars are not rigid rules, nor are they universal. They are as flexible as humans, but each party has to understand enough about how another person communicates for communication to occur. In companies with a strong culture, communication is heavily influenced by underlying beliefs that translate into cultural rules. Verbal and nonverbal expressions have specific meanings that only individuals within the company understand.

Because every craft is affected by the social environment, by culture and by change, corporate communication constantly becomes outdated and is renewed. Office practices of one generation differ in the next, much like men wearing, and later discarding, a hat as part of a work uniform.

Figure 1.4
The Crafts of Communication

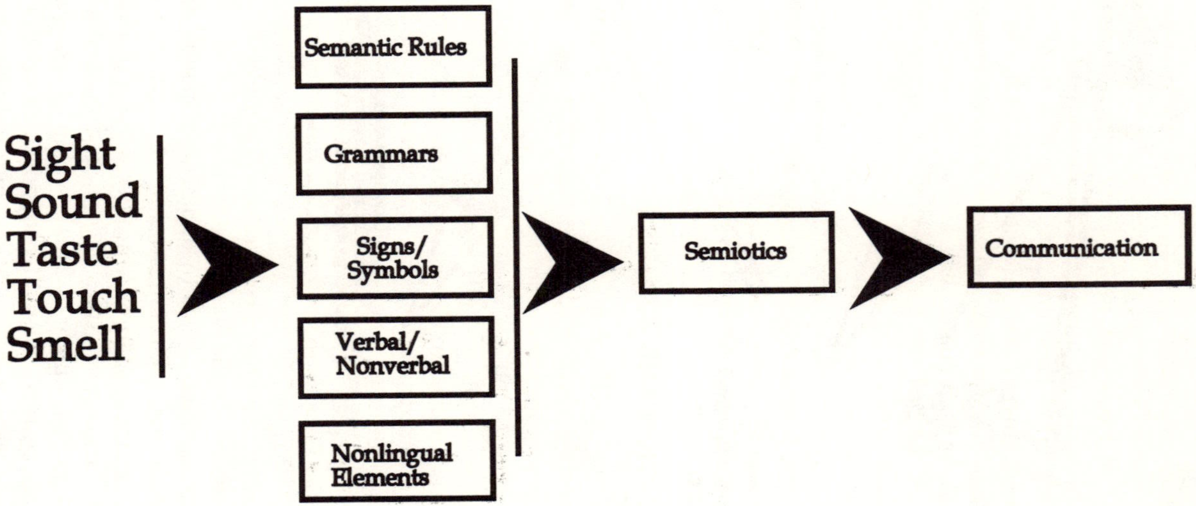

Because corporate communication uses all grammars of the senses, a working knowledge of verbal and nonverbal grammars is fundamental to avoiding communication failure. Corporate communication has signs or symbols, such as letters, numbers, movements and sounds. It has rules for assembling signs into messages with meaning and rules that denote strict meaning or connote "meaning assigned to symbols on the basis of attitudes or emotions."[4] In a business, where every form of communication is used, there is an avalanche of messages and meaning, some of which change constantly. Nonverbal communication changes from office to office and company to company. A stare in one office might connote concentration while in another office it signals disapproval. There are so many uses for communication and language that neither message senders nor message receivers can be sure of the particular use at any point in time. Thus, a message sent only once and through only one medium can be misinterpreted. The broad uses of communication often force managers into repetition and training to avoid communication failure. Messages grow old and language changes. Multicultural, multilingual, multigeographical and multi-educational variants constantly affect communication. Managers lead within this shifting environment of meaning, symbol and media.

COMMUNICATION AND BUSINESS

No one can buy or sell a good or service without communication. Among the earliest writings discovered are communications about business, such as records of inventories and transactions.[5]

Business uses informational communication to learn what to say and effective communication to say it and produce results (Figure 1.5). Successful businesses are learning organizations that gather the information needed to build and deliver effective messages.[6] To complete an economic transaction, there must be a message sender, or seller of goods and services; a message receiver, or buyer of goods and services; and a message that effectively communicates the following (see also Figure 1.6):

- information about a proffered good or service (one cannot buy what one does not know about);
- value of goods and services (one cannot buy without knowing the price or terms of exchange);
- trust between the buyer and seller that equivalent value is being exchanged, that the seller has the power to deliver goods or services and that the buyer has the means to pay for them.[7]

Communication in an economic transaction is effective because it intends a specific result—the exchange of goods and services for wealth—and it requires verification of the intended result. Business communication also is

Figure 1.5
Informational and Effective Communication

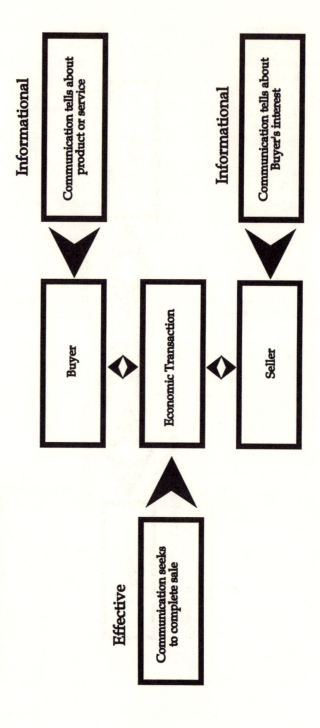

Figure 1.6
Communication and the Economic Transaction

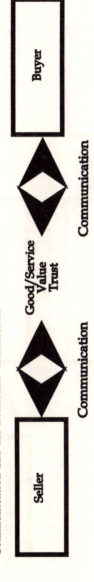

Seller

Communication

Good/Service
Value
Trust

Communication

Buyer

9

economic. It requires time, people, material and the consumption of wealth. Managers regularly judge the point at which communication is sufficient for economic purposes. One can become more informed about a good or service, but rarely can one be completely informed. At some point, the cost of getting more information outweighs the gain of acting. Adequacy of information is a judgment that buyers and sellers make in every exchange of goods or services. As one author wrote:

In actuality, the human being never has more than a fragmentary knowledge of the conditions surrounding his action, nor more than a slight insight into the regularities and laws that would permit him to induce future consequences from a knowledge of present circumstances.[8]

Effective business communication depends greatly on persuasion because some information always remains unknown. What a person does is to induce another to believe an intended message is right and should be acted upon. Persuasion relies on acceptance by the message receiver and on persuasive techniques that are older than the first philosophers. The Greek philosopher Aristotle (384–322 B.C.) defined rhetoric as "an ability . . . to see the available means of persuasion."[9]

Persuasion does not abandon fact. Rather, it uses fact to facilitate the induction of a belief or of credibility. One powerful business publication advertisement played off persuasion and fact in the following manner. The ad showed a grim-faced, balding man sitting in an office chair and staring at the reader. The ad copy read:

> "I don't know who you are.
> I don't know your company.
> I don't your company's product.
> I don't know what your company stands for.
> I don't know your company's customers.
> I don't know your company's record.
> I don't know your company's reputation.
> Now—what was it you wanted to sell me?"
> Moral: Sales start before your salesperson calls—with business publication advertising.[10]

The advertisement highlights that trust is required between the buyer and seller, which cannot be coerced. Persuasive communication requires that one person convince another to do something. As one executive put it:

An organization comes into being when (1) there are persons able to communicate with each other (2) who are willing to contribute action (3) to accomplish a common purpose. The elements of an organization are therefore (1) communication; (2) willingness to serve; and (3) common purpose.[11]

In this view, every organization is a kind of democracy of individuals performing the actions necessary for an organization to survive and succeed. Even in business autocracies, employees must submit willingly, if not happily. A black athlete who had played professional football under coach Vince Lombardi was once asked if Lombardi was racist. The player replied that Lombardi was not racist because he treated everybody the same, "like shit." Nonetheless, Lombardi's iron-fisted methods brought one championship after another to the Green Bay Packers. Lombardi's players tolerated him because they believed he would make them winners.

Businesses have a clear purpose—to increase the wealth of owners and operators—but achieving that purpose is not always a straightforward process. Diffuse data flooding into a business often carry clues to the policies, directions and controls that a business should adopt, in response to a changing environment, in order to reach greater wealth. A large part of a manager's reading in trade publications, attendance at conferences, gossip with colleagues, dinners with clients, walks around the office and chats with employees is intended to elicit information that can help the manager glimpse the direction of a business, the industry and the competitors.

Value is at the core of business. Wealth must have accepted value. Value, however, is a function of communication that depends on individual judgments by buyers and sellers made at the time of each economic transaction. Even a medium of exchange is a communication. Money has value because it is backed by an issuer whose credit is communicated to, and accepted by, the buyers and sellers. During the economic transaction, value is directly affected by the persuasive abilities of the buyer and seller. There is no good, service or other medium of exchange whose value is fixed and immutable and does not need communication of some kind to establish worth.

A good or service itself might express part of its value built on common belief. Gold is an example. It is common during crises for individuals to buy gold. However, what is gold, other than an easily worked element with an atomic weight of 197.2 and atomic number of 79? To a prospector dying of thirst in a desert, gold no longer has the value it had when it drove him there in the first place.

Among the robust media in business are counting and accounting, because they assign value. Both are languages with strict rules of use and meaning. Accounting occurs after events, such as manufacturing or economic transactions. It communicates that transactions have occurred and wealth has been earned. Accountants even describe themselves as communicators.

[Accounting is]: (1) communication of information about (2) economic entities to (3) interested persons. . . . Financial Accounting is the process that culminates in the preparation of financial reports relative to the enterprise as a whole for use by parties both internal and external to the enterprise. In contrast, managerial ac-

Figure 1.7
Accounting: A Limited Language

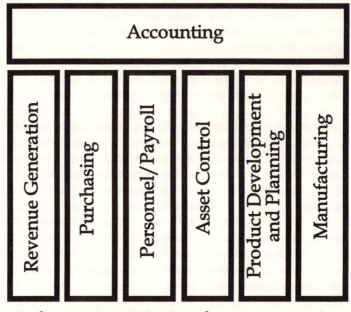

Accounting

Revenue Generation

Purchasing

Personnel/Payroll

Asset Control

Product Development and Planning

Manufacturing

Information Missing from Accounting

Morale	Customer Perceptions	News Affecting Business
Supplier Quality	Policies and Procedures	Schedules/Meetings
Product Failures	Competitive Moves	Government Regulations
New Product Uses	New Product Uses	Customer Needs/Wants
Customer Complaints	R&D Breakthrough	Interest Group Support/Resistance

counting pertains most directly to the accumulation and communication of information relative to subsystems of the entity for use by internal parties (management).

Accounting is a system that feeds back information to organizations and individuals, which they can use to reshape their environment.[12]

Accounting is not an exact language, although the illusion exists that it is. Accounting is a language with a syntax built on conventions. Moreover, the language of accounting is limited. Numbers are a pallid painting of a rich communications environment in which economic transactions occur (Figure 1.7). Managers who forget that accounting is just one of many business languages divorce themselves from the real business of a company and become monolingual in a multilingual environment. They are captives of seemingly precise numbers that describe a narrow version of a complex past.

To define business in terms of one buyer and one seller in a deserted location is a simplistic analysis. There are usually many buyers and sellers, all competing in one way or another for a buyer's wealth. Around buyers and sellers are colliding signals—messages and meanings that create noise and distract and confuse message receivers. Message encoding, transport and meaning become complex, chaotic and chancy. If a seller's message is worthless to a buyer, no economic transaction is possible, no matter how well a message has been communicated. On the other hand, if a seller's message has value to a buyer, the buyer might still fail to grasp it because of the surroundings in which a message is delivered, the condition and appearance of the seller and sociocultural barriers such as language differences.

The communication of trust underlies any value estimate and any possible transaction. Through information transfer, a seller must believe that a buyer can exchange goods and services, while a buyer must believe that a seller can deliver them. Economic transactions require bidirectional credibility, and the greater the perceived risk, injury or loss to either party, the greater becomes the need to be satisfied that a proper exchange can take place. Trust grows or diminishes with each economic exchange along two dimensions: the credibility required for one transaction at one point in time, and the credibility required for transactions over periods of time. Before an exchange can occur, both buyer and seller must accept an ability to transfer ownership. The exchange itself validates the assertion that the buyer and seller had the power to make it. The power to complete an exchange has no relationship to ethics or legality. Power is of three kinds:

- Absolute: a person has (or does not have) the ability to exchange wealth or products.
- Relative: a buyer has leverage over a seller or vice versa. That is, either there is one buyer and many sellers or one seller and many buyers. In each case, the leverage to complete a transaction swings from one party to the other.
- Perceptual: one person believes another has an ability to make an exchange, whether or not there is evidence that the latter actually has the ability.

Power is an idea built through communication and from actual or perceived need. It is a concept with as much variation as that of worth, and it includes a large perceptual component. Indeed, in politics, it is said that the perception of power is power.

In business, an image of success is used to enhance selling. Sales representatives dress smartly, wear the right clothes and jewelry, drive the right cars, hobnob with the right people. The "rub-off" (implied) communication is that the person possesses power to get things done, make a sale and satisfy needs. In an organization, being seen with the boss communicates power. Much corporate gamesmanship is built on this.

Most buyers and sellers work in public. Business is conducted in a market environment and not in a vacuum. As a result, the communication between

Figure 1.8
Most Buyers and Sellers Work in Public

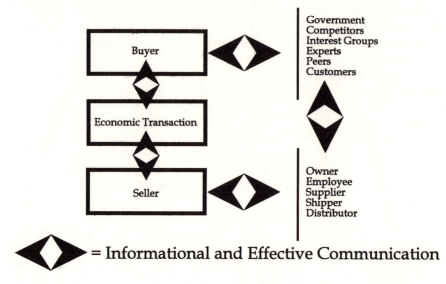

= Informational and Effective Communication

buyers and sellers is observed by others (Figure 1.8). The others may be potential buyers, sellers, uninterested parties, political representatives and regulators, friends or enemies. Each person may interpret an economic transaction in a way that only incidentally agrees with that of another observer and not at all with that of the buyer and seller. Interpretations may be benign, neutral or hostile. As a result, public communication of a transaction may have ramifications beyond the transaction. While the seller and buyer may say that others have no interest in their exchange decisions, the observers may impose themselves as official representatives of the public or self-appointed guardians, such as interest groups (Figure 1.9). The following example came from the *New York Times:*

A Street Vendor's Harried Day: "Quality of Life" Campaign
Makes a Tough Job Tougher

It was not quite noon when Gopal Saha, Mobile Food Vendor No. 18575, made his first sale of the day: a $2 Haagen-Dazs Cookie Dough Dynamo sandwich. . . . Suddenly, Mr. Saha's worst nightmare began to come true. "The alphas are coming," yelled the hot-dog vendor down the block. That is street-seller argot for the police who have begun a crackdown on food cars in congested midtown neighborhoods the city has declared off limits.[13]

There are hundreds of examples of third-party presence in economic transactions, including the U.S. Food and Drug Administration, bureaus of

Figure 1.9
Communication Links: A Simplified View

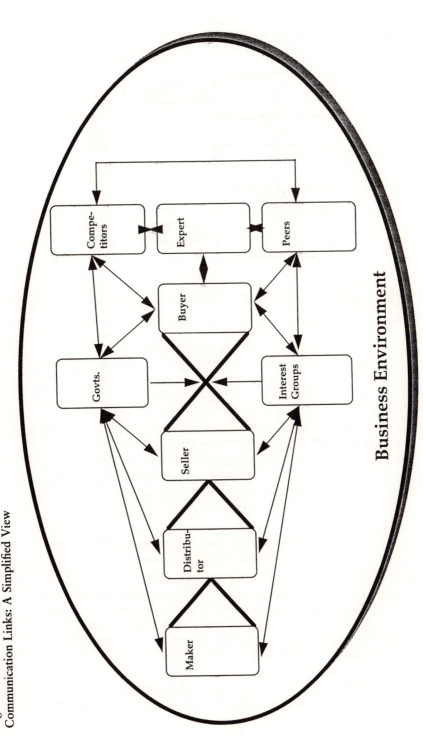

Business Environment

weights and measures, Underwriter's Laboratories, the Good Housekeeping Seal of Approval, the Consumer's Union, transportation inspection units, the U.S. Environmental Protection Agency, the U.S. Federal Aviation Administration, medical and dental societies, and so on.

Buyers and sellers have a mutual interest in controlling such communication "spillover" if they perceive it as harming completion of a sale. On the other hand, if spillover has no evident impact, they may also ignore it. Some sellers welcome outsiders into the economic transaction because they add to credibility. Others have no choice but to accept third parties in business transactions. Finally, there are always sellers and buyers who try to "end-run" (avoid) third-party oversight.

The challenge that buyers and sellers face is the future. Neither can know the outcomes of economic communication. Chance and chaos may intervene and impose an interpretation that is inimical to either or both parties. Most businesses are not large enough for unfair opinions to become a problem, but some are. A mom-and-pop dime store in a small town hardly attracts the attention of local or other government agencies as long as it pays taxes, licenses and other permits. On the other hand, the chemical plant on the edge of town that employs 5,000 workers will attract attention because of its products, its impact on the tax base, its size of employment and other factors. The instances of third-party impact on economic transactions are numerous, and they may include news stories that may be erroneous and require rebuttal, such as the staging of an exploding General Motors truck that appeared on NBC television.[14] They include rumors that cut into a company's business, such as rumors that Equitable Life Assurance Society was going bankrupt.[15] They also involve the loss or gain of government support, such as the waning of the tobacco lobby's influence in Washington, D.C. and its continued strong support in Japan, where the government owns tobacco production.[16]

Most businesses do not have a perceived public interest, but some do. Public regulation of geographically monopolistic utilities came directly from the perceived importance of electrical, gas and water services to society. Government influence extends to price controls, service requirements and return on investment. Every business has a different and unique need for communication, which is based on the business environment in which it exists. Some companies can be minimalists, communicating only to customers, while others must invest heavily in communications to stay in business.

The influence of third parties on communication works inside organizations, too. An order given to one group is observed by others whose interpretation may differ. A group for which a message was *not* intended may, because of the message, act in unintended ways. A communication might solve one problem but create another. A common example is layoffs. When people are let go in one part of a company, it often affects morale and output in another part as surviving workers interpret the meaning of

Figure 1.10
The Fragmentation of Communication in Business

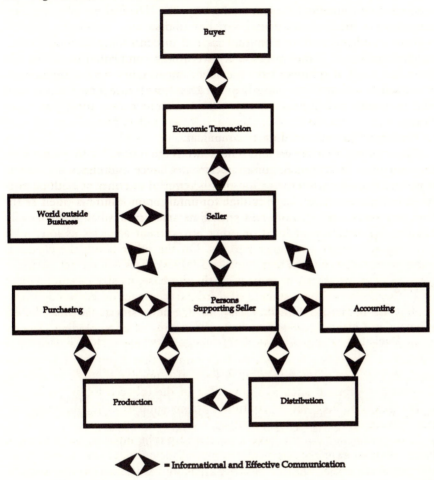

= Informational and Effective Communication

the layoffs to themselves and their interests. Especially in companies with a tradition of retention, firings can be a traumatic message with both intended and unintended consequences. The larger the organization, the greater the chance of misinterpretation.

The ways in which communication is used in business splinters into multiple and, often, uncoordinated fragments (Figure 1.10). Corporate communications has many roles. Participants express consent to be part of an organization. Managers provide and maintain a focus and sense of purpose. Organizations form communication subgroups, divisions, departments and teams. Businesses communicate to coordinate purchasing, production, distribution, sales, consumption and wealth creation. The worlds outside and inside the organization express agreement or disagreement with goods, services and policies. The worlds outside and inside the organization also communicate social concerns into the business. There is one-on-one communication; small- and large-group communication; communication to owners, managers and employees; supplier and customer communication; communication to communities and governments; and communication systems. There is communication security and communication direction—downward, upward, horizontal, inward and outward. There are formal and informal communication networks, communication media and distance.

The challenge of corporate communication is its ubiquity. It is, as one manager called it, "the flux" in organization—the flow that keeps business together and profitable. Because it permeates every organizational action, it is often buried within the task itself and overlooked until something goes wrong. Managers learn quickly that communication failure is often at the root of business disaster whereas strong communication lies at the root of business success.

NOTES

1. Niccolò Machiavelli, *The Prince,* ed. Quentin Skinner and Russell Price (Cambridge: Cambridge University Press, 1994), p. 82.

2. Daniel R. Kimble, *Biological Psychology* (New York: Holt, Rinehart and Winston, 1988).

3. Vincent M. Colapietro, *Glossary of Semiotics* (New York: Paragon House, 1993).

4. Cassandra L. Book, Terrance L. Albrecht, Charles Atkin, Erwin P. Bettinghaus, William A. Donohue, Richard V. Farace, Bradley S. Greenberg, Hal W. Hepler, Mark Milkovich, Gerald R. Miller, David C. Ralph, and Ted J. Smith III, *Human Communication: Principles, Contexts, and Skills* (New York: St. Martin's Press, 1980), p. 44.

5. Daniel C. Snell, *Ledgers and Prices: Early Mesopotamian Merchant Accounts* (New Haven, CT: Yale University Press, 1982). This is a study of cuneiform ledgers from the Ur III period (2112–2004 B.C.E.). The author examines the accounting techniques used in that era. The commodities traded included resin, salt, seeds, refined bitumen, gypsum and copper.

6. Greene, *Global Quality,* p. 229.

7. Philip Kotler, *Marketing Management: Analysis, Planning and Control* (Englewood Cliffs, NJ: Prentice-Hall, 1984), p. 8.

8. Herbert A. Simon, *Administrative Behavior: A Study of Decision-Making Processes in Administrative Organization* (New York: The Free Press, 1957), p. 81.

9. Aristotle, *On Rhetoric: A Theory of Civic Discourse* (New York: Oxford University Press, 1991), p. 36.

10. McGraw-Hill Magazines, as reprinted in *Data Communications,* November 1993, p. 106.

11. Chester I. Barnard, *The Functions of the Executive* (Cambridge, MA: Harvard University Press, 1950), p. 82.

12. Donald E. Kieso and Jerry J. Weygandt, *Intermediate Accounting*, 2d ed. (New York: John Wiley & Sons: 1977), pp. 3, 4, 7.

13. James Barron, "A Street Vendor's Harried Day," *New York Times*, April 24, 1994, metro sect., p. 37.

14. Elizabeth Jensen, Douglas Lavin, and Neal Templin, "Tale of the Tape: How GM One-Upped An Embarrassed NBC on a Staged News Event," *Wall Street Journal* 221, no. 29 (February 11, 1993): A1.

15. Larry Light, with Mark Landler, "Killing a Rumor before It Kills a Company," *Business Week*, December 24, 1990, p. 23.

16. Eben Shapiro and Rick Wartzman, "Smoked Out: Tobacco Lobby Finds Its Influence Waning as Health Issue Grows," *Wall Street Journal* 223, no. 58 (March 24, 1994): A1. See also James Sterngold, "When Smoking Is a Patriotic Duty," *New York Times*, October 17, 1993, sect. 3, p. 1.

2

Describing Corporate Communication

Think of the tools in a tool-box: there is a hammer, pliers, a saw, a screwdriver, a rule, a glue-pot, glue, nails and screws. . . . The functions of words are as diverse as the functions of these objects.
—Ludwig Wittgenstein, *Philosophical Investigations*[1]

A shared understanding of the meaning of words is absolutely necessary as people set out on a complex undertaking. . . . Think of the impact of what you say. The casual aside or pleasantry at the head office can have huge rippling impacts out there in the organization.
—Lt. General William G. Pagonis, *Moving Mountains: Lessons in Leadership and Logistics from the Gulf War*[2]

WHERE WE ARE

So far, we have summarized the roots of communication and defined business as a subset of effective and informational communication. We have positioned persuasion as a part of effective business communication, and we have noted the fragmentation of corporate communication.

This chapter describes corporate communication in greater detail. It outlines corporate communication with internal and external individuals who directly affect business success or failure. It ties organizational behavior, marketing and business structure to corporate communication, and it clarifies why communication is pervasive in everything a corporation does.

A DEFINITION OF CORPORATE COMMUNICATION

Corporate communication is the process that collects information from the business environment, develops messages from the information and transmits them to get specific economic results.

Figure 2.1
Two Forms of Corporate Communication: Internal and External

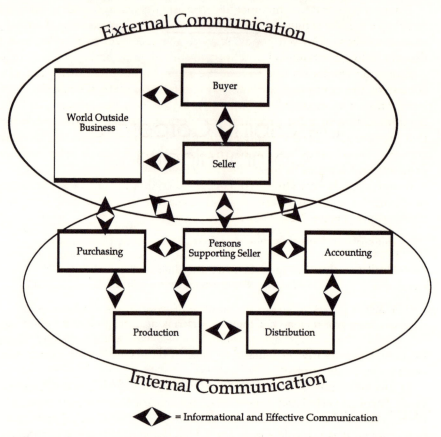

Corporate communication uses multiple messages and media, both verbal and nonverbal. It is called informational communication when it collects and transmits data from the business environment and effective
communication when it defines and sends messages for a specific purpose.
Corporate communication moves in every direction from the top, the bottom, across, outside in and inside out of the business. Corporate communication does not guarantee results because message receivers are free to
comply (or not) with the messages.

There are two forms of corporate communication—internal and external. Each depends on the other to achieve economic transactions (Figure
2.1). Of the two, however, external communication is more important because it results directly in an economic transaction and the transfer of
wealth into the organization. Looked at simplistically, a single seller does

not need internal communication. The seller is dependent on him- or herself to make the sale.

External corporate communication consists of message sending intended to achieve specific economic results from those who buy goods and services, as well as those who sell goods, services and resources to a seller, and it directly influences how well a seller will survive in a market.

Economic results do not have to be sales. For example, they can also consist of the continued societal permission to operate a business. Communication with customers is not the only, or even the primary, external communication in most organizations. Business satisfies needs and wants that are communicated verbally and nonverbally by potential customers. It conveys[3] those needs and wants internally to individuals who produce products and services to meet external demand.[4]

Business rarely acts alone. To achieve its goal, a business communicates to a range of actors who are essential to making and sustaining economic transactions (Figure 2.2). They include:

- suppliers;
- intermediaries: distributors, service agencies and financial companies;
- customers;
- competitors;
- publics, from governments and trade associations to journalists to interest groups.

Business is constantly responding to other forces as well, such as potential entrants and substitutes.[5]

At any time, one or all actors might possess a key to a company's survival. Through verbal and nonverbal communication, a company persuades them to cooperate, but it usually has little leverage over external individuals except when it is the sole source for a high-demand item.

The role of each external actor may change at any time, moving along a continuum from opposition to support. Managers can never be sure for long where a market and its players stand. This is why the first task in corporate communication is observation. A manager observes the business environment and then translates the information into messages that are tailored to the needs of external individuals who directly affect a company's survival and success. The manager uses the same messages to direct internal action toward the completion of economic transactions with buyers. How managers communicate externally relates directly to a learning model—comprising a cycle of observation, assessment, design, implementation and building shared assumptions about what the organization should do to survive and succeed.[6]

Managers are interpreters of the external business environment to the internal organization. They understand and direct the internal and external

Figure 2.2
Business Rarely Acts Alone

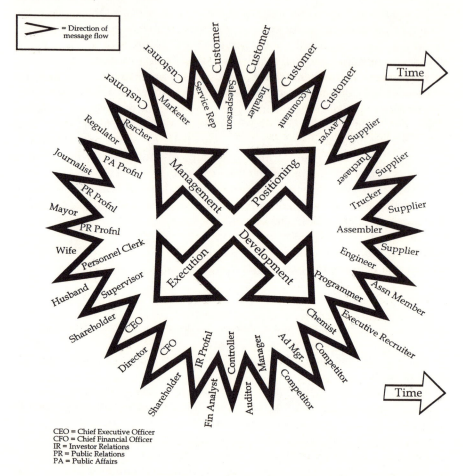

CEO = Chief Executive Officer
CFO = Chief Financial Officer
IR = Investor Relations
PR = Public Relations
PA = Public Affairs

chain of communication. However, anyone who has translated information from an external environment to an internal one knows that the task is not easy. Employees are not automatons. They do not change behavior instantly when a new message comes from a manager, and they resist changes that threaten their personal well-being.

The threat of job loss can disrupt external corporate communication because employees often balk, leaving the company unable to deliver on its promises. Even in high-productivity and strongly disciplined companies, employees resist change that they feel pushes them too far, as the following excerpt from the *Wall Street Journal* describes.

Driving Harder: As UPS Tries to Deliver More to Its Customers, Labor Problems Grow

United Parcel Service of America Inc. has stood as a model of corporate efficiency. It knows exactly how many workers it needs to deliver its 10 million packages a day. It tells drivers how fast to walk (three feet per second), how many packages to pick up and deliver a day (400, on average), even how to hold their keys (teeth up, third finger). This attention to detail has always been at the core of Big Brown's success. . . . UPS, though, like much of the rest of corporate America, has been pushing to get even more productive. In recent months, it has rolled out a slew of new products and services: computerized tracking systems, bulk discounts on large shipments, higher limits on package weights and earlier "guaranteed arrival" times. Customers love the changes. But inside UPS, the overhaul is causing problems, especially with the company's heavily unionized workers.[7]

From the start of external communication, a manager is faced with a challenge—that of making messages and meanings real in the economic transaction. Frequently, internal activity does not equal the external rate of change. As a result, a manager might communicate in order to anticipate a mismatch between the marketplace and company, restructure to match a market's rate of change, or slow or freeze the market to give a company time to catch up.

Guessing the direction of clothing demand six months in advance of shipping is an example of anticipating a mismatch between fashion trends and productive capacity. This practice lay at the root of the fashion industry for decades. Designers sold fall lines in the spring and spring lines in the fall. Buyers committed themselves to purchase goods well in advance of the time when customers began thinking about them. Today, with real-time reporting, buyers purchase less and instead replenish stocks quickly to reduce the risk of overstock.

Restructuring a company to match market speed is the essence of time-based competition.[8] Chrysler Corporation took this course to compete in the auto market and thus overcame the disadvantage of its small size. The "freezing" option attempts to confuse a market in order to get customers and suppliers to wait. IBM used this communication tactic against Control Data Corporation in the 1960s, and Microsoft employed it in the early 1980s with its early version of Windows. This technique is called the "fud" factor, with "fud" standing for Fear, Uncertainty and Doubt.

Each industry has a different rate of change. Some are glacial, while others are hyperactive, and the tempo can also change over time. Where automakers once produced a new car every five years, now the aim is two years or less. One corporation, Hanson, played off rates of change in its advertising.[9] The company displayed a computer microprocessor and a brick on a page. Under the processor were the words, "This is the latest thing in microprocessors. In 12 months it will be obsolete." Under the brick were the words, "This is a brick. In 12 months it will still be the latest thing in bricks." The body copy for the ad began: "At Hanson, we prefer to own things a little more solid than the latest trend in solid state."

Because the external marketplace changes constantly, a manager can never know the precise status of individuals, a market or an industry. Skillful managers, however, can gain a better understanding than others and capitalize on this advantage in their actions and messages.

Environmental observation is a craft in itself, and success in practicing the craft has a direct impact on the messages that a corporation can develop and send. Environmental observation has:

- psychological dimensions: consumer behavior and product positioning by individuals and groups;[10]
- measurement: dimensions of needs and demands, segmentation, and product and service measurements against needs and demands;[11]
- political calculations;
- process and modeling systems.[12]

A manager examines purchasers and other influential actors in several ways to determine how best to communicate to them. There are high-involvement purchases that carry risks for buyers and low-involvement sales of "impulse" items. There are complexities in decision making involving information search, brand loyalty, variety seeking and inertia. There are stimuli, or data, to be communicated to buyers and influentials. There are buyer and influential variables, including perceptions of a good or service, needs for its benefits and attitudes toward a brand. Perceptual variables intertwine with behavior variables, including the early or late adoption of new products and services. There are environmental variables that influence buyers and pressures from culture, social class, face-to-face or reference groups, opinion leaders and the situation in which a product or service is encountered. Finally, in some markets, interdependency between the company and customer is profound because of product complexity, the buying process and economic relationships that remain after a transaction has been completed.[13]

The process of observation is so tangled that at times, managers communicate out of personal conviction without basing their arguments on facts, which may be too expensive or elusive to obtain. In some industries, experience is the only way in which one learns how to communicate effectively.

To most managers, understanding is intuitive. They cannot explain how they know what to do. They simply have "a feel for a business." They know who initiates a transaction, who influences it, who decides and who buys. They know who uses a product or service and who is important to support and reinforce after a sale.[14] Just as important, they know who does not do these things. They carry this localized knowledge in their heads and add to it as they work and learn.

Business knowledge does not require library study. For most people, it comes from direct observation over time. As a result, knowledge is often fragmentary. Managers know enough to compete in a niche but know other market participants poorly or not at all, even if the others may be potential customers or key influentials.

Managers run into trouble communicating externally when they distance themselves from the external environment. It is more difficult to see from afar subtle changes in the market, in customers' minds or among competitors. "The act of designing the company's product and marketing mix to fit a given place in the consumer's mind" requires constant and close attention.[15]

There are many events that change the makeup of a marketplace and the messages to which a marketplace will listen:

- demographics evolve;
- energy sources run out;
- new technologies appear and old ones fade;
- economies falter or take off;
- legislators enter and leave office;
- new laws go on the books;
- managers become self-important and believe they know everything one needs to know;
- entire markets lose touch with sociocultural trends.

Without constant attention to the external business environment, managers also lose their feel for resources needed to communicate effectively— the exposure a product or service needs, as well as the amount of attention customers pay to a good or service and communications about it and how much they understand and retain messages about its benefits.[16] Managers may also distance themselves from experts that customers listen to as well as word of mouth opinion about a product or service.[17]

The manager's challenge is to monitor all key participants in an economic transaction. In large and multilocation companies, this is impossible to do. Managers depend on communication systems to tell them what is going on, but they can never be sure about what they are told. Systems are limited in two ways: they depend on humans and they are selective in observation.

Point-of-sale information systems were a major advance in retailing. Data capture takes place at a cash register where bar codes, stock unit numbers or other identifiers are scanned or keyed into the system. From that point, the information is routed by computer through a store's inventory and financial accounting systems to regional and corporate warehouses, where stock reorder is automatic.

A point-of-sale system tells a manager whether one store sells more teddy bears than another, but the system cannot explain why store A sold 100 teddy bears last week and store B sold only 50. That requires more observation. The manager might discover that store A uses a more prominent display or that the stores are in different ethnic neighborhoods. Before the manager can communicate clearly how to increase the sales of teddy bears in store B—if sales can be increased—he or she has to add to the information reported at the point of sale.

Nor can a manager dispense completely with judgments about restocking teddy bears. Theoretically, point-of-sale information systems dispense with a manager's need to decide how many teddy bears to reorder: the system has taken over a human activity by *informating* the inventory process. *Informating* (a coined term) uses technology to automate work and "simultaneously generate information about the underlying productive and administrative processes through which an organization accomplishes its work."[18] However, such systems are mindless. For example, "make 10 toys to replace the 10 sold." Such system messages assume that another 10 toys will sell if they are placed on the shelves. Another ten toys might sell, but the sales could also number 20 toys—or none. Further, the 10 toys that have been moved off the shelf and through the point of sale system might not account for five other toys that were spirited out of the store or wrecked when a child spilled a soft drink on them.

The difficulty in obtaining good readings of the business environment is a major reason why executives retain colleagues with whom they have worked for many years. They need individuals whose observations they trust or can adjust with accuracy. Even so, managers need to ground themselves regularly in the reality and perceptions of their markets, especially those of competitors.

Competitors are unpredictable actors whose avowed mission is to take away customers, and competitors are not always who you think they are. The five competitive forces—entry, threat of substitution, bargaining power of buyers, bargaining power of suppliers, and rivalry among current competitors—reflect the fact that competition in an industry goes well beyond established players. Customers, suppliers, substitutes, and potential entrants are all "competitors" to firms in the industry and may be more or less prominent depending on particular circumstances. Competition in this broader sense might be termed extended rivalry.[19]

Moreover, like it or not, a company communicates with extended rivals both verbally and nonverbally through market signals.

A market signal is an action that provides a direct or indirect indication of a company's intentions, motives, goals or internal situation. The behavior of competitors provides signals in a myriad of ways. Some signals are bluffs, some are warnings and some are earnest commitments to a course of action. Market signals are indirect means of communicating in the marketplace, and most, if not all, of a competitor's behavior carries information that can aid in competitor analysis and strategy formulation.[20]

External communication can preempt or threaten competitors, test ideas, express agreement or disagreement, boost stock price, gain internal support for action, minimize retaliation and guard against simultaneous moves, such as major capital expenditures leading to over-capacity.[21] Inevitably, no matter what a company communicates externally, its messages may have peripheral effects with Wall Street; local, state, national and international governments; journalists; and citizen action groups. Society may willfully misinterpret a communication and turn it against the person who made it. An often-quoted expression of corporate arrogance, "The public be damned," was a reasonable response used against the one who said it.

Billy Vanderbilt, a man of much softer mold than his father, has been represented as a paragon of capitalist despotism. In reality he had simply been explaining why the fast extra-fare mail train between New York and Chicago was being eliminated. It wasn't paying, he asserted. But the public found it both useful and convenient; should he not accommodate them? "The public be damned. I am working for the stockholders," he had answered his interlocutor. "If the public want the train why don't they pay for it?"[22]

Frank Lorenzo, the builder of Continental Airlines (which he later took into bankruptcy), was prevented from reentering the airline business by the animosity he had created among Continental employees. The unions crusaded against him and convinced one legal authority after another to deny Lorenzo permission to operate another carrier.

The larger a company is, the more likely it is that its external communications will have peripheral impacts, especially in terms of social questions, crises, layoffs, plant closings and withdrawal from a market. "In many important ways, the United States appears to have become a corporate state, where the institutions of government and economy are intimately related."[23] The authors of the quotation see a socially responsible role for the corporation as citizen, producer, employer, resource manager, investment and investor, neighbor, fair competitor and social designer, with a direct influence on culture and mores.[24] In fact, any one business may be all, some or none of these things, but a manager cannot assume to know a company's position in the external environment without investigation.

By nature, managers are directed inwards in their thinking, toward the firm. They prefer the structured, authoritarian, quantitatively organized world they were trained for. "The business of business is business," says Nobel Prize-winning economist Milton Friedman. But in fact, top corporate managers have found it necessary to spend more and more of their time dealing with the noneconomic environment.[25]

Although a company may not choose to be active in one or more roles, it communicates verbally and nonverbally its attitudes about them. Moreover, it may be legally constrained to act in certain ways. For example, pension plans come under law, and health plans may also be regulated. There are family leave policies, labor relations requirements and other regulations that define how a company treats its work force. In a truly free economy, such policies would not exist.

For law-abiding companies, an economic transaction is rarely free and untouched by society. Law-abiding companies must communicate to influentials and third parties to continue to do business. On the other hand, managers decide how much to abide by societal demands, and with what commitment. Organizations can skirt or transgress the law and make no effort to communicate except to manipulate perceptions about their actions. Colombian drug lords built hospitals and schools to win the loyalty of peasants in the communities where they operated and to offset the savagery of their business practices. Outside their immediate communities, however, they were enemies of the state.

Corporate advertising, public affairs and public relations deal with many external issues that threaten or hinder a company from completing economic transactions. However, there are no rules saying that company A must use corporate advertising yet company B can get along without it. Although size is a criterion, it is not a definitive reason for formal communications structures, especially for privately owned companies. Major multinational firms in grain trading, oil exploration, finance, accounting and legal services, to list a few, for decades kept to themselves, their owners and their customers without advertising, public relations departments or public affairs officers. They successfully avoided public involvement and, through chance or design, public perception did not force them to act beyond the dictates of law and regulations. These companies were virtually invisible. This is why one commentator on American journalism, Walter Lippmann, concluded that the media could never be a primary tool for societal control:

[The press] is like the beam of a searchlight that moves restlessly about, bringing one episode and then another out of darkness into vision. Men cannot do the work of the world by this light alone. They cannot govern society by episodes, incidents and eruptions. It is only when they work by a steady light of their own, that the press, when it is turned upon them, reveals a situation intelligible enough for a popular decision.[26]

Lippmann stressed that the press makes no effort to watch everything in society but only scrutinizes those areas where aberrations regularly appear, such as at the police station and courthouse. What this means is that some businesses that work quietly may go for years without news coverage. The author once worked with a highly successful New York real estate developer who had avoided the New York news media for 30 years. One newspaper, the *New York Post,* wrote a story on the developer only after a reporter sat in the developer's reception room and refused to leave without an interview. The developer valued his privacy and the fact that he could walk the streets of New York without being recognized.

For other companies, the case is exactly the opposite. They are visible and cannot avoid social involvement. They are designated spokespersons for an industry, whether they wish to be or not. These are firms like General Motors and IBM, Citicorp and Chase, Procter & Gamble and McDonald's. In companies that need corporate advertising, public relations and public affairs, the kinds of issues they confront are many and include:

- diversity of company structure, products and services;
- technology;
- productivity;
- energy use and conservation;
- ecology and environmentalism;
- social responsibility;
- consumerism;
- capital investment;
- financial performance;
- economics and regulation;
- recruiting and labor relations;
- acquisitions and mergers;
- name change announcements and protection of trademarks;
- general information about corporate activities.[27]

What a corporation communicates externally is not necessarily isolated from individuals working internally. Employees can observe and react as third parties to external messages in ways that support or harm a company. That is why some corporate advertising campaigns have been targeted more to employees than to customers.

Ford Motor Company's long-running "Quality Is Job One" advertising campaign is an example of a message targeted to both employees and customers. By having employees speak for Ford quality, the company sought to have employees buy in to quality policies. Ford understood if those who make, deliver and sell a good or service are skeptical about it or the company, they can do direct economic damage.

Sometimes, no matter how hard a company tries, messages carry no weight with marketplace participants who have already made up their minds about a subject. There is little a U.S. tobacco company can say today to justify its position on smoking. Similarly, there is little a weapons maker of inexpensive handguns can communicate to offset criticism that such weapons are "Saturday night specials" (easily obtained for use in crimes). Fears about the genetic alteration of plants and animals also intrude directly into business and have led to boycotts of milk and crusades against tomatoes. As one group of researchers expressed it:

We believe that . . . research and examples drawn from everyday life show that some kinds of information that the scientist considers highly pertinent and logically compelling are habitually ignored by people. Other kinds of information, logically much weaker, trigger strong inferences and action tendencies.[28]

Any marketing, public relations or public affairs professional can tell war stories of journalists, interest groups and politicos who were not ready to listen to reason. Sometimes, facts had nothing to do with a case:

When laypeople are asked to evaluate risks, they seldom have statistical evidence on hand. In most cases, they must make inferences based on what they remember hearing or observing about the risk in question. Psychological research . . . has identified a number of very general inferential rules that people seem to use in such situations. These judgmental rules, known as heuristics, are employed to reduce difficult mental tasks to simpler ones. Although they are valid in some circumstances, in others they lead to large and persistent biases with serious implications for decision making in areas as diverse as financial analysis and the management of natural hazards.[29]

Managers resort to heuristics just as anyone else does. They learn rules of thumb that help them guide business activity. However, they may not be able to explain them logically or in the context of external environments. An odd but interesting work on rules of thumb listed examples of the kinds of mental shortcuts humans take.

- Rule 281: If a phone rings more than six times it probably won't be answered.
- Rule 660: The idea for a new venture is likely to be strategically unsound if it can't be put into one coherent sentence.
- Rule 809: Always expect to find at least one error when you proofread your own statistics. If you don't, you are probably making the same mistake twice.[30]

The problem with these methods occurs when managers use or communicate heuristic rules outside the environments in which they work. To outsiders, rules of thumb may seem contradictory and even injurious.

Conflict arises when organizational processes run afoul of changing so-

Figure 2.3
Organizational Processes and Changing Societal Mores

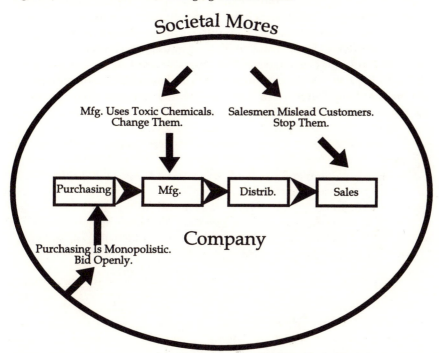

cietal mores. Society may demand instant change, but this might not be possible until new technologies and rules of thumb have been developed to manage a new market environment (Figure 2.3). Meanwhile, the company may appear to communicate arrogance and attempts to resist doing what is best for the public. There are numerous instances of this conflict. For example, laws enforce unreachable fuel efficiency standards using present technologies. Similarly, laws mandate racial and gender equality when neither minorities nor women have been trained for the positions for which they have a right to compete. There are demands for environmental protection for which there are no technologies. The societal agenda can motivate or retard a company. Often, the difference lies in the attitudes and perceptions of the message receivers—top executives who must accept or reject the social principles.

External corporate communication does not have to be rational and in fact, frequently it is not. Communication can be built on heuristics, on prejudices or biases, on political power or leverage and on culture. A manager will be pragmatic about the persuasive techniques used as long as they work and do not jeopardize a company's aim to survive and succeed in the marketplace. Even suspect research studies can, and have, been employed to offset environmental charges and justify such products as, for example, disposable versus cloth diapers.[31]

What managers must remember is that external communication frequently fails because of noise in the business environment, competing claims, embedded biases, the heuristics of message receivers and other factors that can blunt even powerfully communicated messages. After the end of the Cold War, all the arguments that defense firms made for weapons systems suddenly sounded hollow, and the industry quickly began to contract. U.S. auto companies fought their Japanese counterparts for years with charges of dumping and unfair trade practices until they saw they had to change and become as competitive. The steel industry used the same arguments to no avail.

No company completely controls its external business environment, and no communication to external individuals can guarantee a result. People have free will, and companies have little control. In the end, managers have two choices in communicating to external audiences: their messages can either lead or follow. If managers follow, they must observe individuals keenly and be prepared to move along with customers or influentials. If managers elect to lead, they must still observe individuals keenly to determine how to persuade customers and influentials to go where the company wants them to go. Either way, the role of the manager is that of observer first and message sender second.

INTERNAL CORPORATE COMMUNICATION

Internal corporate communication transfers information from the business environment into the organization and directs specific activities that result in economic transactions. It is difficult to develop and send effective internal corporate communications for all the same reasons it is difficult to communicate to external individuals. Most conditions of the external environment apply internally, and there are the added stresses of coordinating the activities of hundreds or thousands of dissimilar individuals. Managers contend with colliding assumptions and messages; multiple command, control and information systems; and communications devices of many types—computers, telephones, faxes, meetings, speeches, memos and more.

A company potentially has more leverage over employees than the external environment, but not much more. Internal corporate communication is often circumscribed by law, by internal politics and by employees who band together for self-protection. This is not to say that the day of the authoritarian or autocratic manager is over—this is far from the case. Such managers will continue to exist as long as they can appeal to a fundamental employee self-interest—survival.

Prison camps in China have built profitable businesses on the backs of their inmates. Immigrants still work in the sweatshops of New York's Chinatown and the Los Angeles Hispanic districts. In each case, however, the conditions under which these individuals labor are counterbalanced by a force or forces keeping each one in place, whether the counterbalance be threats or the desire to earn a wage. Even in socially acceptable businesses, autocratic managers continue to thrive. They demand obedience, adherence to strict procedure and loyalty. Such managers say that the success of a business depends on fealty, and employees must agree—or leave.

Internal corporate communication coordinates the activities that are necessary to complete economic transactions and transfer wealth to owners. It uses both the informational and effective forms of communication. Large enterprises of the nineteenth and twentieth centuries developed massive systems of internal communication to maintain coordination and control, and these are still in use.

Before the nineteenth century, business enterprises were generally small. Internal operations were controlled and coordinated through informal communication—principally by word of mouth except when letters were needed to span a greater distance.[32] Today, corporations are held together by networks of internal communication that extend up, down and across hierarchies. Employees at all levels read and write countless memoranda, letters and reports and spend untold hours in meetings.[33]

This is not to say that large enterprises did not exist before the nineteenth century. The Mesopotamians, Egyptians, Greeks and Romans all built massive public works projects and kept public archives of official internal communication in cities such as Rome and Alexandria. These enterprises must have used formal internal communication and control systems, but for the most part, records of these systems appear to have been lost. Even before the rise of railroads and the electric telegraph, in the 1790s, optical telegraph networks were constructed and used across France and Sweden as internal communication media.[34]

The large growth of internal corporate communication media, however, occurred in the nineteenth century. At least one researcher traced the rise of formal internal communication systems to the development of the American railroads, which needed to conduct safe and efficient operations over large operating areas. Formal communication traveled from the bottom up in order to give management an accurate view of operations and to maintain accountability along the line. This gave birth to the theory of systematic management, which was a precursor to scientific management.

Many different themes were intertwined in the writings of systematizers, but central to the idea of systematic management were . . . two principles[:] . . . (1) a reliance on systems mandated by top management rather than individuals, and (2) the need for each level of management to monitor and evaluate performance at lower levels.[35]

Internal corporate communication sought to gain control over foremen, craftspersons and contractors and put them to work efficiently in a far-flung organization. This involved the transfer of knowledge about the workings of the enterprise from the shop floor to the executive suite. In the executive suite, knowledge was turned into written records and other communications used to control activities. This practice extended naturally to monitoring and evaluating performance by means of written reports and records, such as cost-accounting and production control systems.

Systematic management generated a backlash from employees because its principles required depersonalizing the workplace in the interests of control and efficiency. Both workers and managers frequently resented and resisted the substitution of impersonal systems for personal relations in communication. In response to this resistance, attempts to repersonalize aspects of the workplace emerged.[36] By 1918, management consultants had published articles calling for in-house magazines, shop newspapers and committees to help reestablish connections between the management and employees. Managers viewed these media as top-down communications intended to improve plant operations through cooperation.

Developing technologies aided the expansion of internal communication—the electrical telegraph, copying techniques, filing methods (from pigeon holes to flat drawers and then vertical cabinets), the typewriter and carbon paper and concepts of information organization based on Dewey's library subject classification system.

Formal internal communication evolved from posted rules to manuals, to orders incorporated in discursive and then tabular forms, and finally, to memos and visual communications, such as graphs and charts. The Gantt chart, which is still used today, was developed by Henry Laurence Gantt in 1917 to help the war effort.[37] Developments were not linear: instead, they were sporadic. Managers adapted technologies only as they found a need for them—a process that remains in effect today.

The efforts of systematic and scientific managers to develop internal communication techniques extend directly to the present:

Just as the telegraph opened possibilities for wider domestic markets and more scattered production facilities[,] . . . worldwide communications systems now do the same for international markets. Historical cases suggest, however, that the potential of internal corporate communication media cannot be realized through a simple extension of communication patterns. Gains from new media await innovative thinking about underlying managerial issues.[38]

Technologists have responded to the need for internal corporate communication in many ways, mostly involving discrete inventions. The telegraph, which was invented in 1838, was joined by the telephone in 1876 and wireless telegraphy, or radio, in 1897. The mechanical calculator led to the cash register, to analog calculators built on telephone relays and, finally, to the digital computer, in 1945.[39] Since then, the computer, in various guises from mainframe and workstation to the personal computer and the portable notebook, has been in the forefront of tools that have fundamentally altered how organizations communicate internally. Telecommunications linking computers have been made digital as well, which increases the amount of data that can be sent over both metallic and fiber optic wires.

At least one author has written of the "Panoptic power of information technology"—the ability of modern information technology to allow one to observe the organization at any time and from anywhere.[40] A *panoptic organization* is a giant message machine that depicts a view of the organization at every level. A panoptic business is theoretically democratic because everyone has the same information at all times. In reality, however, a panoptic organization is limited by the enormous amount of data it captures, stores and makes available. High-speed processing systems with sophisticated search and compilation capacities are needed simply to interpret the information flow from a chain of grocery stores. Managers must still distill and channel informational and effective communication to the right places at the right time and in the most persuasive ways in order to promote action that supports the company's economic survival.

Managers control internal communication only in part. Indeed, no individual, group or department can organize all verbal and nonverbal communication elements at all times. There are too many elements, and humans find new ways to send and receive messages constantly. Part of the challenge is that internal communication is multidirectional. What is said in confidence to an assistant may be repeated in a lunchroom or affect the behavior of the assistant toward others in the department. Even basic instructions with seemingly neutral implications, such as, "Would you look up the numbers for last month?" can have subtexts, implicit meanings that may either reinforce or destroy the cooperation that is necessary to complete economic transactions. Words gain connotations based on history among individuals, the business environment and expectations. If I tell someone whom:

- I do not trust to look up the numbers, I exercise control;
- I trust to look up the numbers, it may be a friendly request to do my job for me;
- I trust to look up the numbers, and the company is failing, my statement may have urgency;
- I am getting ready to compensate, the request symbolizes payday.

Corporate communication implies positive or negative consequences, which are based on results of messages that were sent. Managers reinforce or punish individuals to, respectively, increase or decrease behavior tied to economic transactions.

Leadership is an interaction between two or more members of a group that often involves a structuring or restructuring of the situation and the perceptions and expectations of the members. Leaders are agents of change—persons whose acts affect other people more than other people's acts affect them. Leadership occurs when one group member modifies the motivation or competencies of others in the group.[41]

Agents of change communicate positive and negative messages through verbal and nonverbal media to get individuals to act as the agent wants them to act. Unfortunately, managers often do not understand the power of nonverbal messages in internal communication. Even the best-written and -spoken words can fall before symbols that denigrate a message. "When nonverbal messages contradict verbal ones, the listener tends to trust the nonverbal message more than the verbal one."[42]

A chief executive officer (CEO) who says, "We are all in this together," while wearing a custom-tailored suit and expensive watch and commanding the attention of fawning assistants might not convince the employees that a pay cut is necessary. To stamp out such symbols, some factories have gone to using identical uniforms for managers and employees.[43]

Adding to the manager's challenge in internal corporate communication is multilingualism. Multilingualism does not mean different languages like English, Spanish, Japanese and Thai, although these can be major barriers in international business. Multilingualism in internal corporate communication defines the shorthand and specialized ways of speech that speed internal and external action but may divorce a department or company from the larger business environment. An engineer may talk to colleagues about "LAN," "WAN," "ISDN," "VLSI" and "OSI" without explaining these acronyms. A cost accountant may talk about breakevens, variable and fixed costs, standard costing, absorption and shrinkage without asking if the other person knows what he or she means. Similarly, a marketer discussing portfolio management will confuse a treasurer, who views the subject differently.

Most organizations do not—and cannot—have one language with precise meanings because the many detailed tasks of the organization require specialized vocabularies (Figure 2.4). As one observer noted, an organization is a series of translations of meaning. It translates:

• observed customer behavior into customer wants;

• customer articulations into customer wants;

• competitor success at meeting customer wants into a threat assessment;

• competitor process capabilities into a threat assessment;

Figure 2.4
Organizations and Translation of Meaning

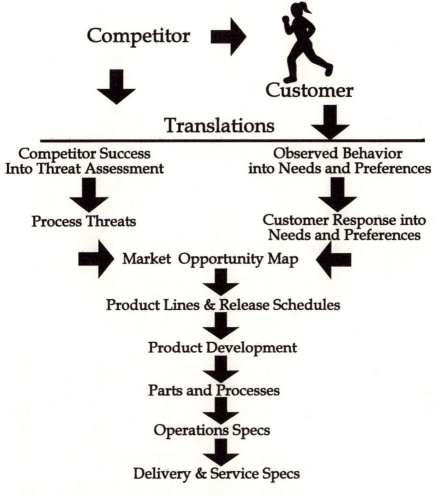

- customer wants and competitor threat assessments into a market opportunity map;
- a market opportunity map into product lines and release schedules;
- product lines and release schedules into product development projects;
- product development projects into part and process specifications;
- part and process specifications into operations specifications;
- operation specifications into delivery and service specifications.[44]

These are but a few of the translations that occur in an economic process. As a result, the first task of a manager is to learn the language of the entity that he or she supervises. The manager cannot talk credibly without knowing the language and may lose credibility for his or her ignorance.

This is a challenge for executives who communicate general company policies. As a CEO's message filters through the ranks, each unit translates (and, often, misinterprets) words into a unit's mission and function. Efforts at *cascading* messages by having each level teach the next are also at risk as language changes. Cascading assumes a fractal organization whose functions remain the same even though department sizes differ.[45] In a fractal organization, each level copies the best practices of the level above it. However, any process in which humans are involved cannot be fractal because of the uniqueness of individuals. Factors as fundamental as literacy will change the cascade process. In cases where workers are illiterate, language and media must be adapted to their ability.

Companies that recognize the danger of misinterpretation during internal communication and supply consistent policy definitions as a remedy may also run afoul of essential activities that do not fit definitions. The term "customer-driven" in quality management often means the next level in the process chain. If my department satisfies my "customer" departments, my department has met quality goals.

A simple case shows why this practice is dangerous. If my department produces customer sales brochures for your department, I measure satisfaction based on your responses. However, your responses might be wrong in relation to those of the actual customers, who may ignore the brochures I produced. While I satisfy your department, I have not satisfied the real customers.

The concept of "customer-driven" quality management is particularly difficult when dealing with some types of departments. Who is the customer of a collections department, the external customer, who has not paid for goods and services, or the company? The answer is not clear-cut. A valued customer who has given, and will continue to give, the company a lot of business is treated differently from a small customer with less potential. Nonetheless, the large customer may have larger and older balances outstanding.

The translation of internal corporate messages also is affected by perception, which is:

the process of interpreting the messages of our senses to provide order and meaning to the environment. . . . The key word is interpreting. . . . People frequently base their actions on the interpretation of reality provided by their perceptual system, rather than the reality itself.[46]

Behavior is a powerful influencer of perception. First-line employees and supervisors may hear a message repeatedly yet may not translate it into behavior because of inertia, resistance, contradiction (they are told to act in a new way yet are rewarded for maintaining old standards), inability to adapt a message to the workplace and lack of credibility. Employees have no faith in management's view. Today, communication systems can reach every employee everywhere in the world at the same time, but these systems still have gaps. They do not translate internal corporate messages into the idioms of the individuals receiving them. They cannot guarantee change in an individual's perception. Thus, they cannot guarantee behavior change, and they can create as much noise as insight.

Executives complain of receiving a huge volume of E-mail every day. Technologists have responded to the glut by developing new filtering, classification and expert software to help executives decide which messages to read. The net result is parity with the older, paper-based systems. Even though an executive physically receives data, he or she never looks at it unless it is captured by filters. Filtering depends on an executive's decision about what he or she needs to know. Problems arise when critical information from outside the normal classification boundaries enters the system and is not picked up by filters. For example, a Fortune 500 company with an organization-wide E-mail system discovered it had 80 electronic bulletin boards for departments and groups. Few individuals knew where or how to obtain the wealth of data on the computer. The company's E-mail had become a barrier rather than a support to internal corporate communication.

Managers and employees also communicate internally for reasons other than the survival and success of a business. They protect themselves against bad decisions, market themselves to superiors and buck decisions to avoid responsibility. Internal corporate communication will not become any easier with the increase of technology. New challenges will arise and new behaviors will be needed to make effective use of information and media.

COMMUNICATION, CLASSICAL STRUCTURE AND HUMAN RELATIONS

Internal corporate communication is intimately tied to business design. Three traditional structures coordinate communication—classical, human relations and systems.[47]

The classical approach is based on activities that must be done to achieve objectives. It uses a chain of command and hierarchical groupings to achieve specific areas of accountability and responsibility. Information is communicated up and down a tree structure in a flow that tends to stay within a specific root. Line relationships establish communication from the top to the bottom of an organization. Managers assign explicit external tasks to specific departments. They establish spans of control to prevent communications failure and to keep activities synchronized.

In the classically structured organization, communication focuses on departmental or chain activities and not the organization as a whole. As the responsibility for meeting goals becomes subdivided and communication lines multiply and lengthen, people with common goals no longer know what their colleagues do.[48] The classical approach recognizes informal lateral communication and the need for cross-departmental communication, but with a different emphasis, as it examines vertical relationships more closely than horizontal ones.

The human relations approach focuses on behavior in organizations, all of which is influenced by verbal and nonverbal communication. Managers employing the human relations approach want to achieve objectives while satisfying the bulk of an organization's members. They focus on individual needs and wants, the behavior of work groups and relations among groups.

Verbal and nonverbal communications are at the core of work group behavior. People within a business do not generally behave as isolated individuals. They are either organized or come together voluntarily and, in consequence, they influence each other's behavior.[49]

A formal or informal work group is more than the sum of its individuals because the members will conform to behaviors approved by the group. The group enforces conformity through communicating rules either explicitly or nonverbally, as customs. When a group solves problems, the process is more difficult and slower than under unidirectional authority because group problem solving requires communication among individuals. However, there remains a strong temptation for group leaders to make decisions without discussion and selling an idea to others.[50]

However, group leaders ultimately are the captives of their groups. To rise to spokesperson, group leaders must conform to accepted behavior and be "heavy contributors to the interactions that take place in their groups. They display more initiation of ideas, express more opinions, and ask more questions than do those members who do not emerge as leaders."[51] However, once in charge, leaders can, and do, seize power and dismiss members who do not conform to their view, as the lives of Hitler and Stalin make clear.[52]

Groups go through life cycles of formation, differentiation, blending and maturity. At every step of the way, verbal and nonverbal communications cue members to the dimensions of the group itself—its activities, interactions and sentiments.[53]

Individual attitudes toward job performance are, for the most part, defined by group communication. A blue-collar worker does not want to be a "rate buster" or "scab." A manager does not want to appear too "free-spirited" lest he or she be banned from the power structure. On the other hand, group self-motivation may exceed all norms through self-induced peer pressure. An early example of group self-motivation occurred during the building of the Panama Canal and was touched off by Joseph Bucklin Bishop, editor of the weekly newspaper, the *Canal Record*.

Bishop began publishing weekly excavation statistics for individual steam shovels and dredges, and at once a fierce rivalry resulted, the gain in output becoming apparent almost immediately. "It wasn't so hard before they began printing the Canal Record," a steam-shovel man explained to a writer for *The Saturday Evening Post.* "We were going along, doing what we thought was a fair day's work . . . [but then] away we went like a pack of idiots trying to get records for ourselves."[54]

Group rivalry remains a potent form of communication and a means to enhance economic transactions. Sales managers will pit one group of salespeople against another, even to the point of forcing a losing group to undertake demeaning tasks such as polishing the winners' shoes. However, group behavior can lead to a condition in which members no longer observe the "business of a business" but instead focus on other group members. This self-focused communication is called *groupthink*. It includes:

- Overestimation of group power and morality, which leads the group to take extreme or morally dubious risks.
- Closed-mindedness: group members rationalize evidence and convince themselves of interpretations that cannot stand up to scrutiny.
- Pressure to conform: the group uses self-censorship and directed pressure on nonconformists.
- Self-appointed protectors who guard against evidence that might contradict the group's view of the world.[55]

With groupthink, communication becomes a weapon deployed against the business environment rather than a means of trying to understand and persuade individuals within it.

Groups have their own cultures. They enter into formal and informal communication networks with attitudes and beliefs that may be far removed from company policy. To find out what a company is doing, managers must tap into its cultural network of groups. "The manager who wants, first, to know what people in their organization are really thinking, and second, to influence their behavior day to day must be deft at working the cultural network."[56]

Cultural networkers use groups for internal communication. They cultivate exposure to people at all levels, reinforce values and seek friendships that help them get the word out. The cultural communication networks that they build can be diagrammed to show real relationships, such as cliques, in which communications flow only within a group of personnel; liaisons, in which persons communicate to, and connect, cliques without belonging to any; bridges, in which persons link cliques and are members of one of them; and isolates, who do not participate in the network (Figure 2.5).[57]

While communicating, managers contend not only with formal structure and formal and informal groups, but also with themselves. Managers are

Figure 2.5
Cultural Communication Networks Can Be Diagrammed

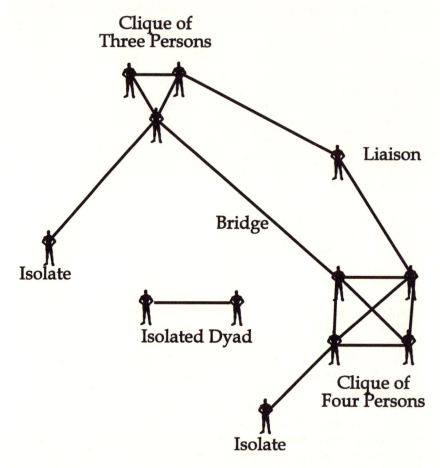

job-centered or employee-centered and, depending on conditions, they may be both. A job-centered manager communicates to an employee as a tool. An employee-centered manager communicates to a subordinate as a person of personal worth with a job to do. Both types of managers can be effective communicators and both recognize that employees work for reward. However, the definition of reward itself results in misunderstanding, miscommunication and conflict.

Employers and employees understand work for wages, but employees also understand the implied message when productivity demands outstrip wage increases and personal security. Management is telling them that they are expendable tools to be pushed to the limit of time and motion efficiency.

This is at the root of Theory X and Theory Y. Theory X assumes that "people generally dislike work, lack ambition, and will avoid responsibility if possible."[58] A Theory X manager assumes that people work because they have to and that punishment, threats and close supervision may be necessary to motivate them. The one powerful motivator is money. A Theory Y manager assumes that work is natural and that workers accept the responsibility to pursue objectives with a self-motivation that is as powerful as close supervision or monetary rewards.

Theory X and Theory Y are both correct for some individuals at some times. There are slackers, self-motivated go-getters and individuals who seesaw between the extremes. A manager who communicates in one way will have trouble unless he or she is surrounded by compliant employees. (When a manager talks about building a team, the team is usually in the manager's image.)

The degree to which a manager communicates to employees as participants in decision making usually depends on how he or she views individuals. Communication style should vary by person rather than by group, but this does not always happen. A manager or group (or both) can be inflexible. In large groups, where individuals are harder to know, trust is jeopardized early on. It is easier for managers to fall back to work rules than account for individuals, and it is easy for groups to fall back on perceptions of management rather than facts about individual managers.

Managers also balance and communicate multiple goals—group goals, individual goals and performance goals. Each goal has expectations and importance attached to it that come from individuals and human behavior.[59] Goals communicate a view of how one decides to interact with the environment and may or may not have a rational basis. High goals may be motivated by greed or fear of competition. Low goals may come from a generous view of a marketplace or from concern for employees.

Managers may communicate not only a goal, but also the reason why a goal was set. If employees accept the reasoning, there is a greater likelihood that they will accept the goal. However, there is no guarantee that they will cooperate. On the other hand, managers may not communicate reasons for goals because they choose not to or cannot.

Communication success and failure also rest on interpersonal relationships. A leader who talks a lot is not necessarily the best leader or communicator. Here, the quality of communication takes precedence over quantity.[60] A subordinate might expect an approach that a manager cannot provide, or sometimes, individuals just do not like each other. A poet wrote an epigram two thousand years ago that described this "bad chemistry." The epigram was translated into English by Thomas Brown as follows:

I do not love thee, Doctor Fell.
The reason why I cannot tell.

But this alone I know full well,
I do not love thee, Doctor Fell.

Henry Ford II, when he led Ford Motor Company, fired Lee Iaccoca using similar words.

Interpersonal relationships are built on feelings and mutual satisfaction, understanding of the business environment and self-understanding or accurate perceptions of reality. They also develop from giving guidance to help one reach a desired change and from getting a task or job done, such as achieving a goal.[61] Individuals expecting one type of interpersonal relationship can misinterpret communication resulting from another type.

In horizontal organizations, with few management levels, interpersonal relationships are broader in number and bidirectional communication is hindered between the manager and employees. That is why in such flat organizations, there is more chance of information overload and slow or bad decisions or no reporting at all. In vertical, task-specific organizations, relationships are structured by unit or department. Information flows well within the chain but is sanitized from level to level. By the time reports reach the top, it may be difficult to learn from them what is happening in the business environment.

With information, or panoptic, technologies, organizational communications are pervasive and multidirectional, but they are not a panacea. Employees can overuse communications by reporting large amounts of diverse information that damages productivity.[62] Alternately, they can establish links outside the formal structure and, sometimes, against its policies. With E-mail systems, there have been tensions between managers and employees based on freewheeling and graphic on-line discussions.[63]

At the core of internal corporate communication is authority—an individual's decision to be guided by the communication of another. Authority is given by a message receiver, and not seized by a message sender. An individual may be persuaded to obey and change behavior in congruence with a message received, or commanded to obey. Authority can extend upward, downward or across. It does not recognize formal organizational structures. In crisis, authority often flows to those who get things done, no matter where they are in a formal organizational structure. After the crisis is past, the formal organization restores the lines of control.

Communication by fiat can be as effective as communication by persuasion. There are times when giving orders is the only thing for which a manager has time, especially in crises, and subordinates are expected to mute their personal opinions. Usually, managers and employees clearly perceive a crisis and automatically adjust their behavior, but there are times when a crisis is not clear, especially if it unfolds slowly. An example of a slow crisis is a societal change in attitudes about smoking, drinking or the possession of firearms that takes place over years rather than minutes. In such cases, communication by fiat is more difficult.

Some managers prefer to communicate in a crisis mode. They create crises where there are none—or should be none. Management-by-crisis depends on poor communication that allows events to get out of control. In some industries, management-by-crisis has been institutionalized, with managers being rewarded for putting in grueling hours when, with planning, everyone could go home on time.

A well-managed relationship between the boss and subordinates can achieve a great deal, but it also can be destructive. Managers vary in their need for communication from employees. Some want to know everything, and others, little or nothing. Employees can be conduits, gatekeepers or both. A manager may not feel free to tell an employee about the employee's errors, especially if the employee has power in the organization. Similarly, employees who are beholden to managers for pay raises or promotions may not feel free to tell managers what the latter need to know. Other dangers include delivering individual evaluations while ignoring group behavior and vice versa. A manager might criticize an individual for actions that are a group norm. Finally, managers may not feel free to rate employees because they consider the ratings a reflection on their management skills.

In such cases, communication becomes distorted. Managers and employees erect "Potemkin Villages"—beautiful shells of message sending and message receiving that cover tensions and ugly realities. Real communication occurs through a grapevine or not at all. The author worked with two companies where aggressive friendliness was part of the culture, while underneath the friendliness was character assassination by grapevine.

In a public case, an employee of Prudential Insurance Company of America reported fraud in the company's real estate funds and then was fired by his manager. Only later was the individual reinstated after a second examination proved that he was right. In the interim, the employee's attempt to communicate nearly destroyed him.

Mark Jorgensen thought he was just being an honest guy, exposing fraud in the real-estate funds he managed for the Prudential Insurance Company of America. Then his world fell apart: The boss who had once been his friend abandoned him. His circle of colleagues at work shunned him. Company lawyers accused him of breaking the law. The once powerful and respected executive soon found himself hiding in the local public library, embarrassed that he had been forbidden to return to the office and hoping not to be seen by his neighbors. His long and successful career seemed to be dwindling to a pathetic end.

Finally, in February, came the bitterest moment, the phone call from a middle manager at Prudential telling him he had been dismissed.[64]

In an extraordinary turnabout, Jorgensen finally received an apology directly from the chairman of Prudential.

SYSTEMS AND INTERNAL CORPORATE COMMUNICATION

The systems approach to organizational structure examines how parts of a business work together. Systems-style managers believe that the role of an organization is to facilitate decision making. Decisions depend on information, and information depends on communication. Systems-style managers see communication as fundamental to enterprise.

Without communication there could be no organization since it would be impossible to get people to act in a coordinated way; people would be linked together by an abstract chain of command but acting without a chain of understanding. Where communication is poor, coordination is poor since coordination implies that people are being informed about each other's plans. Furthermore, cooperation presupposes coordination so that cooperation depends on communication.[65]

As a result, systems-style managers analyze information needs and communication networks.[66] They specify objectives, list subsystems or main decision areas, establish information needs and design communications channels and group decision areas to minimize communications burdens. A management information system has as its goal an integrated system of reports that gives each level the "right" information at the "right" time, enabling decisions to be based on the best information available, as far as the provision of such information can be justified on economic grounds.[67]

Part of the success of the "lean" production style pioneered at Toyota Motors was based on a communication process that developed the right choices at the right time from teams representing all aspects of the enterprise. Toyota used:

- The boss: the large project team leader—who moves a new car through the design and manufacturing system.
- The team: a tightly knit unit reporting to the boss and responsible for carrying out design and production.
- Simultaneous development: the ability to design production machinery at the same time as body design.

Communication was the glue that held together these three factors.[68]

The matrix system was a western approach to internal communication. It assigned specialists to guide projects horizontally through the organization with reporting responsibilities to vertical departments and to a team that drew on the functional resources of manufacturing, marketing, purchasing, and so forth.

Systems look at process and linkages—the point at which one activity feeds into another and the information that each process must have for the next activity in the chain to do its job. Process defines feedback as comparison of actual outcomes to preset standards, followed by corrective action if necessary. Process fosters a closed-loop system. Most of the quality control approaches to business are based on this premise. Systems of control communication keep an organization on course while planning systems look ahead to possible courses of action. Managers identify and communicate actions and processes based on possible outcomes. If the managers can simplify decisions, they can make them routine. Decision rules standardize communication and relieve managers of unnecessary judgment calls, and they also simplify complex problems so that managers can make and communicate adequate decisions.

A major consideration in the systems approach is the communication network. Systems managers believe that decisions should be made by the persons with the greatest information to make them. Examinations of internal information flow have identified three options (see also Figure 2.6):

- All information going to one person, an authoritarian mode of operation.
- Information flowing to persons linked to at least two others in a circle of communications.
- Communication to every person linked to every other.

Information systems match each of these flows. The mainframe computer is an example of centrality where everything flows to a central processing unit. Stand-alone personal computers are an example of a circle of communications. Each person has a bit of information and is responsible for communicating it to others. Distributed information systems are an example of general linkage. Each point of the network holds the necessary information, but the information is available to every part of the network as well, so everyone uses the same data.

Exogenous variables can affect any communication channel and outdate it, shut it off or send it awry. A perfectly functioning plant may turn out products for which, suddenly, there is no demand. This means that system managers need to include flexibility in interdependent systems. System rigidity is a ticket to failure because even an all-seeing information "Panopticon" is limited to a total view of a closed environment. A panoptic system is like a person in a cave who can view and analyze every part of a landscape outside the cave opening but cannot see behind or above the cave. No matter how much the person analyzes, there is still a mountain above the cave. What is on the other side of that mountain is invisible.

Figure 2.6
Communications Networks: Three Options

Option One: All information going to one person

Option Two: Information flowing to persons linked to at least two others in a circle of communications.

THE CONFUSION OF CORPORATE COMMUNICATION

Corporate communication starts with the economic transaction and builds continuously into machines, relationships and directions of the enterprise. Each message is multidirectional, with impacts and outcomes that cannot be foreseen by a communicator. Moreover, as messages collide within the organization, they set off vortices of chaos that momentarily misdirect the organization. Managers are blinded by the data flowing at them. They make guesses based on data, their propensities and training. Sometimes they are right, sometimes not.

No system is perfect, nor can it be. Perfect communication can be attained in a small way in a small place for a time, but inevitably, events change messages and media. Vital system inputs become extraneous, and inputs that a system needs are lacking. Last, for every rule there are exceptions. In every country and industry, there are organizations that seem to span generations successfully by continuing to do the same things in the same way. They succeed because market dynamics have never changed. Either their business environment is stable, which allows for stable organizational policies and departments similar in structure; they have never been big enough for market dynamics to influence their organizations;[69] managers have adapted over decades to change but visible shifts have not been large; or, finally, the companies have been protected by society so that they can operate as they always have. Such companies, however, are in the minority.

SUMMARY

- Corporate communication collects information from the business environment, develops messages from the information and transmits messages to achieve specific economic results.

- External corporate communication involves message sending to achieve specific economic results from those who buy goods and services, provide them or directly influence how a seller survives in a market.

- Internal corporate communication transfers information from the business environment into the organization and directs specific activities that result in economic transactions.

- Both external and internal communication rely on informational and effective communication.

- Both external and internal communication use both verbal and nonverbal, multidirectional messages and media.

- Both external and internal communication depend on observation of the message receivers for effectiveness.

- Both external and internal communication are affected by heuristics, prejudices, culture, persuasion and political power.

- Both external and internal communication have been affected by the growth of technology.

- Internal communication is tied directly to business organization and design, to human relations and to information systems.

- Both external and internal corporate communication are inherently chaotic because they start from a simple economic transaction and expand into thousands of complex and interacting processes.

NOTES

1. Ludwig Wittgenstein, in *Philosophical Investigations. A Dictionary of Philosophical Quotations,* edited by A. J. Ayer and Jane O'Grady (Oxford: Blackwell Reference, 1992), p. 465.

2. William G. Pagonis with Jeffrey L. Cruikshank, *Moving Mountains: Lessons in Leadership and Logistics from the Gulf War* (Boston: Harvard University Business School Press, 1992), p. 174.

3. J. M. Juran, *Juran on Planning for Quality* (New York: The Free Press, 1988), p. 61.

4. Philip Kotler, *Marketing Management: Analysis, Planning and Control* (Englewood Cliffs, NJ: Prentice-Hall, 1984), p. 5.

5. Michael E. Porter, *Competitive Strategy: Techniques for Analyzing Industries and Competitors* (New York: The Free Press, 1980), p. 4.

6. Daniel H. Kim, "The Link between Individual and Organizational Learning," *Sloan Management Review* 35, no. 1 (Fall 1993): 37–49.

7. Robert Frank, "Driving Harder: As UPS Tries to Deliver More to Its Customers, Labor Problems Grow," *Wall Street Journal* 223, no. 100 (May 23, 1994): A1.

8. George Stalk, Jr., and Thomas M. Hout, *Competing against Time: How Time-Based Competition Is Reshaping Global Markets* (New York: The Free Press, 1990).

9. *The Economist,* n.d.

10. Henry Assael, *Consumer Behavior and Marketing Action* (Boston: Kent Publishing Company, 1984).

11. Glen L. Urban and John R. Hauser, *Design and Marketing of New Products* (Englewood Cliffs, NJ: Prentice-Hall, 1980).

12. Ibid.

13. Frederick E. Webster, Jr., *Industrial Marketing Strategy* (New York: John Wiley & Sons, 1979), p. 18.

14. Ibid., pp. 143, 157.

15. Ibid., p. 272.

16. Assael, *Consumer Behavior,* p. 139.

17. Ibid., pp. 412–14.

18. Shoshanna Zuboff, *In the Age of the Smart Machine: The Future of Work and Power* (New York: Basic Books, 1988), p. 9.

19. Porter, *Competitive Strategy,* p. 6.

20. Ibid., p. 75.

21. Ibid., pp. 75–87.

22. Matthew Josephson, *The Robber Barons* (San Diego, CA: Harcourt Brace Jovanovich, 1962), p. 187.

23. R. Scarpitti and Margaret L. Andersen, *Social Problems* (New York: Harper and Row, 1989), p. 447.

24. Ibid., p. 472.

25. Frank M. Corrado, *Media for Managers: Communications Strategy for the Eighties* (Englewood Cliffs, NJ: Prentice-Hall, 1984), pp. 3–4.

26. Walter Lippmann, *Public Opinion* (New York: MacMillan, 1965), p. 229. This key work on the development of public opinion and the role of newspapers was written in 1922.

27. Thomas F. Garbett, *Corporate Advertising: The What, the Why and the How* (New York: McGraw-Hill, 1981).

28. Richard E. Nisbett, Eugene Borgida, Rick Crandall, and Harvey Reed, "Popular Induction: Information Is Not Necessarily Informative," in *Judgement under Uncertainty: Heuristics and Biases,* edited by Daniel Kahneman, Paul Slovic, and Amos Tversky (Cambridge, UK: Cambridge University Press, 1985), p. 116.

29. Paul Slovic, Baruch Fischhoff, and Sarah Lichtenstein, "Facts versus Fears: Understanding Perceived Risk," in *Judgement under Uncertainty: Heuristics and Biases,* edited by Daniel Kahneman, Paul Slovic, and Amos tuersky (Cambridge: Cambridge University Press, 1985), p. 464.

30. Tom Parker, *Rules of Thumb* (Boston: Houghton Mifflin Company, 1983), pp. 44, 102, 124.

31. Cynthia Crossen, "How 'Tactical Research' Muddied Diaper Debate," *Wall Street Journal,* May 17, 1994), p. B1.

32. JoAnne Yates, *Control through Communication: The Rise of System in American Management* (Baltimore, MD: Johns Hopkins University Press, 1989), p. xv.

33. Gerard J. Holzmann and Bjorn Pehrson, "The First Data Networks," *Scientific American* 270, no. 1 (January 1994): 124–29.

34. Yates, *Control through Communication,* p. 10.

35. Ibid., pp. 15–16.

36. Ibid., p. 88.

37. Ibid., p. 275.

38. Steven Lubar, *InfoCulture: The Smithsonian Book of Information Age Inventions* (Boston: Houghton Mifflin Company, 1993).

39. Zuboff, *Age of the Smart Machine,* p. 322.

40. Bernard M. Bass, *Bass & Stogdill's Handbook of Leadership: Theory, Research, and Managerial Applications,* 3d ed. (New York: The Free Press, 1990), pp. 19–20.

41. Ibid., p. 114. On nonverbal communications, Bass notes: "Remland (1981) pointed out that when nonverbal messages contradict verbal ones, the listener tends to trust the nonverbal message more than the verbal one." See M. Remland, "Developing Skills in Nonverbal Communication: A Situational Perspective," *Journal of Business Communication* 18, no. 3 (1981): 17–29.

42. Peter J. Frost, Vance F. Mitchell, and Walter R. Nord, ed., *Organizational Reality: Reports from the Firing Line* (New York: HarperCollins Publishers, 1993). This is a collection of essays and excerpts about corporate life, two of which focus on nonverbal messages: "Games Mother Never Taught You," by Betty Lehan Harragan, and "Symbols of Power," by Michael Korda.

43. Richard Tabor Greene, *Global Quality: A Synthesis of the World's Best Management Methods* (Milwaukee, WI: ASQC Quality Press, 1993), p. 65.

44. Ibid., p. 154.

45. Gary Johns, *Organizational Behavior: Understanding Life at Work* (New York: HarperCollins Publishers, 1988), p. 81.

46. John O'Shaughnessy, *Business Organization* (London: George Allen & Unwin, 1969).

47. Ibid., p. 41.

48. Ibid., p. 77.

49. Alfred P. Sloan, Jr., *My Years with General Motors* (Garden City, NY: Doubleday and Company, 1964), p. 435.

50. Bass, *Bass & Stogdill's Handbook,* p. 340.

51. Alan Bullock, *Hitler and Stalin: Parallel Lives* (New York: Alfred A. Knopf, 1992).

52. Robert Albanese, *Managing: Toward Accountability for Performance,* 3d ed. (Homewood, IL: Richard D. Irwin, 1981), p. 377.

53. David McCullough, *The Path between the Seas: The Creation of the Panama Canal—1870–1914* (New York: Simon and Schuster/Touchstone Book, 1977), p. 537.

54. Irving L. Janis, *Groupthink: Psychological Studies of Policy Decisions and Fiascoes* (Boston: Houghton Mifflin Company, 1983), pp. 174–75.

55. Terrence E. Deal and Allan A. Kennedy, *Corporate Cultures: The Rites and Rituals of Corporate Life* (Reading, MA: Addison-Wesley Publishing Company, 1982), pp. 100–101.

56. O'Shaughnessy, *Business Organization,* p. 89.

57. Albanese, *Managing,* pp. 446–48.

58. Johns, *Organizational Behavior,* pp. 149–50. The developer of Theory X and Theory Y was Douglas McGregor.

59. Albanese, *Managing,* p. 48.

60. Bass, *Bass & Stogdill's Handbook,* p. 111.

61. Albanese, *Managing,* pp. 334–38.

62. Bass, *Bass & Stogdill's Handbook,* p. 105.

63. Zuboff, *Age of the Smart Machine,* ch. 10.

64. Kurt Eichenwald, "He Told. He Suffered. Now He's a Hero," *New York Times,* May 29, 1994, Sect. 3, p. 1.

65. O'Shaughnessy, *Business Organization,* p. 143.

66. Ibid., p. 127.

67. Ibid., p. 135.

68. James P. Womack, Daniel T. Jones, and Daniel Roos, *The Machine That Changed the World: The Story of Lean Production* (New York: HarperPerennial, 1991), p. 115.

69. Bass, *Bass & Stogdill's Handbook,* p. 566.

3

An Approach to Corporate Communication

Communication may be formally defined as any process whereby decisional premises are transmitted from one member of an organization to another. It is obvious that without communication there can be no organization, for there is no possibility then of the group influencing the behavior of the individual.

—Herbert A. Simon, *Administrative Behavior*[1]

WHERE WE ARE

Thus far, we have discussed communication and defined business as one of its functions. We defined corporate communication as a function of informational and effective communication. We tied learning, organizational behavior, marketing, structure and information technology to corporate communication. We ended by pointing out the complexity of corporate communication, which starts with a simple event—the economic transaction—and then, like mathematical chaos, develops into ramifications (some supportive and some conflicting). As a result, our discussion has stressed the need for judgment in communication because much is unknown.

Chapter 3 will provide eight guidelines to assess communication, and the rest of this book will apply these guidelines to the elements of corporate communication. The eight guidelines are not definitive. They provide a way to attack communication challenges and come to reasonable decisions (Figure 3.1). They do not guarantee success, but they provide a better than average chance that communication will measurably succeed.

Corporate communication accepts partial knowledge as a human condition. Managers are momentary observers, message senders and regula-

Figure 3.1
An Approach to Corporate Communication: Eight Guidelines

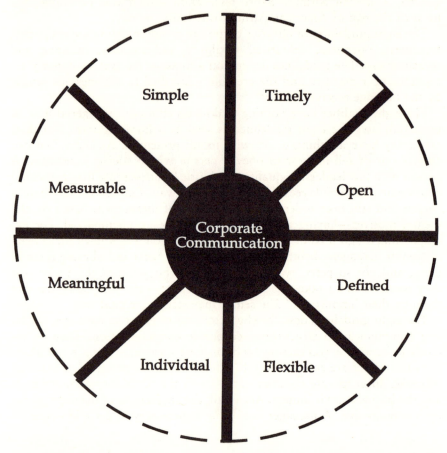

tors. Their insights may advance a company, let it drift or hold it back. Their messages may improve a company or hurt it. Their controls may be too tight or too loose. The business environment may favor them no matter how they blunder or, possibly, work against them no matter what they know. One of the most skilled executives in transportation, Robert Crandall, the CEO of American Airlines, once felt so baffled that he was quoted as saying:

Unless the world changes, we will never buy another airplane. We won't replace the airplanes that wear out. We will never buy an airplane for growth. We can't. We don't make any money with it. So, if you look far enough down the road, when all the airplanes are worn out, the company simply won't be here anymore.[2]

Crandall was widely acclaimed for his farsightedness in understanding how to use information technology as a competitive weapon by placing reservation terminals on travel agents' desks. At the time when Crandall was quoted, American Airlines' Sabre reservation system was profitable, but most of the rest of American Airlines was losing money.

The eight guidelines of effective corporate communication are simplicity, timeliness, openness, definition, flexibility, individuality, meaning and measurement. The guidelines depend on a message receiver's voluntary acceptance of a message and the credibility ascribed to the message sender by the message receiver.

The eight qualities have nothing to do with ethics or managerial style. A barbarian uses the eight guidelines as well as a humanitarian. Nor does credibility have anything to do with moral principles. An individual can choose out of self-interest to obey a person whom society condemns. A person with few leadership qualities and little business sense may command a company, yet employees do their jobs anyway. Employees may hate a person and still take orders. The acceptance of messages is based on elemental motives—having a job is better than being unemployed. For example, one tough boss of an American corporation was known for cursing his senior managers, belittling them in front of peers and abusing them in petty, and not so petty, ways. An observer who watched these men (for they were all men) take this abuse commented, "He [the CEO] has got them by their limousines." The senior managers were paid well.

The eight guidelines describe characteristics of effective messages, media and communication structure in corporate communication. They tie directly to economic transactions and business survival. They are not absolutes but rather are rules of thumb. They balance the precision of material processes in corporate communication with the variability of individuals and the business environment. Above all, the application of the eight guidelines is pragmatic. A manager does what is necessary to get a job done.

SIMPLICITY AND CORPORATE COMMUNICATION

Simplicity means the singular focus of messages and media on survival and success of a company. Simple corporate communication uses both informational and effective message sending. Simplicity:

- Captures every message, perception, fact, response and nuance related to company survival and success;

- Formulates clear, focused and credible messages to gain action supporting company survival and success;

- Builds and maintains the least number of media with the highest carrying capacity to transmit and receive messages that are key to company survival and success;

- Eliminates noise and irrelevant information.

Simplicity relates directly to process design. One looks for the minimum number of processes necessary to stay in business and the maximal information content in each process or set of processes. Simplicity strives to get rid of processes that add no value to final customers and constituencies.[3]

Economically, a business uses the least amount of resources to earn the greatest possible return to maximize wealth. By extension, corporate communication uses the least number of messages and media to capture information, formulate and transmit messages and gain action to maximize wealth.

Simplicity does not ignore human nature. Business process recognizes that one must build into the goal of the organization "ingredients sufficient to change human behavior,"[4] commonality (if possible) and a balance of social and business action.

Simplicity sees corporate communication as a pipeline with a continuous two-way circulation of message and response between the individuals who are key to survival and success and those acting to ensure it. Packets of information and instruction flow through the pipeline in two directions. Some are directly related to one another and some are not. Some are easily manipulated by a manager to gain results, and some are not. All are either directly related to the survival and success of a business or are filtered out as noise.

Simplicity in corporate communication accounts for both verbal and nonverbal communication and for uncertainty and risk. Keeping the medium, message and process simple avoids distortion.

Simplicity works for the clear expression of meaning to give internal and external individuals the best chance of understanding and acting with the least effort. Simple corporate communication is easy to use. Ideally, every user finds, in a simple corporate communication pipeline, the information that he or she needs in order to act. In actuality, few organizations capture all the information needed all of the time because it is difficult to do, expensive and, eventually, is of marginal value. Corporate communication already transmits many kinds of information about:

- accounting and finance
- marketing and customers
- suppliers
- distributors
- competitors
- employees
- company policies, missions, and strategies
- business environment data
- regulatory data

Simplicity uses verbal and nonverbal media and focuses signs, symbols, grammar and semantics on meaning and clarity. It considers organizational and personal geography (one's physical location), personal territory (what one considers to belong to oneself), speech qualities, body language, pragmatics, media, meaning and the nonlingual uses of language.

Simple corporate communication accepts uncertainty, risk and the lack of precise rules by which employees, customers and others make decisions about messages. Corporate communication does not "engineer" consent by manipulating inanimate and unthinking materials. Individuals cannot be constrained to interpret evidence or restrained from accepting facts that are declared out of bounds. There need not be facts, only hearsay, and there need not be rational consideration, only perception. Anyone can vilify an organization fairly or unfairly. No judge will intervene.

That is why simple corporate communication focuses its highest persuasive powers on key individuals and lets the rest of the populace go. Simple corporate communication recognizes that only a few individuals ultimately decide a company's fate and that it must deal with those individuals to survive.

Two factors work against simplicity—the amount of data and data structure. Data floods can wipe out systems that are ill-equipped to handle them. Some information is structured, easily captured and easily stored, such as bookkeeping data. Other information is poorly structured, difficult to capture and almost impossible to classify, such as gossip about competitors and interest groups. Simple corporate communication captures both.

Change complicates simplicity. A simple process implies stability, which change upsets. Corporate communication is like a vascular system, starting with the heart and aortas and then splitting into arteries, which shrink to less than threads before returning the blood, by way of the veins, to the heart. Within this pipeline is constant change and response to change as blood nourishes the tissue and carries away substances that can harm the body. The vascular and corporate communication systems are simple structures with complex tasks.

One might argue this justifies different messages and overlapping media. However, contradictory messages help no one. If messages conflict, misinterpretation grows. If messages contradict each other, the organization goes awry, and if messages are ambiguous, no one will know what to do. The author once reported to two bosses who shared his time, an arrangement that quickly became untenable. Boss A would give the author an order, and then, moments later, Boss B would countermand Boss A and give the author a different order. The standoff was resolved only after the author was assigned permanently to one boss.

Finally, organizations are not simple. They tend toward complexity. It is only through the effort of managers that they remain simple and focused.

Managers may send one clear message to employees, departments, customer segments and interest groups, but individual responses to the message will be diverse and, frequently, at odds with its intent. Simplicity requires ongoing, hard work to adjust messages effectively among message receivers until the feedback agrees with the intent. This is why executing behavioral change in an organization is a matter of years and why simple messages focus on ideals, such as customer service, that are resistant to environmental shifts. It takes time to achieve simplicity with even a simple message. With a complex message, it is more difficult.

Time and Corporate Communication

Time is a fundamental business performance variable. Listen to the ways in which managers talk about what is important to the success of their companies: response *time,* lead *time,* up *time,* on *time.* Time may sometimes be a more important performance parameter than money. In fact, as a strategic weapon, time is the equivalent of money, productivity, quality, and even innovation.[5]

Achieving response time, lead time, up time and on-time depends on timely communication that transmits the parameters in which an activity must be done to achieve economic transactions in time.

• a buyer and seller meet in time;
• goods and value depend on time;
• communication occurs in time.

  In corporate communication, ideal timing delivers information at the exact moment needed to support economic transactions and employees. For example, manufacturers use video terminals that indicate each assembly step as an employee does it, along with help for troubleshooting if something goes wrong. This is perfect timing. Companies can reach ideal timing in structured activity only in cases where all information is known. Delivery companies, for example, have systems that trace packages from pickup to drop-off. A customer can find out where a package is—in a truck, on a plane or in a messenger's pouch and even who signed for it. What a company cannot do, however, is guarantee against the unknown—a delivery truck has an accident, an airplane drops from the sky or an employee simply fails to deliver a package. Some years ago, the author flew into Chicago during a snowstorm. His luggage did not make the plane because of the weather, so the airline promised to deliver his luggage directly to his door the next day. Two weeks later, the luggage still had not arrived. Upon investigation, airline managers discovered that an employee who was charged with returning the luggage had left it in his home while he went away on vacation. One unknown—the employee's vacation—defeated the best efforts of the airline in customer service.

Expanding telecommunications networks have reduced the time needed to transmit messages and elicit feedback. Since the invention of the telegraph and telephone, and with the advent of E-mail, work-group automation, real-time databases, electronic group scheduling and video and audio conferencing, physical, if not cultural, distance has collapsed. Minimizing queue and transport time in message sending maximizes value-added time in understanding, and acting on, a message. Moreover, the results of an action may be known at once when feedback is built into the response.

For example, not long ago, clerks in financial services companies took two or three days to answer customers' questions. In an insurance company, for example, someone would first go to a file room to get a customer's paperwork. This would take a day or more. The clerk had to examine the paperwork, which might take only seconds or minutes, but with other cases under examination, any one customer's paperwork could sit in a file tray for hours. The clerk then phoned the customer, who might or might not be reachable. The clerk would communicate with the customer and answer the question, but if the response generated other questions, the process might begin again. With optical storage and on-line data, however, a customer calls, gets an answer in seconds from one or more clerks and hangs up. The communication is captured immediately on-line for the next clerk who deals with the customer, even if it involves the same question. The author had a wonderful experience with American Express after his charge card was stolen. Each clerk to whom he spoke by phone had a perfect record of his information, including a letter he had written the company explaining the theft. American Express had built a system that immediately put everything about a customer into one database. Gear-up time for communication was eliminated using this system, and the value-added time of communicating with customers and resolving their problems was greatly increased.

Paradoxically, timely communication takes time to achieve. Systems are difficult to build and require huge assets. As databases and processing and storage demands grow, the information technologist must scramble to expand, reorganize and handle the data flows.

In most corporate communication, timing is far from ideal. For example, stores depend on laser scanning to speed checkout and communicate good service to customers. Inevitably, with thousands of stock unit numbers from small screws to plywood panels in a hardware or home center store, there will be uncoded parts that a clerk does not recognize. When this happens, the clerk stops the checkout until someone identifies the item. Short lines become long and waiting periods rise.

Communication timing fails when the business environment changes in chaotic ways, when a competitor changes, when interest groups and in-fluentials change, when systems fail and when credibility questions disrupt timing. In a bank, a branch manager measures customer flow so that an adequate number of tellers can be on duty at peak hours. This is part of a bank's communication of customer service. However, on any given day, customers arrive randomly in clusters. The population standing on line is a jagged curve that rises and falls chaotically and can overburden tellers at one moment and leave them without work the next.

Competitors rush to be first on the market with a new product to com-municate leadership and capture market share, but only one company can be first. The company that comes in second or third must use another rationale to communicate superiority. The author served a company that built a new product for video-on-demand switching. The company had a working prototype before anyone else, but it delayed its announcement for legitimate reasons. During the six-month delay, another company arrived with the same product. The new architecture was suddenly old news, and the company had to work hard to stay ahead.

Until the 1980s, AT&T was known for its record of uptime and faithful, 24-hour-a-day service. Several nationally publicized system failures under-mined the company's record and scared telecommunications professionals who began to search for backup providers—a situation that delighted AT&T's competitor, MCI.

Time is relative in corporate communication. An overwhelming amount of real-time data floods a communication system. Resources devoted to capturing it become enormous and uneconomical. The analytical programs needed to turn data into useful information become increasingly complex and expensive. At some point, the cost of communicating information in real time outweighs the benefit gained from it.

Secondly, real-time communication does not mean that a message re-ceiver can perform a real-time action. Only with preprogrammed actions can responses be instantaneous. Actions requiring an understanding of an out-of-parameter message, such as a broken machine, may require a great deal of delay. Further, some messages do not require instant action, and some actions in response to messages have longer time frames than others.

Periodicity is an important part of timeliness. When a company com-municates daily, weekly, monthly and quarterly results, it transmits the same information in four different time spans. It makes little sense to com-municate a quarterly report at the beginning of a quarter, when little in-formation is known, but daily and weekly reports have great usefulness at that time. Each hour of a normal selling day is a significant fraction of that day. Each day equals 20 percent of a normal five-day week or 14 percent of a calendar week. Even this percentage can be influenced by timing in the business environment. In a restaurant, lunch trade might equal 20 percent of a ten-hour day but 40 percent of total revenue. Downtimes before lunch, after lunch and before dinner have little significance. Here, five or six hours of a ten-hour day may represent 100 percent of revenue.

Because time is relative, analyses covering time spans of months or years may be as critical to communicate as minutes and hours. In design, construction and development, as well as in marketing and public affairs, communication time crosses several business cycles. The development of an oil field may be measured in decades while gas sales from the field may be measured in hours. Similarly, the passage of a law may be measured in years yet the extent of lobbying for or against it is measured in days. Managers simultaneously balance corporate communication against time spans ranging from seconds to years.

The timing of corporate communication requires an intimate understanding of business cycles and the market environment. To assume that all business can benefit from the immediate capture and delivery of data ignores reality. Timeliness is as much a matter of judgment as of fact.

OPENNESS AND CORPORATE COMMUNICATIONS

In corporate communication, openness means that information collected anywhere can be communicated anywhere, and in any direction, to internal or external individuals who need it to support or complete economic transactions. Corporate communication openness is not the same as technological openness. In a management information system (MIS), *open* means common computer and telecommunications hardware so that any manufacturer's equipment and software can work with any other. In the U.S. power industry, there are standard alternating current (AC) wall sockets. Machines run on standard voltages. The wires connecting machines to power are standard in sizes and power ratings. Thus, power delivery and measurement are standard.

An open *technology* organization can be a closed *corporate communication* organization because information is kept from individuals, even though communication media and technology are common to all. One of the prime contributors to closed corporate communication is the "need to know" philosophy, which segments information. Each individual gets only the data needed to do a given task. On the surface, "need to know" appears to be an application of simplicity and timeliness in corporation communication, but it is not. The reason is that managers decide what individuals need to know, and they inevitably focus narrowly on tasks at hand. For organizations to advance, an individual's understanding should broaden to include links among tasks and a sense of a whole process. When individuals are prevented from achieving such an understanding, they cannot contribute more than a given task. There is little room for creative input that might improve a process.

Openness in corporate communication means an ability, when variance intrudes, to reach outside need-to-know barriers and pull in the necessary information. A person who performs a job that is linked to the chaos of the business environment may need information from many sources at any given moment. A sales person calling on a new account will have a sudden need to know as much as possible about the company, its products, the contact person and the decision maker in purchasing. A factory based on just-in-time materials delivery does not work well when systems are subject to large fluctuations of unforeseen demand or supply. For example, toy industry executives learned how poorly just-in-time inventory techniques worked when they underestimated the demand for a popular new toy spawned from a children's television show, *Mighty Morphin Power Rangers*. "The shortage reflects the difficulty of divining the minds of children. Who would have thought that an idea for a TV show repeatedly ridiculed by networks execs for eight years would become the rage?"[6]

Open corporate communication means accessibility, in which the right message reaches the external or internal individual through a proper medium, no matter the need. A corollary of openness is to let individuals speak for themselves about the information, feedback and directions they need. Managers should not assume levels of understanding or capacities of individuals to learn. On the other hand, employees and customers often do not know what communications they need. They may have worked or used a product or service in only one way. Asking such individuals what they need may draw blank expressions or erroneous answers.

For example, marketers know that customers cannot evaluate a product or service they have never seen before. Customers will say they do not need it. Only after trying a product or service will they realize the benefits and provide accurate opinions. A large part of *beta testing* of high-technology products gathers testimony from satisfied customers who act as credible witnesses. Beta testing occurs when a product is first tried with customers in a prerelease version, usually in small numbers to see what works and what does not. It also has been used as a marketing weapon to forestall competitive products, as Bill Gates of Microsoft once did with an early version of the company's Windows product.[7]

Openness is relative based on environment, security, managerial preference and individuals with whom a company communicates. Openness fails when systems fail, when owners are uncomfortable giving out information and employees horde it, when individuals do not know what their tasks are and when there is no clear sense of direction. Openness can expose a company to competitive assault and to criticism from those who disagree with its way of operating.

Openness is dependent on individuals. Some employees handle information well. Others do not, and still others grow from ignorance to understanding. An open system encompasses and integrates all of them. This not only builds a degree of lag into the system, it requires constant managerial attention. With self-managed teams in open work environments, openness presents unusual challenges, such as:

- "Tasks like adding new people get harder not easier."[8] Self-managed teams become closed to communication. They are focused on output and do not want to take time to bring new members up to speed.
- "Supervisors are sorely missed—but not for reasons you'd expect."[9] Managers preserve openness within and among self-managed teams. Teams are supposed to handle all human relations, but when groups spat, either within a team or among teams, they need managers to separate them and communicate with the combatants.
- "Team building doesn't go neatly from one stage to the next."[10] Some teams fail to form because participants cannot work or communicate openly together, while other teams deviate and hide their failures by failing to communicate.

Open communication requires a disciplined examination of the organization and its customers and publics to detect changes that affect survival and success. Analytical techniques become outdated, search engines can no longer cope with masses of data and individuals do not understand what they should be looking for. One of the largest challenges to an open system is that individuals must be trained to use it to their advantage. An open system requires constant self-education, and the manager is as much an educator as a controller.

Open communication means yielding responsibility to subordinates to the extent that they can handle tasks and get the desired results for survival and success. Openness recognizes that individuals learn from experience and should be given information reflecting their abilities and knowledge.

DEFINITION AND CORPORATE COMMUNICATIONS

Defined corporate communication is purposeful communication. It determines who communicates what messages through which media to message receivers who are individually identified both inside and outside an organization. Defined corporate communication is linked directly to the actions needed for survival and success. Definition includes verbal and nonverbal corporate communication, and it divides the merely helpful messages and media from key messages and media. It lets managers focus on fundamentals and cut away communication that wastes time and resources.

Definition starts outside an organization with key customers and constituencies and then progresses toward the inside. The definition of message senders, receivers, messages and media is essential even in a simple economic transaction. The buyer and seller must define themselves as targets for mutual communication. They also define a good or service being sold and the type of wealth to be exchanged. Moreover, by making such definitions, they allow the matching of media and message for maximum effectiveness in completing the sale. Definition has the same purpose as the customer-aided design of products and services, which results in a tailored response to a customer's needs. "It has to do with discerning customer wants better with less intermediate processing, and with less information loss due to a lot of hand-offs of information from one party to another."[11]

If messages and media are not defined continuously in relation to business survival and success, they begin to fail. Committees and meetings proliferate; memos and E-mail spike in number. The system goes into a spiral of messages and responses without action. In a major U.S. financial services firm, mid-level managers once held meetings to define the agendas for meetings. To get anything done, one had to get on the agenda and then into the meeting. The results of the meeting became a communication input to another meeting at a higher or wider level. Thus, the process was divorced from the business of the firm—credit card services.

Definition accepts muddling as a necessary condition of management. Muddling occurs when neither the message nor the medium are precisely clear or defined because the external market environment is unclear. Even the ideally defined communication is only relatively clear. Managers juggle the volume of messages and media against investment, returns and opportunity. A great deal of management is opportunism rather than calculated foresight.

Definition in corporate communication goes wrong when too much time is spent in definition and not enough time in action. Definition is incremental and occurs over time. It is never complete because media, messages and message receivers change before the process of communication is fully defined. Particularly in industries tied to transient phenomena, such as entertainment and fashion, social patterns may change at speeds that do not allow for much more than a swift reaction. Teenagers' tastes in clothing and music may change in a period of only months. Industries selling to teenagers survive through trend spotting and fast footwork or, if they are fortunate, through becoming arbiters of taste who define a message and medium that customers willingly adopt.

Defined corporate communication is also tied to outcomes—economic transactions occurring today and in the future. This requires forecasting and risk, some of which is high. For example, a Hollywood movie studio may spend $50 million on a film and more millions defining audiences, messages and media in order to promote it. The studio executives then wait to see the box office receipts. Hollywood is used to grand slams that carry a studio for years and debacles that return barely a cent.

Defined corporate communication attempts to make risk explicit and easier to manage, but definition deals with two unknowns—the *known unknown* and the *unknown unknown*.

The known unknown might be a person who is a target for media and messages to buy a new product. We may know a great deal about where the ideal customer is located and what the person is like but we do not know the particular individual. Advertising, public relations and promotion try to persuade these people to identify and define themselves in the economic transaction and to become regular customers.

The unknown unknown events are those we cannot forecast or prepare for. These might include an event that destroys any need for our product or service or the loss of an essential supplier. For example, a retailer might stock up on snow shovels in preparation for a snowy winter that may turn out to be unusually mild. Similarly, in the late 1980s, an explosion at a chemical plant in Japan wiped out the only producer in the world of computer chip packaging material. No one had forecasted such an event. Chip manufacturers had to rapidly redefine messages and media to account for the sudden shortages and a rapid rise in prices.

Because messages and media change constantly in response to the environment, definition is always out of date to some degree. That is why manuals with fixed rules have only limited usefulness. Manuals express an ideal of how a company operates, but actual operations, messages and media may be different. Unused manuals are clean, well-preserved communication failures. Messages in manuals only become real in behavior, and it is the managers who instill proper behavior. To the degree that managers do not, they communicate the impression that messages in a manual have marginal usefulness.

The same is true for operating instructions for products and services. Few people read directions, so these are marginal media from the start. That is why engineers put "help" systems on computer screens to encourage users to consult messages about the hardware or software they are using while they are using it. Even so, however, it is still more common for someone with a computer problem to telephone for help rather than click an on-screen help button.

Most of the definition of messages and media is part of oral culture handed from one employee to another. In the U.S. Army the author witnessed the oral culture of supply sergeants on how to run a supply room. The definitions that were passed from one supply sergeant to the next were effective but had little relationship to the well-defined policies of the formal supply system. Noncommissioned officers relied on material swapping and barter, with the result that the army never knew what it had in inventory, or where its inventory was.

Well-defined corporate communication transforms policy into system functionality. Communication becomes part of intended action. This is called designing for human factors—or ergonomics. Human factors designers devise systems that are natural to use in the right way and difficult to manipulate incorrectly. To achieve this physical expression of communication requires knowledge from psychology, engineering, medicine, physiology, anthropology, biology and education.[12]

Training is a part of well-defined communication and serves to guide individuals through the proper behavior until it becomes automatic. For high-risk and critical activities, companies spend millions on simulators to create normal and abnormal events. This is why, for example, astronauts train for a year to undertake a five-day mission in space.

THE INDIVIDUAL AND CORPORATE COMMUNICATION

Corporate communication does not persuade groups. Rather, it persuades individuals, who accept a definition of self and of group norms. Individuals act together in groups but remain individuals.

An unfortunate misnomer of corporate communication is mass media. As newspaper, radio and television ratings show, individuals select mass media individually, as each person buys a paper, turns on a radio or changes a television channel. With abundant media choices, individuals segment themselves by self-interest, tastes, needs and desires. The extent of self-segmentation is visible at any newsstand. There, one finds hobbyist publications, personal computer magazines, fashion books, military pursuits, general information, opinion and hundreds of other topics. As cable television channels grow in number, self-segmentation is occurring in this mass medium as well. Radio splintered long ago, and major cities now have more than 50 AM and FM stations with different formats and listeners.

Mass media describes the distribution of messages but not their reception. To achieve a specified action in accordance with a message, managers should think in terms of individual media. Individual media are ways of sending messages that most persuasively appeal to a specific person and motivate him or her to act in accordance with a seller's or manager's message. This process is well underway in marketing and advertising, as one book on the new methods of research noted: "Technology is returning the individual to the focus of marketing strategy. Technology allows the collection, storage and use of disaggregated data in integrated databases, which has fostered a shift from macro to micro marketing."[13]

Managers can appeal to group norms for action, but they should never forget that below norms and abstractions are unique persons who freely accept or reject messages based on calculations of self-interest and who will either act or not act. Some individuals place their self-interest in the group and organization, while others believe it lies in individual powers of achievement. An organization encompasses both types of person and keeps them linked to a coordinated effort of the whole. Individual corporate communication allows each person to configure information as he or she prefers to receive it and to continue to work for the survival and success of a business.

Figure 3.2
Individual Communication

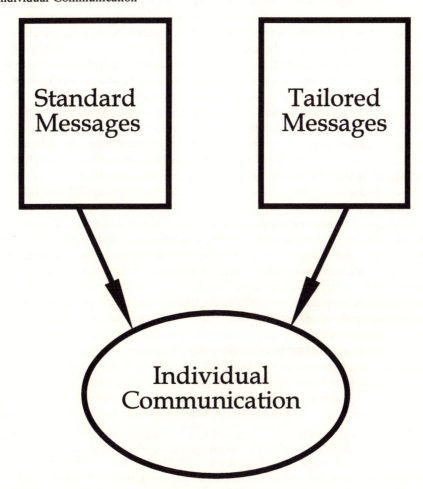

Individual media place personal preference into a mass distribution network. A useful example comes from software that turns text from an online information service into an on-screen newsletter. The software creates headlines, columns, tables of contents and so forth, while the contents of the newsletter can be tailored by each person. Your newsletter tracking the competition in the on-line database may have nothing to do with my newsletter that tracks evolving human relations and benefits policies, yet both look the same.

Individualized corporate communication has some standard messages, but most are tailored to specific needs and desires (Figure 3.2). Among standard messages are company policies, missions and strategies; descriptions and definitions; products and services; personnel roster; addresses and phone numbers; tax identification (ID) numbers; and benefits packages. Individual messages include personal performance measures, customer service contacts, departmental goals and activities, data collection and analysis and links with team members or customers.

In individual corporate communication, managers control two-way communication by person and provide networks and databases whereby individuals can get messages delivered in the way each needs in order to do a job. The field of work-group computing provides hardware and software solutions that allow individuals to communicate in unstructured and ad hoc ways. Managers can schedule events while accounting for individuals and available resources. They can make meetings productive through providing tools that individuals can use at their desks, such as videoconferencing. Managers can conduct conferences and collect information in personalized ways.

One important invention in this field was a software package called Lotus Notes, which is "a document-oriented database system designed to handle loosely structured information."[14] Lotus Notes already allows more than a million employees to structure customized information portfolios for their work.

For some companies, individual communication is not practical, but increasingly, with the decline in cost of central processing units (CPUs), memory storage and media, companies are moving in that direction—and sometimes in surprising ways, as the following excerpt from the *Wall Street Journal* indicates:

Metal Buttons Carried by Crop Pickers Serve as Mini Databases for Farmers

NEW YORK—As much a part of farm life as the bushels of strawberries trucked each spring from Bob Jones Ranch are the dime-sized metal buttons that crop pickers pin to their shirts or drop in a pocket.

Stuffed with a compact semiconductor, the buttons serve as mini databases, telling payroll computers how many boxes of fruit each field worker gathered.[15]

Individual communication fails when managers forget they are dealing with discrete persons, when the medium used does not allow for individualized message sending and when timing does not allow for customization, such as in a crisis or rapidly changing market environment. When managers forget individuals, they become unidimensional in messages and media, but they can still build successful businesses this way by finding like-minded persons. This approach affirms individuality by extracting from a larger population just those persons who agree with a manager's view. On the other hand, individual communication with diverse groups requires close observation, practical psychology and a variety of communication styles. A manager's communication methods can verge on the crude, such as curing a slacker by hanging him out of a window.[16] At other times, one can be deeply sympathetic with the plight of an individual and still order the person to act in a particular way.

FLEXIBILITY AND CORPORATE COMMUNICATION

Flexible corporate communication means that organizations adapt messages, media and audiences, as necessary, to achieve results. An organization avoids committing itself so heavily that it is locked into specific messages and media without fall back.

A major reason for communication flexibility is to change course. When an environment shifts, companies change or die. Firms like Kodak, IBM, American Express, General Motors, Xerox, Honda, Chrysler and USX have restructured, laid off workers and fired CEOs in order to become competitive again.

Regaining flexibility has been at the root of much downsizing and reengineering. For example, major sources of corporate communication, such as marketing, are doing away with hallowed positions like the brand manager.

A recent study by the London branch of Coopers & Lybrand, an accountancy firm, concluded that "marketing as a discipline is more vital than ever" but that the marketing department itself is "critically ill." And in an essay last year, consultants at McKinsey argued that large marketing departments are "often a millstone around an organization's neck." Most companies that have "re-engineered" their production department are now applying the same process-driven logic to their marketing department.[17]

Messages have changed radically inside many corporations. One no longer talks of loyalty, but of efficiency:

The current euphemism is "reengineering"—a bloodless term for corporate bloodletting on an unprecedented scale. In the year's (1994) first quarter, employers announced an average of 3,106 cutbacks per day.

The sight of so many bodies on the corporate scrap heap is sparking a complex debate—about profits and loyalty, and about benefits and unforeseen consequences of layoffs. . . .

Today's corporation is no longer a secure or stable place. It's an uncertain, turbulent environment where managers often find their compassion and humanity in conflict with the pressures of competition and ambition. Fear is almost palpable in the corridors of the reengineered workplace, where loyalty takes a backseat to survival and personal advancement.[18]

Flexibility in corporate communication is an ability to adapt messages and media without jeopardizing survival or success (Figure 3.3). Sometimes, flexibility requires brutal action. Most of the time, however, managers maintain flexibility through daily activity.

Corporate communication is never perfectly flexible. Every message and medium has inertia. Inertia comes from the time, resources and labor invested or affected because of a message. A transmission medium usually cannot be replaced overnight, and individuals often coopt messages directed to them. They become a constituency that can influence company direction. For example, one cannot abandon loyal customers or dedicated employees and expect them not to fight.

Major policy decisions carry enormous inertia and a proportionate loss of flexibility. Even with "downsizing," "rightsizing" or "reengineering," asset sales, layoffs and process changes preclude a company from courses of action that it could have taken. If the environment changes as the company takes a new course, the company may find itself in trouble.[19]

Managers judge the speed of change and design messages and communications accordingly. Their challenge is like that of the captain of an oil tanker who sends orders from the bridge to the engine room for immediate execution but watches the ship respond only minutes later. Captains adjust for the lag in communicating through the system, and managers do so as well. However, when it is possible to redesign the system and reduce lag, the competitive nature of the business environment will almost force this action.

Flexible communication allows for serendipity, fortuitous connections and unfortunate outcomes from using information and media in novel ways. Good managers exploit the opportunities and guard against the threats. Personal computers are an example. Applications of word-processing and graphics systems were discovered and implemented that no one had foreseen when the systems were originally installed. The new applications directly affected the jobs of secretaries and graphic designers. As managers began to use the systems, the numbers of secretaries shrank and their tasks changed from what they were before the 1980s. As graphics programs proliferated, design boards disappeared, and with them, jobs for layout artists. As personal computers (PCs) and software became more powerful, the number of managers needed to control activities diminished. In all cases, the communication distance, response time and flexibility between the CEO and the person working directly with customers and key constituents shrank as the middle was discarded.

Communication flexibility comes from both initial system design and continuous improvement. Continuous improvement comes through systematic examination, feedback and measurement. Managers use several techniques to keep communication systems flexible, such as:

Figure 3.3
Flexibility in Corporate Communication

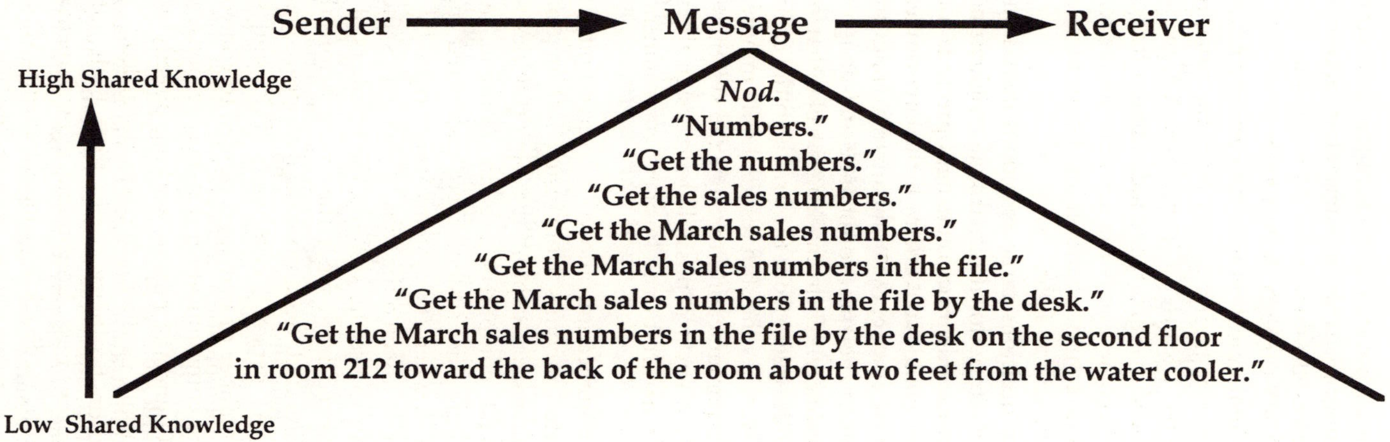

Sender ——▶ Message ——▶ Receiver

High Shared Knowledge

Nod.

"Numbers."

"Get the numbers."

"Get the sales numbers."

"Get the March sales numbers."

"Get the March sales numbers in the file."

"Get the March sales numbers in the file by the desk."

"Get the March sales numbers in the file by the desk on the second floor

in room 212 toward the back of the room about two feet from the water cooler."

Low Shared Knowledge

- Stress testing: managers push communication to see what they can—and cannot—do at the extremes of a crisis or competition. Rehearsal is similar to war gaming or time spent in a simulator.
- Play: this involves experimenting and practicing with productive tools to see what else they do. With new media and technologies, most system capability is never put to use.
- Training: some tasks lend themselves to limited information and maximum activity, while others, such as research and development, are precisely the opposite. Managers train employees to act without thinking sometimes and to think without acting at others.

Communication flexibility accepts diverse skills and management styles. A salesperson is often a loner pitted against the environment. A self-directed manufacturing team depends on group norms and behavior. A CEO may have abundant public duties, while a chief operating officer (COO) may be invisible. Some companies are molded in the image of a top executive, while in other companies, players are the stars. There are also companies that do both, depending on the task. Managers decide on the best approaches and adjust communication accordingly. Flexible communication allows for modification without throwing out messages, media or behavior.

Flexibility in communication goes wrong when tasks require precise communication for long periods, when individuals are inflexible by nature, when customer demands do not allow for flexibility, where materials or events do not allow variance and when a product/service is jeopardized by seeming inconsistency.

Accounting is a precise language in which the medium conveying the message does not change, even though messages do (such as how to account for derivatives in a financial portfolio). Individuals with rigid personalities also show rigidity in communicating, but, if rigidity contributes to successful economic transactions, it can be useful. When customers have a great deal invested in a product or service, they may be inflexible in the type of communication they want to support it. For example, a customer may demand 24-hour-a-day phone service even though the reliability of a machine makes that unnecessary. Some materials and resources demand inflexibility in handling, such as changing uranium rods in a nuclear power–generating station or transporting highly toxic chemicals. In these cases, rigid communication according to strict guidelines is essential. Finally, any product or service in which a seeming inconsistency can harm sales requires inflexibility. Pharmaceuticals are an example. The U.S. Food and Drug Administration precisely regulates what can be said about the efficacy of a drug, and variance opens a company to regulatory retaliation.

Organizations, like all physical processes, tend toward inertia of embedded behaviors, assumed customer needs and wants and self-interest that no longer coincides with the survival of the organization. It takes a great deal of managerial effort to maintain flexibility in observing and communicating both externally and internally.

MEANING AND CORPORATE COMMUNICATION

Meaning is message content—the intent and purpose of a communication. Managers waste time and resources to send messages with no meaning or unclear meaning and no intent. Ideally, every message has one meaning, one subtext and one intent linked to corporate survival and success. However, in practice this is never the case. Every message has multiple meanings and subtexts that come from the message sender, the environment in which a message is sent and the receiver. The manager has two tasks when dealing with meaning: to emphasize the explicit intent of a message and to combat or hammer down subtexts that harm intent.

Meaning, by definition, involves two parties—message senders and message receivers. Both must have enough awareness of each other such that the messages sent have a high likelihood of being received and, once received, of being understood. This is the reason why corporate communication begins with observation. Meaning has the following characteristics:

- it contains the intent and purpose of the message sender;
- it recognizes the capacities, psychology and culture of a message receiver;
- it refers to a task or activity for which the message sender and receiver have mutual interest or responsibility;
- it contributes to an organization's survival and success;
- it is bounded by a mutually understood place and time.

A *meaningful* message is, literally, full of meaning. Managers strip away content that does not contribute to immediate and clear understanding, intent and action. Ideal meaning in corporate communication is directly related to survival and success and ties directly to simplicity and specificity. For example:

- Say the following to the customer because it helps make the sale.
- Run the machine at 1,000 revolutions per minute (rpm) because it increases total output with less maintenance cost.
- Answer the phone before it rings three times because our customers do not like to wait.

Meaningful is a relative term. Sometimes it equals elaborate exercises in message transmission, while at other times, it means using the fewest words. Two examples highlight the differences.

A beer baron held an annual distributor's meeting in San Francisco. The baron had every billboard from the airport to midtown San Francisco—a distance of some 15 miles—plastered with a welcome sign to arriving distributors. When asked why he engaged in such extravagant communication, the baron replied that distributors were the heart of his business. The act of renting every billboard was a meaningful message to distributors of their importance. On the other hand, in a surgery suite, a surgeon will often speak in terse language, saying, "Forceps," or "Clamp." To participants in the surgery, the meaning of the message is clear based on the activity at hand and prior training.

Meaningful communication is tied directly to clear, focused and credible messages. Meaningful content cuts down the number of possible misinterpretations and increases the chances for understanding and compliance. Noise in corporate communication partially comes from a failure of meaningful message transmission, such as:

- communication without clear purpose and targeted ends;
- legacy communication inherited from the past that has not been removed;
- ego communication, designed to bolster an individual;
- ignored communication that nonetheless continues.

Specificity is a part of meaningful messages. Ideally, the message sender identifies and sends the exact content that carries the most meaning in the least time. When understanding is lacking, meaning is lost or message senders and recipients speak in parallel: "He said . . . , but I thought he meant. . . . Meanwhile, he thought I meant. . . . We went round and round for a while." Specificity is bounded by:

- Space: sending messages from a distance increases the chance of misunderstanding.
- Time: message content either matches the activities of message receivers or is data without value.
- Individuals: message content directed to individual understanding and perception has the highest chance of reception.
- Content: some messages carry more meaning than others, especially messages that deal with immediate and fundamental issues such as personal security.
- Intent: the message receiver must understand enough of a message sender's intentions for a message to have meaning.
- Medium: the verbal and nonverbal means of message sending define the detail necessary to transmit it. Face-to-face communication is superior to all other forms because the transmission communicates a symphony of verbal and nonverbal cues with immediate feedback. As one moves away from direct transmission, specificity demands different levels of detail based on the medium and complexity of a mes-

sage. Economy in the use of the medium also amplifies the message content that the medium carries. For example:

Data graphics should draw the viewer's attention to the sense and substance of the data, not to something else. The data graphical form should present the quantitative contents. Occasionally artfulness of design makes a graphic worthy of the Museum of Modern Art, but essentially statistical graphics are instruments to help people reason about quantitative information.[20]

Much communication founders on a failure to define terms and meanings. On the other hand, negotiation, which is an essential part of business communication, often depends on the avoidance of exact meanings over which parties cannot agree. Two companies may consent to a cooperative merger but avoid questions concerning who will lead the combined entities and what departments and activities will survive or be closed or spun off. The communicators know, or should know, that hard decisions lie ahead, but to gain acceptance for the merger, they obscure its consequences.

At task levels, meaning has to specify where individuals take explicit actions contributing directly to company survival and success. At policy levels, meaning can be generic, with leeway for individuals to apply content to their tasks. Generally, detail is preferable because it leaves little doubt about what one is to do. However, specificity can be stultifying and resented when it treats individuals like machines rather than thinking beings. Too much detail carries with it a subtext that a message recipient is not to be trusted.

The level of detail is a manager's judgment call. When one is learning to operate a machine, a detailed step-by-step guide is often necessary. However, once a person has learned to operate the machine, he or she will prefer a more generic guide or no guide at all. The benefit of self-paced task learning is that it lets individuals proceed without holding them to average group speed or, worse, the pace of the slowest person. Meaning calls on all a manager's skills in observation and message formulation.

Meaning fails when there are mismatches of sender and receiver, media, or of the common understanding between sender and receiver. It fails when there are subcultures that interfere with a company's overall mission, when there is a credibility gap and when there is poor message encoding and decoding.

The avoidance of mismatches is the major reason for observation before message formulation and communication. The presence of subcultures in business is part of multilingualism discussed earlier. Subcultures continue to plague business communication.

Management gurus of the 1980s did their best to convince corporate America that corporate culture is a uniform force, a single rudder that guides organizations. . . .

Enter the pragmatic 1990s. The same consultants now realize that corporate culture isn't a single engine driving the boat; it more closely resembles a collection of oars paddled by employees who have conflicting ideas about the daily course of business.[21]

Any act to clarify intent is open to question when there is a credibility gap between managers and employees. The successful owner of an auto-body company, Jim Graley, discovered this the hard way in his effort to transform his company into an "employee-involved" organization with state-of-the-art technology.

In the spring of 1989 Jim introduced a program that tipped the scales—from a few missteps to a question of character, as his employees saw it. The innovation was part of Jim's master plan: computerizing the workplace. He wanted to use information technology to gain a competitive advantage, just as he had read countless companies had done to great bottom-line benefit. It was a decision that sealed his fate with most of his longtime employees. "He thought the computer was a secret weapon," says body man Greg Ellis, who had been at Graley's for a year. To Ellis, however, it appeared to be "a clever way to lie."[22]

Graley lost five of his eight original employees in the upheaval that followed. Graley's employees saw the computer as a way of cutting compensation for work rather than boosting efficiency, and when employees saw a paper shredder installed in the office, they decoded its presence as proving their worst fears. The effort to improve the company nearly sank it because of misunderstandings over meaning. Meaningful communication requires constant effort, refinement and modification to fit the circumstances.

MEASUREMENT AND COMMUNICATION

Communication either contributes to, or detracts from, economic transactions and corporate survival. There is no neutral communication. All communication uses resources and competes for attention. If messages have no value, they waste time and money and distract individuals from communication that results in economic transactions and survival. A continuing challenge faced by advertisers is to get consumers to pay attention to advertisements *and* to buy the product. Television commercials that consumers prefer do not necessarily translate into sales at the checkout counter.

Seven packaged-goods brands were among the 25 consumer products identified by Video Storyboard Tests Inc. as having the most popular and best remembered commercials of 1993. Five of those brands, however, had either flat or declining sales last year in supermarkets, drugstores and mass-merchandise outlets, according to Information Resources Inc.'s InfoScan service.[23]

Measurement is the only way to learn what corporate communication works and what does not. Ideally, managers boost expenditures for communication that works and eliminate communication that fails. In actuality, it is never easy to isolate any one communication or medium as there is too much intertwining of audiences, media and messages.

Measurement is evidence about which two or more independent observers can reach agreement. In science, the proof of an experiment is that it can be replicated in more than one laboratory. The ultimate business measurement is a sale or support from key constituencies. The challenge managers face is to measure how *this* corporate communication works compared to other types. Measurement requires:

- Simplicity: what is measured should connect directly to corporate survival and success.
- Definition: what is measured must first be defined.
- Openness: what is measured must be known to those who are held responsible for its accomplishment.
- Individuality: a person held responsible for communicating effectively has to know what he or she is held to.
- Timeliness: late measurement is no measurement at all. Measurement is simply a basis for further action and not an end in itself.
- Meaning: it is easy to measure elements of corporate communication. However, it is difficult to measure contributions to survival and success.

The challenge of achieving these parameters in corporate communication lends credence to sunset provisions for communication. Sunset provisions get rid of media or messages after a specific time period to check their usefulness. If a company can operate successfully without a communication, it is evidence that the communication was never, or is no longer, needed. However, measurement by subtraction, which is what sunset provisions amount to, is a blunt instrument.

There are three challenges to measurement: inertia, management preference and deciding what to measure. Media and messages take on lives of their own and roll on long after their usefulness ends. Company magazines and newsletters are an example. Many have no value beyond someone's desire to have a publication. Editors write, print and distribute them with little idea of who reads the information, whether readers believe the stories and whether the information supports company goals. The excuse for keeping such publications is that they take little time and cost, but publications take time for editors to produce, and they can distract managers, employees and customers from more important tasks. Increasingly, editors of internal media have taken steps to ensure that publications support organizational goals, yet many still do not.

Management preference is a tough challenge. A CEO may order something to be communicated in a certain way without a clear reason for doing
so and with little apparent understanding of the impact on target individuals. The net result may be wasted time and effort, an audience that fails
to get a message and a risk of a message backfiring into conflicting interpretations.

Annual reports to shareholders are an example of a medium in which
management preference frequently overrides measurement. An annual report reprises results of the previous year. In reality, these reports are often
exercises in self-justification and art design, with little thought given to
readers or credibility. There are time-honored approaches, such as:

- The bad year report: a simple, black-and-white publication is used to avoid criticism of expenses and imply a company's desire to do better.

- The division report: each division takes a section to recite accomplishments, explain failures and announce direction.

- The product report: copy and photos feature glamour shots of company goods
  and services.

- The theme report: copy and photos focus on an announced company policy or
  direction and show how each sector of the organization supports it.

- The compliance report: A mandated 10-K report to the U.S. Securities and
  Exchange Commission is stapled into a cover along with bare-bones text and
  little explanation.

Writers, designers and CEOs pay little attention to what target audiences
are likely to accept. Often, they attempt to sell a viewpoint unilaterally
without measurement.

Deciding what to measure is probably the greatest challenge. One can
measure the wrong elements precisely and the right elements not at all.
Managers have only partial control over a message and medium. Since the
understanding and acceptance of messages relies on the free will of the
message receivers, a sender can do everything right but still fail to communicate effectively (Figure 3.4). A communicator has to be persistent and
be ready to try more than one message and medium until an audience
understands, if it is going to. Measurement may distinguish a fruitful from
a fruitless approach, but it also might not if the measurement incorporates
extraneous elements. One might credit a brilliant marketing campaign for
the rise in sales of four-wheel-drive utility vehicles and ignore the fact that
it was the worst winter on record that lifted sales of all four-wheel-drive
utility vehicles.

Measurement should isolate the medium and the message from the environment, which is not easy. Consumer products are launched with advertising and promotion campaigns yet fail miserably in the market. In fact,

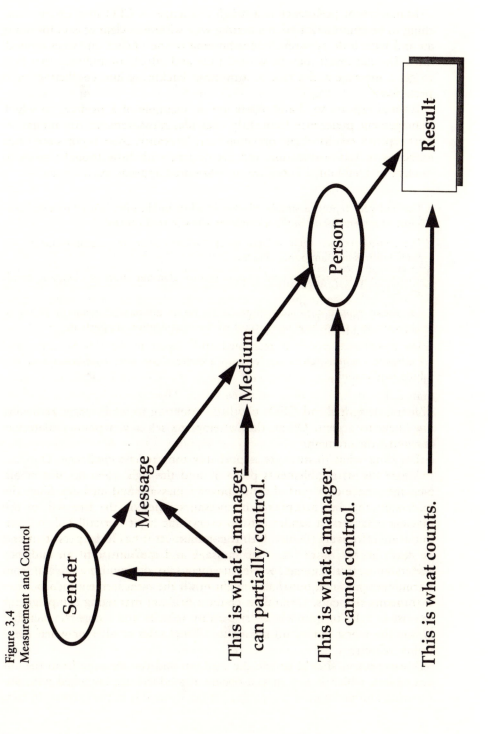

Figure 3.4
Measurement and Control

Sender

Message

Medium

This is what a manager
can partially control.

Person

This is what a manager
cannot control.

Result

This is what counts.

most new products fail to find a permanent spot on a store shelf. A manager could blame the failure on communication or the company, for launching the product to begin with. Measurement may not indicate precisely where the failure occurred.

There are two times for measurement—before sending a message and after. Before transmission, measures are forecasts. Afterwards, measures are historical. Managers use both types to reduce risk, but they do not necessarily increase certitude. Pretransmission measurement can actually increase risk, if not carefully done. An oft-cited example of prelaunch mismeasurement was the introduction of a new formulation of Coca-Cola. The company claimed it had conducted a million taste tests that showed a clear preference for the new Coke. Apparently, however, it did not realize that it had built a strong constituency for the traditional taste. It was the traditionalists who raised the outcry that brought back "classic" Coca-Cola.

Posttransmission measurement becomes miscommunication if managers spin theories for failure or success without adequate evidence. Engineers have learned in failure analysis that the reason why a system broke may be subtle at best and thus may require a great deal of observation before a probable answer is found, but the market and public opinion may not provide enough time to learn probable reasons why something did not work.

Union Carbide assembled a team of chemists and engineers after the Bhopal, India, chemical spill and charged the team to find out how more than 2,000 Indian citizens had been killed. The team did arrive at a plausible answer which involved sabotage by an employee. By then, however, it was months too late. The Indian government and public opinion had convicted the company of direct responsibility for the worst industrial accident in recorded history. Thus, measurement had little meaning.

Measurement establishes a point of evidence in a universe of possible messages and media. The point helps managers adjust communications directionally toward effective results. Negative outcomes are as good as positive ones. However, behavioral measurement is never precise. It is relative to the environment in which the target audiences live. Human nature is not as static as the properties of materials. One can measure a carbon atom and make a statement that will be true years from now, but with humans, a communication approach that works today may fail tomorrow.

Measurement does not have to be formal. It can be a matter of observing an audience while speaking, by talking informally to message recipients or in any number of other ad-hoc ways. The danger of such informal measurement is that it becomes more inaccurate as the number of message receivers grows. With large groups, a quick, nonscientific sample of opinion can be less useful than no measurement at all. Nonetheless, managers take personal observation more seriously than randomly selected interviews with faceless survey subjects, and they have good reason to do so. All measurement instruments look for certain answers, but direct observation provides undifferentiated data that may contain clues that measurement instruments miss. This is a reason why "management by walking about" involves simultaneous communications and measurement. Managers see for themselves how work is done, and they have a chance to communicate policy and direction as employees act.

Measurement goes wrong for all the reasons cited here, but also for a more fundamental reason. The people who measure can bring biases to their work that distort how they operate. Measurement requires a careful and objective analysis of the facts at hand. Questions asked in a leading manner will get exactly the results to which an interview subject was led. Unasked questions do not get answered. Overreliance on techniques can cause bias if the technique is pushed beyond its limits. For example, focus groups have often been used as the basis for action when it has long been clear that at best, they are trend indicators of how some people are thinking at a point in time and not necessarily indicative of how all individuals in a target group are thinking at the present time. In measurement, as in other professional disciplines, the manager must retain a sense of judgment about the results being presented.

SUMMARY

If there is one message to take from this chapter, it is to investigate before you speak.

Managers avoid much failure in corporate communication when they build messages on facts rather than perceptions of the business environment. Corporate communication is built on patterns of thinking that "have not altered substantially since emergence of the human race."[24] These include assessing and clarifying, identifying cause and effect, making choices and anticipating the future. The guidelines resting on these patterns are:

- simplicity
- timeliness
- openness
- definition
- flexibility
- individuality
- meaningfulness
- measurement

NOTES

1. Herbert A. Simon, *Administrative Behavior: A Study of Decision-Making Processes in Administrative Organization*, 2d ed. (New York: The Free Press, 1957), p. 154.

2. Stephen D. Solomon, "The Bully of the Skies Cries Uncle," *New York Times Magazine*, September 5, 1993, Sect. 6, p. 13.

3. Richard Tabor Greene, *Global Quality: A Synthesis of the World's Best Management Methods* (Milwaukee, WI: ASQC Quality Press, 1993), p. 69.

4. Ibid., p. 75.

5. George Stalk, Jr., and Thomas M. Hout, *Competing against Time: How Time-Based Competition Is Reshaping Global Markets* (New York: The Free Press, 1990), p. 39.

6. Joseph Pereira, "Tough Game: Toy Industry Finds It's Harder and Harder to Pick the Winners," *Wall Street Journal* 222, no. 121 (December 21, 1993): A1.

7. Stephen Manes and Paul Andrews, *Gates: How Microsoft's Mogul Reinvented an Industry—and Made Himself the Richest Man in America* (New York: Doubleday, 1993), p. 227.

8. John Case, "What the Experts Forgot to Mention," *Inc.* 15, no. 9 (September 1993): 66. For an examination of self-managing teams at XEL Communications, Inc.—a maker of custom circuit boards—see p. 67.

9. Ibid., p. 68.

10. Ibid., p. 70.

11. Greene, *Global Quality*, p. 79.

12. Peggy Tillman and Barry Tillman, *Human Factors Essentials: An Ergonomic Guide for Designers, Engineers, Scientists, and Managers* (New York: McGraw-Hill, 1991), pp. 4–13.

13. David J. Curry, *The New Marketing Research Systems: How to Use Strategic Database Information for Better Marketing Decisions* (New York: John Wiley and Sons, 1993), p. 4.

14. Gail Shaffer, "Coping with Change," *PC Magazine* 13, no. 11 (June 14, 1994): 146.

15. Mark Boslet, "Metal Buttons Carried by Crop Pickers Serve as Mini Databases for Farmers," *Wall Street Journal,* May 31, 1994, p. A11A.

16. General H. Norman Schwarzkopf, *The Autobiography: It Doesn't Take a Hero* (New York: Bantam Books, 1993), p. 89.

17. "Business: Death of the Brand Manager," *Economist* 331, no. 7858 (April 9, 1994): 67–68.

18. John A. Byrne, "The Pain of Downsizing: What It's Really Like to Live through the Struggle to Remake a Company," *Business Week*, no. 3370 (May 9, 1994): 61.

19. Solomon, "Bully of the Skies." Robert Crandall's experience at American Airlines, mentioned previously, is a near-perfect example of a company committing itself to a direction that proved wrong in the end.

20. Edward R. Tufte, *The Visual Display of Quantitative Information* (Cheshire, CT: Graphics Press, 1984), p. 91. See also Edward R. Tufte, *Envisioning Information* (Cheshire, CT: Graphics Press, 1990). These books analyze details and di-

mensionality of graphical excellence. Tufte espouses integrity in information transmission and minimalism.

21. Shari Caudron, "Subculture Strife Hinders Productivity," *Personnel Journal,* December 1992, p. 60.

22. Elizabeth Conlin, "Collision Course," *Inc.,* December 1992, p. 140.

23. Laura Bird, "Marketscan: Loved the Ad. May (or May Not) Buy the Product," *Wall Street Journal,* April 7, 1994, p. B1.

24. Charles H. Kepner and Benjamin B. Tregoe, *The New Rational Manager* (Princeton, NJ: Princeton Research Press, 1981), p. 21.

4

Understanding the Business Environment

Managers may be conductors, but, if so, they are as much controlled by the orchestra, the audience, and the sponsors as they are the controllers. Managers live in a world of tensions, constantly balancing one factor against another.
—David Kroenke, *Management Information Systems*[1]

WHERE WE ARE

We have described eight guidelines to help managers assess and select effective corporate communication messages and media. These eight guidelines connect directly to effective and informational communication. They also connect to internal and external characteristics of corporate communication.

The remainder of this book looks at components of corporate communication in greater detail. We start with the business environment because that is the location of:

- wealth and resources
- customers
- power bases of key constituencies
- competitors
- economic transactions

Environment describes the internal or external persons, events, ideas, behavior or perceptions that present barriers and opportunities to wealth.

Inevitably, the marketplace is unfriendly, if not hostile. A seller starting out in business has no record of success or proof that his or her product or service is as good or better than others in the market. A seller first has to build credibility. Only later does selling become easier—but it rarely stays easy. To paraphrase Clausewitz, the commentator on war, business is an effort to persuade a customer to do our will: To quote Clausewitz, it is also "an act of force to compel our enemy to do our will."[2] "Our enemy" is a competitor, or other social or economic force, that would take a customer from us through superior persuasion. Corporate communication is part of competitive strategy, and "the essence of formulating competitive strategy is relating a company to its environment."[3]

However, unlike those who see competitive strategy primarily as opposition of industries, a corporate communicator speaks to all the social and economic forces that have direct power over a company's survival and success. The corporate communicator is responsible for fostering friendship, where it can be had, and for reducing opposition.

CORPORATE COMMUNICATION AND ENVIRONMENTAL CHANGE

The first step in corporate communication is observation. Corporate communication interprets the business environment to help sellers adapt and succeed. Observation is both proactive and reactive. Reactive observation captures and classifies data as profitable opportunities or threats, while proactive observation reaches into the business environment to find profitable ways to take advantage of it and reduce threats to company survival. Both types of observation require analysis. The reactive observer must understand how to classify data, while the proactive observer must understand how to put data together for strategic advantage. Proactive and reactive observation thus work together.

For example, managers use computerized decision support systems, which combine analytics and information, to understand how to set pricing. Decision support systems work partly from data gathered reactively during transaction processing. The tasks that decision support systems perform, however, are pro-active. They familiarize managers with the scope of a business challenge by defining the links between work processes. Moreover, they define the extent of change in results when a manager manipulates one or more variables behind the result. They also:

- identify patterns in data;
- predict outcomes;
- develop models of business processes;
- calculate optimum mixes of labor, resources and equipment;

• make communications easier among disparate groups through defining common-alities to which all can agree.

Each of these tasks results in corporate communication directing economic action.

The difficulty with observation is that everything in the marketplace is in a state of flux. Corporate communication cannot afford to assume that any environmental element will remain stable. Therefore, it monitors any internal or external persons, events, ideas, behavior or perceptions that may threaten or enhance a company's survival and success. However, corporate communication must work within economic limitations. No company has the resources, time or need to document or monitor everything.

The challenge with collecting, storing and analyzing data is that one can gather an enormous amount of useless information and yet miss what is necessary. A company can never know what it will need in the future nor what events might change its need for data. Nor is data alone satisfactory. What is done with the data makes the difference between success and fail-ure. Analysis ultimately requires humans who know what to look for: tech-nology will never completely replace human judgment.

The same person is rarely suitable for both reactive and proactive ob-servation. That is why organizations need personalities who dedicate them-selves to one type of analysis. Even highly educated individuals cannot make the transition from one mode to the other, as the medical profession learned when it tried to retrain medical specialists to work as general pri-mary care doctors.[4]

Information from the environment is either hard or soft. Hard infor-mation falls into logical and rational structures, like numbers; soft infor-mation does not. Business deals with both the rational and irrational: "It is impossible for the behavior of a single, isolated individual to reach any high degree of rationality."[5] The reason is that a person must examine too many alternatives requiring too much information. As a result, people work with assumptions and adjust behaviors within these assumptions. Only oc-casionally are individuals able to break out of the limitations of assump-tions and pursue entirely new directions.

Every organization has limits imposed on its rational processes. Some information cannot be verified through logical analyses, statistics, cause-and-effect diagrams, control plots, pareto charts, matrices or surveys. Cause-and-effect thinking frequently reaches data limits in observation, and usually there is not enough time to gather missing information, even with enormous research sources at hand. Clausewitz, in his treatise on war, de-scribed the challenges that generals face with environmental observation. His description applies as well to managers trying to formulate proper mes-sages to guide organizations.

Many intelligence reports in war are contradictory; even more are false, and most are uncertain. What one can reasonably ask of an officer is that he should possess a standard of judgment, which he can gain only from knowledge of men and affairs and common sense.[6]

A manager uses judgment to create enough information at any one time in order to maintain economic transactions and ensure survival and success. The information generated is often local knowledge—specific observations that subtly tilt probabilities for or against the effort to communicate persuasively. For example, a CEO of a major computer software company would not listen to a presentation that did not make its case in three points. Any more than three points, the CEO believed, was excessive. Outsiders who did not know the CEO's belief fared badly in communicating to him. One role of an organization's information technology system is to be a well of structured and unstructured environmental observations, out of which actionable messages can be drawn.

Observation itself is not knowledge. The primary definition of knowledge is a clear and certain perception of something. The tertiary definition of knowledge is practical experience, or skill. Business is a practical skill that translates data into profitable activity. Knowledge in business includes an ability to make economic transactions based on certitude about observations (Figure 4.1). Ability requires practice, and managers are responsible for maintaining business knowledge through training and leadership.

Knowledge becomes a message that directs specific economic action. Learning without economic result has value only insofar as it is perceived as an exploitable economic resource. Knowing the moon is rich in silicates and iron is useless if one cannot mine the moon to make steel and glass. Similarly, knowing that manganese nodules lie on the bottom of deep ocean trenches is useless unless the nodules can be dredged and then sold at a price greater than the cost of dredging. Many discoveries are put on a shelf until a company decides what it can do with them. This presents a conundrum. One never knows when a business opportunity might arise from seemingly valueless knowledge. To limit environmental observation is to cut off potentially profitable avenues, but a company has limited resources and so must limit its activity in order to survive. A greater conundrum involves limiting investigation within boundaries. A company might limit market research to competitors' communication activities. Then, it might limit investigation to competitors' share of voice—the amount spent on advertising—and miss promotional, public relations, direct and other forms of communication. Developing business knowledge, even within boundaries, is like peeling an onion: there is always another layer below.

Because a company is limited in resources, learning is incremental. A company starts at some point, often with little preplanning. Over time, a seller learns the subtle facts of the marketplace. Some sellers strike paydirt

Figure 4.1
Knowledge in Business

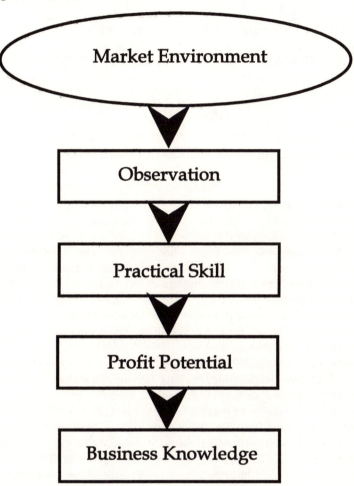

and build large companies, but they are few. Most sellers either grow slowly, stagnate, wither or die.

CORPORATE COMMUNICATION AND CHANGE

Business environmental change may be negligible, immediate (as in a crisis) or delayed. A classic example of delayed change involves IBM, which degenerated from fearsome competitiveness to committees that "nonconcurred" in the face of fast-moving technological developments.[7] Because knowledge is relative and limited, change is a normal part of business and does not represent a loss of control. Change differs by division, department and individual. A manager can never be satisfied that all change has been directed to productive ends, and in fact, the opposite is true.

A manager's attitude about change distorts environmental observation because managers have power over the livelihood of the employees who tell managers about shifting events. Managers who:

• fear change, communicate fear;

• reject change, communicate rigidity;

• welcome change as opportunity, communicate false optimism;

• balance good and bad in change, communicate a need to think about the meaning of events.

Managers' stances toward change may be involuntary, due to their natures, or deliberate, to get results. A manager may appear to fear change in order to energize employees for major decisions. Managers can reject messages about change because a fledgling direction might be stifled too soon. They may adapt a sense of false optimism to buck up employees or take a balanced approach because the environment allows it. Change with large, immediate effects, such as disaster, is more beneficial from a management communication point of view because clear and present danger sends an overpowering message. Subtle change is nearly invisible and, as a result, can be dangerous.

Managers keep mental change and watch lists and update both constantly. A change list documents shifts among individuals inside or outside an organization and among events, ideas, behavior or perceptions that directly affect a company or market in the present. A watch list includes shifts among those individuals inside or outside an organization and among events, ideas, behavior or perceptions that might affect a company or market at any time in the near future. Although such lists should be written, many managers rarely have time to record observations and, regrettably, it means that they leave employees and customers uninformed and less able to act.

Companies possess many environmental observations in recorded form, but records are rarely synthesized and communicated. There is too much data and too much isolation among divisions, departments and individuals. Expert knowledge that might be useful to many never leaves the department in which it originated.

A case in point occurred in a Big Six accounting firm. An accountant who needed a valuation service hired an outside firm. A few days later, the accountant received a phone call from a partner in another city who asked why the accountant had hired an outside firm when valuation services existed in-house. The accountant had not known that services existed in-house, and the firm had no directory that one could consult to find out. Organizational learning involves relearning as much as new subjects.

Change includes unknown outcomes. Because unknown outcomes carry both risk and opportunity, managers balance the two factors in communication. They avoid communicating positions that lock them into a future. Proclamations to "stand or die" make great theater but not necessarily great survival. Usually, such statements are made when the hope of survival has dimmed. Change usually induces caution in leadership, but not always. A tenet of warfare and business alike is to take an enemy by surprise through the unforeseen disposition of forces and resources. This requires secrecy and speed.[8]

Mature managers welcome change and master it. However, all managers bring with them personality differences, quirks and behavioral patterns that can change how employees react.

One ex-employee recalls that [Steve] Jobs [cofounder of Apple Computer and founder of Next Computer] was so demanding that, on principle, he would often reject anyone's work the first time it was shown to him. To cope with this unreasonableness, workers deliberately proffered their worst work first, saving their best for subsequent presentation, when it would have a better change of satisfying the boss's expectations. Says a former Next executive: "Being around Steve is a reality distortion."[9]

Managers' conclusions about the business environment are the basis of the messages they shape and send. They use induction and deduction built on fact and perception. Facts are verifiable persons, events, ideas, behaviors or perceptions. A fact is historical: it has occurred and been substantiated. Two or more independent observers can agree that the same meaning is contained in it. Perception is awareness of the business environment through the media of the senses. It is based on immediacy—what I currently see, hear, taste, touch and smell, as interpreted through my personal behaviors and biases. It is not based on historical facts. Perception may be accurate, inaccurate or distorted.

It is a fact that the Sears Tower in Chicago is 110 stories tall. Two or more people can count the floors and arrive at 110. It is also a fact that the Sears Tower is 1,454 feet in height. However, it is perception to assert that the Sears Tower does not look tall or that it dominates the Chicago skyline.

Managers must be careful to distinguish what it is they do. Perceptions are not laws, but facts can be. Especially concerning humans, there are few, if any, laws of motivation or action on which managers can depend. If one knows the height of the Sears Tower, one can draw conclusions about the parameters of wind resistance, load-bearing structure and transportation needs. However, one cannot conclude how people will elect to travel between floors or how they will react to the tower's sway in high winds or fears about building collapse should a terrorist explode a bomb in the basement.

In the haste to get business tasks done, basic distinctions are often forgotten and failures of logic are common. Most managers deal with hypotheses in daily activity because they have insufficient time to gather facts they need. A manager can often, but not always, safely speculate with some accuracy about survival, social acceptance and personal growth motivations in specific individuals. However, there are persons for whom basic needs and extrinsic motivation have little meaning, and they pursue their own visions.

A manager's job is not to understand others but to get them to act. The seller's job is not to understand the buyer but to complete an economic transaction. When theories prove useful, managers use them in communication. When they do not, managers drop them. Hypotheses are limited in what they explain. They are abstract and represent potential directions. Abstraction can rise to many levels, but each rise causes a loss of environmental data. Managers who deal only at abstract levels lose touch with business. This may be one reason why the field of strategic planning has had ups and downs. Strategic planners who are isolated from direct contact with the business environment often derive abstract conclusions so divorced from daily reality that movement in a particular direction is difficult, if not impossible. Hence, corporate communication based on these conclusions is doomed from the start.

The author remembers a lecture on strategic planning given by a planner from a major paper company. This person used a four-box matrix in which market shares were represented by diameters of circles. Observers noticed that the dimensions of circles changed dramatically from year to year, which seemed unlikely because of the size of the business. When asked why this was so, the planner commented that business managers kept redefining market share in order to move out of the low-growth/low-return quadrant of the four-box matrix. Strategic planning in this case was gamesmanship, which had little to do with running the business. The game was how to communicate to the strategic planner the importance of a business segment.

When there is consensus on environmental facts, communication is easier, but there will rarely be consensus. However, there is a process for moving toward agreement. The first step is to collect and store relevant facts continually about key areas. The second step is emphasize rational investigation and decision making within the limits of the information that one has available. A constant effort to remain objective will cut through opinion and hypothesis. Rationality focuses on the known without dismissing the possibility of the unknown. Objectivity also accepts occasions when perceptions are factual. The third step is to rank information. Some

Figure 4.2
Message Decision Sheet

Message:_____

_____

Facts Needed	Consensus	Open	Sources

Open Issues: _____

_____

_____

_____

facts are essential, and the manager should focus on them. For example, on a "message decision sheet," place critical facts under the headings "Facts Needed" (Figure 4.2). Mark your colleagues' agreements under a "consensus" column. If critical information is missing, mark the "open" column. Use the "sources" column to note where facts might be found. "Open issues," at the bottom of each sheet, lists policy disagreements that may change the facts and messages. The fourth step is to stay action-oriented. Managers must make and communicate decisions, even when key facts are not available by any economic or ethical means. In these cases, managers must listen, make judgment calls and act.

Managers fly blind more often than they wish. However, when they do so, they should know that this is the case. There is nothing worse than running headlong into a problem without the slightest idea of what to communicate. Maintaining a rational and balanced focus is a partial solution to observing the business environment. Individuals and departments are inexhaustible in developing business environment interpretations. The endless stream of scenarios and possible outcomes can bog down a business and stop all action. It is the manager's job to keep things moving.

There are many instances in business in which competitors bluff opponents by manipulating perception. Everything seems to be as it appears, but it is not. One may be fooled by canvas tanks and rubber cannons, as were German aviators over England during World War II. Several kinds of perceptual distortion inhibit corporate communication, including:

- Sense: eyewitnesses rarely agree. Usually, events happen too quickly to perceive or an individual's brain does not accept an experience. Investigators know to question the accuracy of eyewitness reports. In accidents or sudden events, most people concur with only the broad outlines of an event, such as, "The plane crashed," "There was shooting and a person fell down," or "A man entered the house with a gun and is still there."

- Sequence: people assign meaning to unfolding events based on how they unfold. Filmmakers learned early that the juxtaposition of images conveyed perceptual meaning. An image of an ugly, old man juxtaposed with a picture of a beautiful, young woman was interpreted by observers as lustful. The same old man juxtaposed with a picture of a table filled with food was read as hunger. Soviet filmmakers were skilled in this form of montage.[10]

- Human nature: humans assign reasons to events in order to maintain control over the unknown or unreasonable. During rapidly occurring events, conclusions are drawn faster than the evidence warrants. This is also known as causative distortion.

- Responsibility: humans assign causes to other humans because chaos is uncomfortable. Much tort law is built on the premise that a manufacturer "should have known" that a product or service could cause harm at some point in the future.

- Wish fulfillment: consciously or unconsciously, humans select perceptions that support their biases. It is unpleasant to deal with facts that question one's personal "answers."

Perception equals fact when a majority of key observers perceive an event in the same way and the perception affects survival and success. This has nothing to do with accuracy. Managers who refuse to accept the power of perception will fail as communicators. They may have facts to support their views, but when customers refuse to buy a product or service, perception wins. For example, chewing gum companies have been victimized by children's rumors about spider eggs in packages of gum. This seems absurd, but children buy gum. Consumer goods companies have been hit by allegations of foreign objects in cans and bottles—syringes, glass, nails, bandages and poison. Sometimes, the companies have been at fault, but other times, they have been the targets of fraud. Companies have been hurt by external interpretations of policies, procedures and even corporate logos on the part of individuals, interest groups and governments. Sometimes, interpretations conform with facts; sometimes not. The degree of conformity makes no difference in the face of a boycott, a lawsuit or general customer disapproval. Companies with a superior product or technology have been beaten by firms with larger marketing budgets and greater influence on distributors, opinion leaders and consumers.

It is difficult for managers who are committed to action to remain objective. Passion and commitment help communicate ideas persuasively and motivate individuals, but if misdirected, they can damage a company. For some managers, their identification with a product or service is complete. They carry in their heads all there is to know about the customer, product and marketplace. Moreover, they refuse to be challenged about the accuracy of their views or messages. They often are successful with their vision and assume that they will continue to be. However, self-deception in such instances can destroy multibillion dollar companies. The author worked with two Fortune 500 companies that failed because the owner-founders would not let facts interfere with personal perception and bias.

Over time, employees tend to identify with a manager's vision and messages. They deny evidence, consciously or unconsciously, to protect their personal security. As a result, one of a manager's important communication tasks is to push for openness. Openness starts at the top and permeates through the entire organization. However, openness has a negative side as well. When employees, customers and others feel free to speak, they do so. Opinion and comment can easily distract a manager from a company's purposes. A truly open manager accepts a flood of opinion yet remains fixed on the primary mission of survival and success.

Managers deal with their own perceptions, with perceptions of others and with facts. Managers work through all three to help a company survive and succeed. All three can exist in parallel without interrupting each other, but they also can cross over and create havoc. Examples of perceptual misinterpretation arise in many corporate areas:

- A male manager might give another male a pat on the back but avoid giving a woman a similar pat out of fear of sexual harassment. The reverse is true for female managers.

- Females of childbearing age working with lead batteries have accused their companies of gender bias after their jobs were taken away out of concern for the safety of children they might bear.

• Qualified minorities have suffered in high corporate positions because they were perceived as tokens appointed to avoid charges of racial discrimination.

Managers are role models and, as a result, their actions are subject to perceptions. A manager might not drink among employees to avoid whispers of alcoholism. A manager might not meet alone with a member of the opposite sex behind closed doors to avoid unpleasantness later. A manager may banish reserved parking spaces to communicate equality of purpose.

Personal restraint also builds a perception of a manager as one whom an employee or customer can trust. This perception of integrity, uprightness and honesty is in itself a strong communication and source of credibility. Integrity, however, is a relative perception. If a manager is given to outrageous behaviors yet is accepted in spite of them, he or she is drawing credibility from other sources. Managers constantly manipulate perception as a form of effective corporate communication.

PRIMARY AND SECONDARY CAPTURE OF ENVIRONMENTAL DATA

Primary data capture comes from direct contact with internal or external persons, events, ideas, behavior or perceptions that may harm or enhance a company' ability to complete economic transactions (Figure 4.3).These include:

• a sales person working with a customer;
• a marketing manager touring booths of competitors at a trade show;
• a service person at a customer's premises;
• a plant manager walking a shop floor;
• a lobbyist visiting senators and representatives;
• a public relations professional conferring with upset homeowners.

Primary data capture grasps unfiltered experience. One sees firsthand the individuals, actions and events that secondary data systems synthesize. Although perceptions are distorted, total data capture is larger and more immediate. Often, such primary data capture is the only source from which company messages are drawn, but it is not easy. Contacts generate paperwork, which clogs filing cabinets and in-boxes. Managers work to keep primary data capture simple and integrated with daily activities, a task in which information technology has helped.

Suppliers now hook up to electronic data interchanges, which automate ordering and payment. Distributors use bar coding and automated reordering systems. Primary data about what is selling, how well and where

Figure 4.3
Primary and Secondary Data Capture

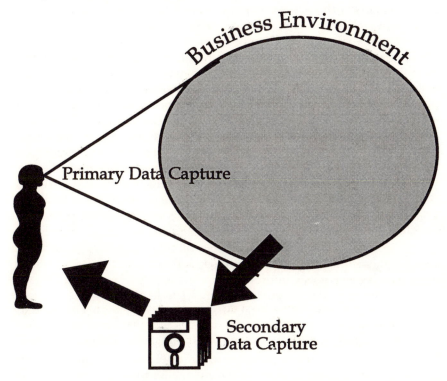

are instantly recorded at the factory level. Employees can access E-mail, groupware and management information systems at the same terminal and can capture environmental data from every level of a company. Marketers watch competitors directly through store-register data purchased directly from data houses. Research and Development (R&D) departments map consumer interests and preferences directly through interactive computer sessions in which target groups enter their preferences directly into terminals that analyze and codify the data. (Home shopping networks and 800-number telemarketers have pioneered instant measures of preference for products of many different kinds.) Public affairs and public relations specialists maintain a direct watch on international, federal, state and local governments through television networks such as Cable News Network, C-Span and local cable channels.

Moreover, monitoring is spreading to include proceedings of community and interest groups, political bodies and courtrooms. Shareholders and the financial community are covered instantly through newswires such as Dow-Jones, Reuters, Knight-Ridder and Bloomberg, which are all delivered to the individual's desk. In addition, financial cable channels, such as CNBC, carry day-long financial broadcasts. Customers' perceptions can be captured instantly with inbound and outbound 800 (toll-free) telephone numbers. Firms maintain computer bulletin boards where one can post questions or write to others with similar problems. Monitoring conversational "threads" helps to find hidden bugs in software, spot new techniques and seal customer relationships. Computer-based training systems capture and store the knowledge and skill levels of individual employees working through interactive tests. Computer systems also monitor typing speed, key entry and errors, time to complete a telephone call and more. News monitoring of stories about a company and its products provides many firms with a quick reputation measure among key audiences and exposure to emerging issues that might pose challenges in the near future.

Data is not as important as the knowledge it conveys. In all the examples cited here, data derived from automated capture provides a base for knowledge that lets a manager enhance a company's survival and success. When automated data capture overwhelms judgment and action, it should be shut off. As in most research, after a number of confirming studies have been completed, additional studies simply support the point that was already made and become noise. Information technology has brought greater efficiency to primary data capture and analysis. It also has made leaps in capturing "soft" or non-numerical information, such as competitor insights or customer gossip.

Secondary data capture is information retrieved from existing databases and libraries. There are hundreds of these in electronic form alone. One corporate communication skill is to know the location of this information and how to reach it quickly. For example, the author uses five commercial on-line databases—Dialog, Nexis, DataTimes, CompuServe and Ziffnet. Each has a proprietary data collection that is not carried on any other source.

Nexis provides general coverage of many fields and detailed coverage of legal and federal regulations through its Lexis counterpart. DataTimes carries many local newspapers and the entire Dow Jones and *Wall Street Journal* news services. It is useful for finding financial information. Dialog has scientific, medical and other journals in a database that covers many countries and languages. CompuServe carries general information from magazines and news services. Finally, Ziffnet has a wealth of computer and high-technology product information.

For all the easily accessible secondary information, there still exists a problem with missing facts. Some companies are practically invisible. They do not issue news releases or their news releases are not distributed through the nationwide public relations (PR) Newswire or Business Wire services that send company information to hundreds of news outlets. Newsletters do not cover these firms, and they do not belong to prominent trade associations. Perhaps, these firms choose to work in secret to gain competitive advantage. As a result, despite access to all the on-line and paper-based libraries in existence, managers are still left without critical facts and must rely on judgment to fill in for missing information.

Action-oriented managers rarely have time to master the numerous facts that cascade from even simple events. Managers get things done. They do not sit all day in an office to think and read. As a result, others must master the facts for the managers. The difficulty with this approach is that it has a distancing effect. Secondary interpretation, even when done by a good analyst, injects a bias between a decision maker and experience. This forces managers to test environmental interpretations for accuracy and common sense. Testing includes checking details—boring into an analysis to see if it supports the conclusions.[11] Japanese manufacturers use a questioning system called the "five why's." Each response is followed by the question "why" in order to progressively uncover root causes. The author watched a similar experience with a board of education in a major midwestern city. One board member reviewed hundreds of appropriations at each meeting. He would ask questions such as, "On page 43, why are we spending so much for light bulbs?" This would set off a scramble as controllers and others would search for a justification for light bulbs. Managers pilot test ideas as well. This can be as simple as asking others, in a disguised way, to respond to a proposed message or as complex as committing time and resources to test ideas. The use of "trial balloons" is a common method of pilot testing messages in politics and companies. A politician or CEO will say that he or she is thinking about doing something in order to see how people respond. Trial balloons, however, can backfire. As a consultant, the author once took a position on the use of E-mail to see how employees would respond. The result was a request for him to be removed from the study "because he was biased." Trial balloons are often taken at face value. Committing resources to test ideas also has positive and negative sides. The positive is that one finds out whether an approach works. The negative is that those who know they are part of a test tend to unconsciously bias it. If possible, one should insulate test participants from a test's true purpose.

Managers also use continuous apprenticeships or on-the-job training to preserve and enhance the skill of environmental observation. Doctors, for example, are taught to watch a patient and detect what is wrong just by observing the breathing, gait, posture and other subtle signs. Construction managers can walk around a work site and know by the disposition and use of equipment whether a job is on time or not. Plant managers can walk a shop floor and know whether operations are in tune or slipping.

Training in environmental observation should concentrate first on accuracy. Accuracy involves exactness in noting elements during an observation. It is learned behavior with no limits. One grows more accurate about causes and effects as one delves more deeply into them.[12] For example, point at the side of a house and ask someone to describe it five different times. The first response might be, "a wall." A second response might be, "a wall with two windows." A third response might be, "a wall with two windows, one of which is cracked." The fourth response might be, "a wall with two windows—one broken—and cracking on the surface plaster." A fifth response might be, "A wall with two windows—one broken—cracking plaster and an evidence of buckling." The fifth response indicates a wall on a slumping foundation—a serious problem. Of course, a trained engineer or carpenter might look at the wall the first time and spot a problem that a layperson would miss.

The second task of training in environmental observation is to focus on the business at hand. Managers regularly lead employees into a deeper understanding of their tasks. A secretary in pursuit of speed may often fail to spell-check documents and, as a result, will be less productive. This often turns into a round-robin of proofing and correction. However, the total time to finish a document using a round-robin approach is greater than if the secretary had slowed down and spell-checked the document carefully the first time. A manager who knows this can help a secretary increase efficiency without straining for speed.

The third training task in environmental observation is to document learning for the benefit of others. A company cannot increase its skills unless individual knowledge and craft are communicated to others. Documenting is done in many forms—writing, videotape, film, audio, demonstrations and studies. One tenet of the time and motion study was to transcribe actions of a worker in detail as a prelude to improving or passing on skills. All time and motion analysis systems rely on measurements of distances, time and action. These are turned into flow diagrams, which document a process from beginning to end. The documentation becomes a basis for applying the process elsewhere.

The fourth training task in environmental observation is to teach incrementalism. Nothing is perfect: everything improves. The methods used today can be improved tomorrow and the day after. Eventually, they can be replaced altogether by new technologies. Demanding perfection from the outset is rarely successful and interferes with accurate observation. Incrementalism, however, depends on the work that one does. An accountant is hardly allowed to vary in accuracy when adding columns of numbers. A doctor is not forgiven if the knife slips in surgery and cuts a vital organ. An airline pilot cannot miss a landing and walk away without injury or retribution. In some skills, accuracy starts at a high level as a condition of work, and then improves.

The final training task in environmental observation is to make it routine—that is, to systematize it. Managers and employees should define fact building as an essential part of their tasks in order to set their company apart from competitors. This enhances marketing and message sending.

Systematic observation allows for incremental improvement, which in turn leads to a continuous increase in the quality of goods and services. A continuous increase in quality will lead directly to the transmission of competitive and persuasive messages to customers and other constituents.

STORAGE AND TRANSMISSION OF ENVIRONMENTAL OBSERVATIONS

Business knowledge must be communicated to the right place for economic transactions to occur. This is the function of organizational media. Some media store information and some transmit it. Business knowledge may be diffused across the organization, directed to specific spots or accessed at will by the individuals needing it. Organizational media may be real-time, but knowledge carried by those media frequently is not. It takes time to transfer knowledge accurately from observers to doers.

Individuals are distributed databases of environmental information. They carry in their heads facts and perceptions of internal or external persons, events, ideas, behavior or perceptions that affect the industry, company or market. Even if they do not carry the specifics, they know where to find them. Debriefing a person is not an optimal method because individuals rarely can relate all they know in an interview setting, even if they are willing to do so. Much information is situational. For example, designers of expert systems observe and debrief skilled persons over weeks or months to capture the heuristics and facts that they apply to their tasks. Then, they code this information into software that others use. However, expert systems are hardly perfect, as one expert noted:

Expert systems cannot solve every problem, nor are they as effective at solving some problems as they are at solving others. Procedural and diagnostic problems are considered easier to solve than configuration and design and scheduling or planning problems. When knowledge greater than rules and facts is needed to solve a problem, expert systems fall down.

Overall, the benefit of knowledge systems, which include expert systems, is that they can:

1. Reduce knowledge acquisition time.
2. Reduce knowledge acquisition cost.
3. Replicate valuable skills.
4. Reduce operational response time.
5. Save valuable knowledge.[13]

A person's knowledge and skills are unique. One might teach a machine to paint, for example, like Pablo Picasso in his Blue period, but could the same machine figure out how to sculpt like Picasso 40 years later? Knowledge transference fixes heuristics and facts at a point in time. Individuals and environments move on, and thus understanding evolves.

Crises show this quickly. For example, suppose a plane crashes and burns. Some passengers and crew have survived: this is the first observation that a manager receives. The manager's next question concerns how many individuals are alive and how many are dead. A medic working on the left side of the plane reports five men, seven women and one child plus two female crew members under treatment. A medic working on the right side of the plane reports three children under treatment and 14 bodies. A manager preparing a public announcement talks to both medics to determine the living and dead. The manager knows the combined count is tentative because a third medic at the rear of the plane may have a different number; moreover, medics might be double counting under the stress of the situation. Finally, reporters swarming the scene also count the living and the dead. Thus, the numbers rise and fall. An accurate count usually comes much later after careful checking against the passenger list, identification, dental records, and so forth.

In ordinary business situations, companies capture customer information in terms of a product or service. A customer's facts might be spread over several databases. A holistic interpretation of a customer is impossible without accessing multiple databases to join information and communicate it to others. Companies often operate in segmented ways because some products and services are not easy to sell in an integrated manner. For example, suppose a computer company makes CPUs, peripherals, software and telecommunications devices. The skill required to understand and sell a mainframe computer is different from that required to sell a high-speed laser printer. Indeed, the salespersons may even work with different engineers when servicing the components at a customer site. However, a printer may be driven by a mainframe, and the two must work together for the system to operate at peak performance.

If a computer links multiple sites, software and telecommunications devices must work in concert. It is unlikely that any one person will understand the whole system. Companies use cross-functional teams to overcome such barriers, but these teams are often ad hoc. They come together to observe and act and then are moved on if it proves uneconomical to keep them in a customer's place of business. Local knowledge of the customer's business is lost when they are moved, even with reporting and debriefing. Service departments reeducate themselves each time a new person touches the machines. Indeed, technicians often spend as much time finding out how a unit was put together as they do fixing it. Even if a technician does learn a system well enough to fix it, there is no guarantee that the learning will be useful in the future because the technician may never work on this type of equipment again. This means that each technician must document the work completely and pass on the information.

That is difficult to do, and cumulative repairs change a system irrevocably from its original state. Unfortunately, the customer is responsible for the whole operation, and variances introduced by the manufacturer send customers a mixed message.

Every organization accumulates contacts with the business environment every hour of the day. The organization decides how many of these contacts must be preserved for the whole company and how many can be stored for local use or discarded permanently. The result is that information about the business environment is never perfect, even if all is stored somewhere.

One critic of information and data capture stated that no company can capture the data it needs without bogging down in considerations about what is, and might be, important.[14] The best that a company should expect is the ability to find information when required. Information technology builds pipelines to vast bodies of information that can be accessed at will. The key challenge, however, is how to catalogue the data for retrieval.

One solution to gaining a total view of a business environment is to capture experiences as records and place them in a common, centralized storage facility where every department can have access for its communication. However, common storage is limited to system capacity and flexibility. It often captures segments of a business environment, but cannot portray the total environment. A credit card company might have everything about their customers on-line but lack information about retailers who accept their card. That information is. stored elsewhere. Similarly, a hotel chain may have system-wide reservation services available through one telephone number yet may not know the state of repair of room 3132 in its suburban Sacramento unit. This information is stored locally, if at all. Should a company commit to integrating such data, it opens itself to an enormous processing task with an uncertain return on its investment.

The decision to cut off knowledge about the business environment at the central storage point is both economic and a matter of point of view. The latter is a larger barrier than investment costs. This is due to a phenomenon whereby humans tend to abstract individuals to represent groups. One thinks more easily about publics than persons. About a public servant given to massive public works projects, it was said he detested individuals. Business uses abstractions constantly and is biased by them.

There is also a question of how much environmental observation an individual can carry out without abstracting the data. Top managers concentrate on the needs of the moment. They select views of the business environment to balance against a constantly changing conceptual whole. Employees who take cues from top managers emphasize some environmental factors and ignore others. This, over time, breeds selective environmental observation and instability if it causes a company to miss trends.

A second question in the storage and transmission of environmental data is, "Who updates the common storage?" Even if the hotel chain's Sacramento unit manager knows that room 3132 has new curtains, chances are that he or she is too busy to report that fact to a main database. The information is more than likely to be stored in a separate work-order system in housekeeping or engineering. If it is joined to the larger system, the organization faces the added challenge of how to classify facts. Should the database be configured by room, by customer or both? Are reservations indexed by customer, by room or both? Is information added twice to the database or to a temporary third file that carries a virtual record of both customer and room information until the customer leaves? The details of data capture are complex and require an intimate understanding of a business and information theory, but most of corporate communication is directly dependent on the correct implementation of these details.

Common storage systems need great flexibility to work well as corporate communication resources. Returning to the example of the insurance company used earlier, a letter sent to the insurance company is stored as an electronic image in a customer's computerized file. The letter is one picture. Therefore, each time a clerk talks to the customer, he or she reads the letter. If that is too slow, someone must rekey the data from the letter into another storage form for easier access.

If a letter contains more than one topic, the organization's classification system will divide the letter's contents or subcode it in a way that preserves, not only the primary source, but multiple topics. To do so, someone codes the letter. However, codes are never exactly accurate, which means that information may be misclassified. The result is that environmental observation held in common storage still needs checking, and communication will still be harmed by insufficient data even when the information is in the system. Few companies have managers who are experts in both business and information storage and retrieval. As a result, common data storage is an incremental task based on needs.

In a perfect world, every pertinent environmental observation would be available at every point in an economic transaction in order to facilitate communication and optimize action. Of course, a perfect world does not exist. Consequently, data design and architecture are key concerns in understanding and communicating messages built from the business environment (Figure 4.4). A company that devises the most efficient means to capture, store and distribute data can outflank its competitors.

Common data storage is part of management information systems (MIS). "MIS is the development and use of effective information systems in organizations."[15] MIS defines three levels of information systems:

- organizational, which encompass all departments and individuals in a company;
- work-group information, to coordinate the activities of individuals devoted to a discrete task within the company;

Figure 4.4
Corporate Communication and MIS

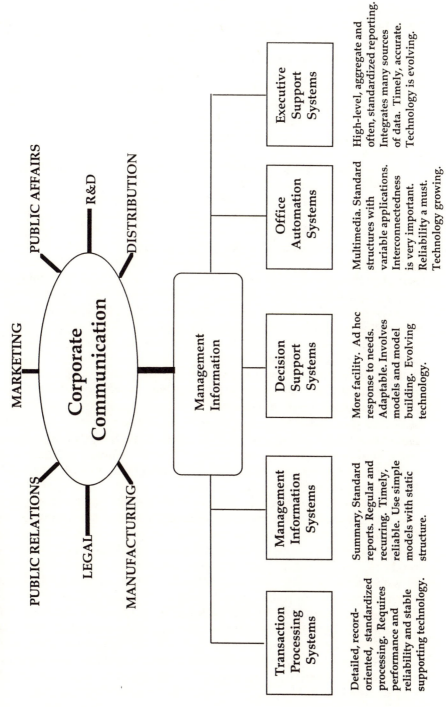

• personal information, to increase individual productivity. These systems include calendars, reminder and to-do programs, electronic notepads, E-mail and more.

Each system captures and stores part of the business environment. In some cases a partial view is enough to communicate, while in other cases, it is not.

Good MIS systems are pertinent. Their information applies to the task at hand. They are timely and accurate. They are factual in that they reduce uncertainty about the environment. Finally, they are informative: they tell a user something new.[16]

Each level of management information differs from the level before it, which poses a challenge for understanding the environment. Organizational systems focus on commonalities—the language of numbers. Usually, such systems are structured according to the financial data each department needs from the general system. Work-group systems handle the hard and soft information of a unit. These systems are frequently built to automate a department's work flow. For example, a system is optimized to capture photos, art and text that flow into it from various points and to join them into a finished magazine that never sees paper until it is printed. Personal systems handle the unique needs and tasks of the individual in the work group. Some personal systems tie to the work group, and others tie strictly to the tasks a person performs. Personal systems are often highly adaptable to an individual's work style.

The different uses of each type of system continue to pose challenges to organizational MIS development. One author listed eight barriers with which information technologists must deal, including differences in viewing data and processing it, as well as differences in terminology, goals and expectations, types of systems desired, levels of competency, departmental competition and fear of organizational change.[17] These discrepancies are enough to bog down any effort to build an integrated understanding of the business environment.

As technology evolves, personal and work-group information can be communicated across an entire organization. An executive support system (ESS) creates links with *drill-down* capabilities built on financial data. *Drill-down* lets a CEO view numerical information at every level down to a single cash register in a particular store. As a result, a CEO can communicate to store managers precisely rather than in generalities, such as questioning why certain product lines did not sell well rather than why overall store revenue stagnated. An ESS system that provides both accounting capabilities and soft, nonquantifiable data would be optimum. For example, if a CEO had access to the weather reports for the month during which store revenues stagnated and knew that severe weather had hampered travel, communications to the store manager could take into account the bad weather.

The ideal is to have all systems construct an integrated environmental profile that reduces need for reinvention and reeducation. One example of such information distribution is a company that maintains a live, on-line information library fed by 25 active databases and newswires. A user fills out an electronic request form which acts as a "smart agent" and searches the databases, pulling out all the relevant information in minutes.

It requires hard work and the ability to see and understand the nature of things in order to find relationships that turn words and numbers into knowledge and trends. Insight depends on an individual's unique gifts. Data relationships can be passive, active, fixed or variable. For passive data, the individual creates parameters for reports that machines then complete. Active data has the "agency" to make relationships to other data and produce information automatically without human intervention other than setting up the original agent. Fixed data has a predefined and fixed set of relationships that individuals set only once. Accounting is an example of fixed data with its system of debits and credits, assets and liabilities and equity.

Finally, variable data has many sets of relationships with infinite connections. This is perhaps the most difficult—and common—type of business environmental change to organize. For example, an important customer may be flirting with the competition. There are signs the customer is doing so, but signs can be read in different ways. Perhaps the customer was seen talking with a salesperson of the competition at a social event. Moreover, the customer has been a little cool lately. That was probably due to the company's big mistake on the last order, but the customer is also having problems at home and with a new boss. The customer has asked for a contract review, which was asked for several times in the past to aid in account planning. There is nothing to indicate that this request is different, but it might be. Here, each fact can be read in either direction. The ultimate interpretation of what the customer is thinking may be revealed in time. However, with care and diligence, a manager may find out if there is anything behind the accumulation of observations or not.

Data should be discrete, reporting the most specific form of a fact about an internal or external person, event, idea, behavior or perception that can be captured for interpretation. The reason is that every step beyond a discrete fact is an abstraction about it and its relationships with other facts. Abstractions are points of view—even when they are carefully formed. To keep the data discrete, one should capture the words of an individual as accurately as possible, along with nonverbal language. (Was he or she scowling or smiling, relaxed or tense?) One should document the participants, locale, timing, actions, purposes and mechanics of an event. One should understand the logic for, and assumptions behind, ideas and the source of, and assumptions behind, perceptions. Discrete data capture has advanced to automation in some parts of business but remains primitive in others.

With some data, capture is difficult and poses challenges that have not been satisfactorily resolved. For example, one can make transcripts of a hearing on patent infringement but written words cannot capture the impact on a jury of an inventor claiming she was denied her due by your heartless company. One may have the law on one's side and yet lose because a good actor in the form of an attorney or witness swayed a jury. Juries have declared policemen innocent who were filmed beating a man on the ground and failed to convict rioters who pulled an innocent passerby from a truck and then nearly beat him to death. In many states, one can videotape hearings and preserve the emotion, but it is difficult to run a tape back and forth in order to skim transcripts for weak points in testimony. Therefore, one captures the same data in two ways—written and visually. This increases both the amount of data and the cost. Further, one type of capture does not link easily with the other. Data storage and classification are done based on the type and frequency of uses to which the data are put.

For many reasons, multiple, linked data files are better, but the challenge lies is in constructing the links. Database structuring is both an art and a science. The questions that must be resolved are complex, and managers generally need specialized help. A typical information matrix might consist of 18 columns by 55 rows, or 990 discrete cells, in which data may or may not be needed for a department to do its task. Moreover, this describes relationships that already exist, and not nonexistent relationships that should exist.[18]

The principle of organization is clear. Customers come first, and other constituencies are then linked to the customer database. Major information systems do that with record systems that deposit hard and soft data about customers into linked databases. Databases for other key constituencies, such as regulators, shareholders, interest groups, employees, suppliers and distributors, are less often linked to customer files.

Customer databases still require classification. For example, to find the number of rhinoplasty surgeries done in the New York Metropolitan area during 1993, one either examines patient records or codes rhinoplasty as a type of medical procedure. With hundreds of medical procedures, there must be hundreds of classifications. This means that one establishes a system under which every procedure has a code that is accessible to users. Alternately, it means that procedures are assigned to broader categories, which are simpler to store but less useful. A count of patients who had rhinoplasties is not finite enough. Counting the number of patient procedures is not discrete enough. Data on patient demographics, diseases, treatment and history of medical procedures begin to approach a level of classification needed. Classifying data for later use is an immensely difficult task.

Managers cannot escape involvement in classification. There are infinite ways to parse data, but only a few are economical and practical based on how environmental data is used in corporate communication. The guideline in classification is flexibility. The atomization of data provides the greatest flexibility for arranging it in different ways; however, discrete classification calls for:

- search engines to filter data from a sea of possibilities;
- high-speed processing units to filter individual data bits quickly enough to be timely;
- time: the more possibilities for interpretation, the more time it takes to decide which approach is best;
- explicit connections among data sets;
- economical and timely methods of updating data.

The difficulties of classification can be shown in a simple example—a list of journalists following an industry. Traditionally, such a list meant fewer than ten discrete items in a database—name, title, organization name, street address, city, state, zip, phone and fax number. However, a media list could grow into more than that. For example, a journalist's list could include reporting assignments. Similarly, in a list of 650 computer and telecommunications reporters, there might be only 25 that follow a particular technology. The list could also include the person's interests. Does he or she like new product stories, breaking news or "people" stories? It could include types of individuals to which this person appeals—opinion leaders, managers, technologists or consumers. It could include references to recent stories that this person has reported. It could also include the last time the company contacted this person. Moreover, it might give the journalist's background to help understand how much this person knows about the company's products and services.

Suddenly, a simple file has become complex. Complexity makes the file more useful, but updating a complex file is more difficult because the more discrete items of information there are, the greater will be the rate of change. A reporter might leave a publication, change assignments on the same publication or change phone numbers or interests. The amount of updating can be as much as one-quarter to one-third of a total file every three months. This is why private data suppliers take over complex databases. Private suppliers can amortize the cost of keeping a system current for a larger number of customers than can one company.

There are levels of environmental data capture based on the economic means of an organization. A low level includes swapping gossip with suppliers, customers, vendors and others who cross a market; reading local and national media, such as *Business Week, Forbes, Fortune* and the *Wall Street Journal* and subscribing and reading key trade journals and newsletters reporting an industry in which a company competes. A mid-range approach to business environmental data scanning would include these actions plus:

- Developing and implementing an integrated organizational information strategy to disseminate business environment information regularly.
- Reviewing information about individuals key to organizational survival and success. Among individuals automatically covered are owners, employees and customers.
- Maintaining a briefing book on key business issues.
- Automating supplier, distributor and customer contacts.
- Maintaining one or more on-line data services focused on the company's business environment.
- Using work-group information systems to place business environmental data on terminals throughout a company for employees to consult as needed.
- Providing company-wide E-mail.
- Appointing an information editor to coordinate and digest data flows to resource files.

A high level of environmental scanning and data capture would add the following to the actions already listed:

- A department to analyze and report business environmental information company-wide. This department would tie into company communications lines as does a wire service. It would maintain a digest of events classified by key business environment variables.
- Company-wide town hall meetings to update employees on the business environment and its implications for the business.
- Key measures for business environmental change and company response.
- Real-time reporting of a company's business environment to special publics and interest groups to help them understand company actions.
- Regular surveys, focus groups and panels with key individuals in the business environment who have direct economic power over a company.
- Ongoing investigations of change in the business environment and how the company should prepare for it.
- Retreats for managers in which the state of the company and business environment is presented.

The cost of data capture and knowledge generation ranges from a few hundred dollars a year to tens of millions, depending on what a manager determines a company needs and can afford. Bigger is not necessarily better. Separate departments increase overhead, which can burden a company that is trying to stay lean and flexible. On the other hand, if the company's future depends on a detailed grasp of the business environment, a department may be a necessary expense. Each manager uniquely determines the data capture of each organization. Formulas such as percentages of sales are simplistic because they give a fixed ratio to a variable need.

One end product of environmental observation is a fact summary. These documents are also called *white papers* or *background papers*. Fact summaries on the business environment can be discursive collections of facts with enough text to tie everything to the business mission or text, such as in a company's annual report or 10-K filing to the U.S. Securities and Exchange Commission. A fact summary is a digest of provable or consensual information about internal or external persons, events, ideas, behavior or perceptions that directly threaten or enhance a company's survival and success in completing economic transactions.

A useful fact summary requires attention and use by top management as a daily working tool. That is why it is best for summaries to reside electronically on a manager's desktop like a library of easily accessible and updated information. Fact summaries often require summation themselves as they tend to be lengthy.

Fact summaries do not explain the whole business environment but only what is generally accepted about it and can be supported. Fact summaries provide a starting point for communicating to internal and external individuals. They provide common ground and reveal how much a company knows about the business environment. Fact summaries focus message creation more quickly because there is less searching for information.

If possible, fact summaries should remain in electronic form so they can be changed readily and can provide for notations without the destruction of the original text. Information technologies such as word processing, on-line bulletin boards and E-mail boxes allow commentary and observations to be added to original text. Fact summaries are not literature but simple, clear and readable documents designed to reduce misunderstanding. They are not ends in themselves but rather the beginnings of the communication process. Fact summaries are often used as a first step in gaining consensus for discussion. Participants review and sign them off. Thus, issues are focused sharply and all parties are placed on a common ground.

The first-time construction of fact summaries can be done by consultants, who bring an impartial view to the process and a knowledge of information sources; by departments dedicated to environmental observation, such as marketing research; or by a cross-functional team. Teams work well as ad-hoc or permanent groups when dealing with many kinds of business challenges. They work just as well in understanding environmental change. Specialists' views are counterbalanced by those of other specialists, and the resulting consensual interpretations will make the best possible sense out of complex events. For example:

- Marketing natural gas as a substitute for gasoline in auto engines combines social attitudes toward the "explosive" nature of gas, distribution problems, political incentives, pollution and the "clean air" lobby. Gas utilities have had to deal with all these business environmental factors in their efforts to use natural gas as vehicle fuel.

- Similarly, persuading citizens about personal health issues (such as giving up smoking) has been a multidecade effort combining science, medicine, social and regulatory pressure and training to reach populations from grade school to senior citizens.

Teams may include engineers, marketers, public relations professionals, public affairs lawyers, assemblers and others.

Last, managers occasionally retain observers who are unfamiliar with a business environment to see what they pick up. Sometimes, this results in insights beyond the scope of an industry. One example is a photocopier company that hired an anthropologist who used a video camera to monitor employees working with the company's machines. The study showed how difficult it was to use copier controls—even for the engineers who designed them. This use of a scientist who would normally study social relationships and customs became the motivation to simplify photocopier interfaces.

SUMMARY

Environmental observation enhances the completion of economic transactions by letting managers form more persuasive and effective communications. Continuous reactive and proactive observation allows a company to adapt, seize themes opportunistically and shuck dated messages without jeopardizing its essential purposes. With inefficient or poor environmental observation, the ability to address change will become damaged or dysfunctional.

Effective environmental observation uses the eight guidelines for corporate communication by being:

- Simple: managers automate data capture and interpretation into business activity as far as economically possible.

- Timely: managers tie business environmental data capture and interpretation to the economic transactions and activities that are essential to business survival and success.

- Open: managers make business environmental data available to all to keep themselves aware of changes that may affect company success.

- Defined: environmental observation focuses on internal or external persons, events, ideas, behavior or perceptions that *directly* threaten or promise to enhance a company's survival and success in completing economic transactions. Managers maintain a "watch" list of issues that might turn into direct threats or opportunities at any time.

- Flexible: managers build organizational, work-group and personal systems that handle both hard and soft environmental information.
- Individual: managers provide tools for access to business environment information and analysis to individuals on the basis of their perceived needs.
- Meaningful: data capture and interpretation are accurate, timely, directly related to company survival and success and in a form allowing easy access.
- Measurable: tracking systems measure and report key environmental indicators bearing directly on company success, such as customer satisfaction, interest group activity, regulatory rule making and positive and negative news.

NOTES

1. David Kroenke, *Management Information Systems* (New York: Mitchell Mc-Graw-Hill, 1989), p. 113.

2. Carl Von Clausewitz, *On War*, ed. and trans., Michael Howard and Peter Paret (Princeton, NJ: Princeton University Press, 1976), p. 75.

3. Michael E. Porter, *Competitive Strategy: Techniques for Analyzing Industries and Competitors* (New York: The Free Press, 1980), p. 3.

4. George Anders and Helene Cooper, "Medicine: Why Specialists Won't Switch to Primary Care," *Wall Street Journal*, June 7, 1994, p. B1.

5. Herbert A. Simon, *Administrative Behavior* (New York: The Free Press, 1987), p. 79.

6. Clausewitz, *On War*, p. 117.

7. Judith H. Dobrzynski, "Rethinking IBM: An Exclusive Account of Lou Gerstner's First Six Months," *Business Week*, no. 3339 (October 4, 1993): 86–97.

8. Clausewitz, *On War*, bk. 3, ch. 9, "Surprise," pp. 198–201.

9. Brian Dumaine, "America's Toughest Bosses," *Fortune* 128, no. 9 (October 18, 1993): 40.

10. Sergei Eisenstein, *Film Form and the Film Sense* (Cleveland, OH: Meridian Books, The World Publishing Company, 1964).

11. James Martin, with Joe Leben, *Strategic Information Planning Methodologies* (Englewood Cliffs, NJ: Prentice-Hall, 1989).

12. Benjamin W. Niebel, *Motion and Time Study*, 9th ed. (Homewood, IL: Irwin, 1993).

13. Kroenke, *Management Information Systems*, pp. 684, 672.

14. J. Patrick Thompson, *Data with Semantics: Data Models and Data Management* (New York: Van Nostrand Reinhold, 1989).

15. Kroenke, *Management Information Systems*, p. 6.

16. Ibid., p. 19.

17. Ibid., p. 564.

18. Martin and Leben, *Strategic Information Planning Management*.

5

Corporate Communication, Strategy and Reputation

The strategist must . . . define an aim for the entire operational side of the war that will be in accordance with its purpose. In other words, he will draft the plan of the war, and the aim will determine the series of actions intended to achieve it. . . . Since most of these matters have to be based on assumptions that may not prove correct, while other, more detailed orders cannot be determined in advance at all, it follows that the strategist must go on the campaign himself. Detailed orders can then be given on the spot, allowing the general plan to be adjusted to the modifications that are continuously required.

—Carl Von Clausewitz, *On War*[1]

WHERE WE ARE

We have tied corporate communication to behavior and organizational structure. We have defined eight guidelines for corporate communication. We have discussed corporate communication in the business environment, business knowledge, persuasive message sending and data interpretation. All these are preludes to the basic message of a business—its strategy for completing economic transactions and surviving. Strategy is a series of decisions that determine behavior over time and must be communicated to others, who act them out. Strategy, as Clausewitz defined it, is a plan of action—a plan communicated to those who effect it. Finally, strategy involves specific choices that are communicated to individuals who could choose to follow other directions. By definition, strategy limits action. For example, one chooses to focus on one part of a marketplace rather than another. Limits are based on a manager's judgment of what it takes to be able to complete profitable economic transactions now and in the future.

Effective communication is based on strategy. A manager communicates the parameters of action to those who must act. The messages and message receivers of effective communication are based on intended economic results. The verification of economic results measures a strategy's success or failure.

Business looks for two outcomes—the transfer of economic wealth into the control of the seller and continued permission to operate. The first result is purely economic, while the second maintains economic potential or capability through preserving a company's reputation among social and political forces with direct power over it.

Reputation is often overlooked in strategic planning. It refers to the estimation in which a person, thing or action is held by others. Reputation is an attributed character that exists outside an organization and is largely independent of it. A company can influence regard for its reputation, but it cannot control it. Reputation is linked directly to credibility and indirectly to esteem:

Esteem is the value of members as persons, regardless of their positions, to their group, to their organization or to society. It is the members' perceived potential to help the group, the organization or society to attain their respective goals, independent of the position the members occupy.[2]

The link between personal esteem for an individual and company reputation is not direct because one might value an individual highly yet dislike the company the individual works for. However, the collective esteem in which individuals of a company are held is a part of a company's reputation and credibility. A company's view of itself and the view of it from the outside may diverge widely.

People who wonder how tobacco company executives can live with themselves conclude they must be in denial. That would explain how they deal with their responsibility for a product that kills more than 420,000 Americans a year—surpassing the combined deaths from homicide, suicide, AIDS, automobile accidents, alcohol and drug abuse. But to be in denial implies that one may not be held accountable, in psychological terms, for one's actions. Tobacco people squarely face the accusation of accountability, and reject it. . . .

In other words, if they experience denial as a psychological response, they also use denial as an aggressive tactic. This mirrors the way they live with themselves in general. Individually, they remove themselves from most of the rest of the country and create their own moral universe or explanations and justification.[3]

The issue of selling a controversial or socioculturally objectionable product or service is just one part of a company's reputation, which affects its strategy. There are political, safety, size, gender, race and other elements that all enter into reputation. Any issue, outside or inside a company, that damages its ability to survive and succeed is a reputation issue with direct bearing on strategy and corporate communication.

The most talked-about advertisement of the 1980s was a 60-second television commercial for Apple Computer that was tied directly to a strategy of getting the company back into the personal computer marketplace, after IBM had buried it with the former's personal computers. The ad was shown just once, during the National Football League 1984 Super Bowl, and it played on George Orwell's novel, *1984*. It showed a young woman carrying a sledgehammer and running into a drab, gray auditorium filled with zombie-like figures listening to a "big brother" figure ranting on a massive screen. The woman runs to the front of the auditorium and heaves the sledgehammer through the screen. Then, a caption appears: "On January 24th, Apple Computer will introduce Macintosh. And you'll see why 1984 won't be like '1984.' " The following was written ten years after the advertisement appeared:

The symbolism was clear: The woman and youth, the hammer and workers of the world and, yes, Big Blue (IBM).

And Apple needed a big bang to get back into the game. IBM Corp. had swept past Apple to take the lead in the personal computer market in 1983. Apple's two most recent product introductions had bombed, and the company's stock was in the tank.

"Apple's future is being questioned as never before," asserted the opening line in Apple's annual report two months before the Macintosh introduction.[4]

That communication, shown only once, not only put Apple computer back into the personal computer game, but won it a reputation that exceeded the capabilities of its original Macintosh—an underpowered machine with "little software, no color monitor and no ability to do letter-quality printing," which had been developed with little insight into who might buy it.[5]

STRATEGY AND EFFECTIVE COMMUNICATION

Strategy has two manifestations—stated and real. Stated strategy is a formal message about choices and directions, whereas real strategy is what a company does (Figure 5.1). What a company does may or may not coincide with its stated strategy. Real strategy, in fact, may be ad hoc, as it was for Apple Computer in 1984. Clausewitz saw a strategist as a rider of events who changes the orders as needed in pursuit of a goal. Others see strategy as a decision process used by managers that is expressed in explicit choice and behavior. Strategy shapes the business environment and is shaped by it.

Strategy is bound together by communication, which transmits goals, purposes and decisions to those who carry them out. The difference be-

Figure 5.1
Strategy: Stated and Real

The Stated Strategy

> We Are a
> Quality Company

Assumption: Customers Define Quality

Purchasing	Mfg.	Quality Control
Customer Desire: Close Tolerances - Parts	Customer Desire: Superior Fit/Finish	Customer Desire: Quality Built in.
Real Strategy: Low Bidder - Std. Tolerances	Real Strategy: Industry Average Defects/Component	Real Strategy: Quality Inspected in.

Shipping	Sales	Service
Customer Desire: Minimal Damage in Transit	Customer Desire: One-Price, Low Pressure Sales	Customer Desire: Evening & Weekend Hours
Real Strategy: Post-transit Repair/Prep	Real Strategy: Deals, High Pressure	Real Strategy: Closed Evenings & Weekends

tween stated and real strategy is reflected in how managers communicate. Stated strategy is a neatly formed, logical series of actions and conclusions. Real strategy often consists of ad-hoc messages to accommodate changing business conditions.

A company proclaims "the year of the customer" as its prime strategy, but nothing happens, or not enough. IBM did this when John Akers, the CEO, attempted to refocus the company. It was widely alleged that IBM's "year of the customer" failed, and Akers was fired. When the stated strategy differs from what happens in the economic transaction and the marketplace, it hurts corporate communication and creates a reputation gap, a dissonance that will cost the company credibility. Customers and employees might not go away, but their level of trust will drop. When they find plausible alternatives, they will drift from the fold. That was part of the experience at IBM. It was also true at General Motors, Ford, Xerox, U.S. Steel and other large firms in the 1970s and 1980s.

Strategy is inevitably bound to individuals comprising an organization and how each person interprets the content of a strategic message. A company may move too quickly at the top and ignore challenges of making strategy work at the bottom. Managers regularly forget about inertia. Strategy rarely penetrates more than a level or two before it is filtered away by the bureaucracy that it sought to change. On the other hand, a company may move too slowly in the execution of strategy and hold back employees who know where it needs to go and are motivated but disconnected from the top.

Strategy is both proactive and reactive. It grows from the minds of managers, the daily activity of economic transactions or both (Figure 5.2). A CEO usually cannot impose goals and plans unilaterally unless he or she is ready to replace workers who do not comply. A company may not have the option of starting over with new employees, which might cause it to fall behind and weaken itself. Long strikes have hastened the death of newspapers. The long strike at International Harvester led to the dismantling of that company, while a strike at Eastern Airlines was partially responsible for the death of that carrier.[6]

One person's vision will usually prevail when a company is small enough for that person to talk directly with those who carry out the orders. As companies grow larger, however, the CEO may lose a clear view of the marketplace because he or she may become distanced from it and also because it may change. Apple Computer lost two visionary CEOs, Steve Jobs and John Sculley. Each man was important to the company for a time, but the business environment continued to shift and neither was able to keep up.

When strategy arises from daily transactions, tactical problem solving builds a body of experience comprised of heuristics, or rules of thumb. Communications are ad hoc and organizational goals are understood, if not articulated. A manager directs employees in ways that make clear the intentions—or the task. A farmhand unloading hay from a truck understands the job. On the other hand, a research scientist might not know what to look for. The scientist might follow interesting lines of inquiry, which might—or might not—lead to profitable products. A scientist might not identify with business strategy at all but rather with recognition from a community of colleagues. It is up to managers to clarify, through communication, individual roles in company strategy.

When strategy comes from the vision of a CEO, there can be two outcomes. Either the CEO builds an organization in his or her image—as entrepreneurs do—or a method of management and problem solving will be imposed on the organization. If a CEO uses both proactive and reactive methods to build strategic messages, chances are that he or she will adapt new techniques to existing processes.

Companies do not need to define their goals and strategies formally. They

Figure 5.2
Strategy: Proactive and Reactive

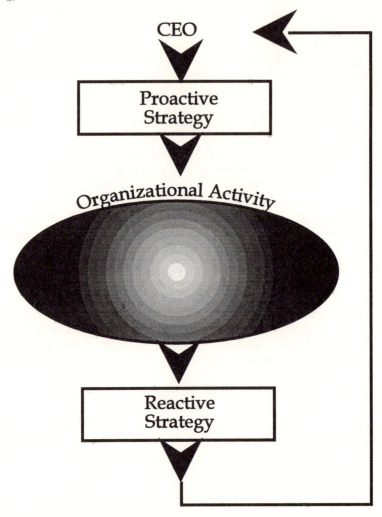

do not need to define them at all as long as they can communicate and gain coordinated action from participants in the economic transaction. Companies that express formal strategies build expectations about accomplishing them. Statements of goals and mission without action open a company and its leaders to criticism and a possible loss of reputation. Many companies have printed mission and strategy statements, distributed them to employees and promptly forgotten that these messages were ever promulgated. Such actions breed cynicism among internal and external observers.

Strategy may be only a limited message. Key participants in an economic transaction only have to know enough to complete a specific task that leads to economic transactions. They do not have to know their roles or their future with the organization. A CEO, for example, may want to sell a company. As a result, advertising for a new product launch may be out of proportion to profitability in order to attract potential investors. Thus, the CEO's real strategy is hidden. The secondary strategy—a successful product launch—*appears* to be primary. As long as the economic transactions are completed and the company succeeds, the formal communication of a CEO's real strategy is not pertinent. However, this can become fertile ground for gossip. One hears speculation frequently among employees about what top management is really doing. The gossip may be idle, but it carries seeds of doubt that can grow quickly if management actions are misunderstood.

Credibility becomes a critical component of strategy when key participants do not believe in a company's goals and plans. Employee resistance to change can stop nearly any strategy, while Wall Street skepticism about announced plans can scuttle a company's effort to pursue a new direction. Stories of companies being disrespected by Wall Street can be heard constantly. Analysts may not trust a CEO, a company's products or the marketplace in which it competes, with the result that the market dumps the stock.

What individuals look for in strategy is what an organization does, and not what it says it did. Companies that engage in misleading message sending about purposes and intents eventually are found out. Few organizations escape detection forever, although they may pursue their goals for decades without serious interruption, because the force of the institution in the marketplace may place it above competition and law for a period.

If a company shouts loudly and long enough, some people will believe its message, but is brand-name aspirin that much better than generic aspirin? Does any one breakfast cereal have clear superiority over all the others? A share of voice—media spending by comparison to competitors—is a time-honored brand strategy. It works, until consumers come to decide that competing products at lower cost are good enough. For example, Kraft, the dairy products company, saw a rapid erosion of cheese sales as no-name generic and house brands pushed it out of the dairy case.

By the 1870s, John D. Rockefeller, had locked up oil refining and distribution on the East Coast and was well on his way to achieving immense riches. It was not until the publication of a year-long expose of Standard Oil, written by Ida Tarbell in 1902, nearly 30 years later, that the company's power began to fade. It was not until May 1911 that the Supreme Court broke up the company. Meanwhile, Standard Oil dominated the oil industry, conducting many of its activities in secrecy.[7]

Standard Oil's strategy was clear to those who ran it and, eventually, transparent to those whom the company crushed. By then, however, it was too late. Rockefeller wanted to bring order to a chaotic market. One could argue that his vision and message of a vertically integrated industry were correct when he started, in 1865. The industry at that time was a welter of small companies and boom-and-bust production that hurt everyone. Later, however, one could argue that Standard Oil became too powerful for its own good and for the good of the societies it served worldwide. The company did not see that its strategy had become self-defeating.

When a company communicates its strategic message, it incorporates its objectives. The mission, strategies and objectives should be clear and simple, with little room for confusion or misinterpretation. Good strategies are usually short, pointed and measurable, such as "Overnight package delivery," "parts to any customer anywhere in the world in 48 hours," or "complete satisfaction or the customer's money back." Simply stated strategies drive objectives at every level. To deliver packages overnight, one must have airplanes, trucks, drivers, pilots, package sorters, loaders, deliverers and administrative machinery to make sure that a package left in a hallway at six P.M. arrives at 10:00 A.M. the next day, 3,000 miles away, consistently, every day and every time. To deliver tractor parts anywhere in the world within 48 hours means that one must have inventory positioned near a customer's machines, whether at a dam in Siberia, a mine in Peru or a street in Los Angeles. To guarantee complete customer satisfaction may mean taking back items that have been used and abused and, maybe, items that the store did not originally sell. There are tales about retailers, past and present, who practice total customer satisfaction. Employees at Marshall Field's department store in Chicago knew that women would "buy" a dress, wear it to a party and then return it to the store. The store would take back the dress without protest. Similarly, a grocer may take back a melon from an angry customer although the store never sold melons. Such "no-hassle" service invites abuse, but it also establishes and communicates the company's strategic message. Strategy expressed in everyday company actions becomes folklore among employees and customers and can serve as a strong communication. Dramatic examples of achieving strategy become part of company culture.

Managers communicate a strategic message in two ways. They either *describe* what a company does or *prescribe* what it ought to do. When one describes what a company does, the assumption is that the company is acting appropriately within its business environment. The manager summarizes the mission and goals. When a manager prescribes strategy, he or she lays out a mission and direction for a company to follow. For example:

A descriptive statement: XYZ company designs and makes automotive brake parts for three original equipment manufacturers in the United States and Canada.

A prescriptive statement: XYZ company will be the market-share leader in the design and production of proprietary parts with superior functionality and cost-benefit ratio for transportation manufacturers.

The descriptive statement defines what a company does today. However, it says nothing about what a company might do tomorrow. The prescriptive statement defines what a company does today *and* tomorrow. A prescriptive statement also may be future-oriented, with no mention of today. Notice that the example does not say "automotive brake parts" because the company does not know whether it will be in the brake part business ten years from today—especially if a new brake outmodes present technology. In fact, this did happen, as U.S. automakers moved from drum to disk brakes. The technologies are different, even though the brakes accomplish the same action. When antilock braking was added, along with microprocessor technology, the distance from mechanical, friction drum brakes to the present brake system became huge.

A prescriptive statement can be as specific as a descriptive one, but by doing so, it shortens its vision of the future. When a company does not know—or care—what it will do in the future, a descriptive statement of strategy will be better. When a company wants to maintain a longer-term focus on technology and marketplace presence, a prescriptive statement has the greater use. When a company wants to describe what it does today and wants to be doing tomorrow, it can combine statements.

XYZ company will be the market-share leader in design and production of proprietary parts with superior functionality and cost-benefit returns for transportation manufacturers. Today, XYZ company is the foremost supplier of automotive brake parts for three original equipment manufacturers in the United States and Canada.

The focus a company takes is dependent on managers, but the actions of a company rely on owners, employees, customers and influentials. Communication bridges them all.

A manager might not have much choice in a strategic message. One might wish to be a visionary and find an industry needing instead the basic management of current processes. Similarly, one might be balanced in focus yet find oneself communicating vision. Pragmatic managers adapt and communicate a strategy needed now for today's environment. Alternately, boards of directors elevate managers as needed for success. Several leaders with contrasting styles were charged, through the late 1970s to the 1990s, to turn around the U.S. auto industry. Of Jack Smith, the CEO of General Motors, *Business Week* wrote:

Smith has been largely invisible to the public eye. Not much of a speaker, he's edgy in the spotlight. He rarely grants interviews and has left most of the speeches to his executive vice president, the affable William E. Hoglund. That's not to say he

hasn't been making friends. Oddly, the last Detroit executive to gain as much pop-
ularity among such a diverse set of constituencies (from Wall Street to the United
Auto Workers) was Lee Iaccoca, Smith's polar opposite. Both are admired for being
straight shooters. But unlike the former Chrysler Corp. chairman, Smith is no cow-
boy.[8]

When a strategic message becomes an ideology that is at odds with the
business environment, a company is headed for trouble. Inevitably, there
is a time when strategy conflicts with the business environment. Usually,
the business environment wins. Above all, a CEO must communicate a
sense of pragmatism—the desire and ability to do what it takes to win.
There is nothing wrong with admitting error and communicating a need
for change. In fact, admitting an error might gain a CEO the credibility to
accomplish change.

A business owner may change directions as many times as he or she
wishes, provided the company stays economically viable. A surrogate manager has to persuade a board of directors. Some CEOs have changed direction and managed to keep their jobs; others have not.

This does not mean that a company should change a strategic message
quickly. It often cannot afford to do so. Companies invest assets, technology and human and material resources to get where they are in the marketplace. These things tie them down. To walk away from employees,
plants and customers and to do something new changes the character of
an organization and forces it to gain credibility in a new marketplace.

When CEOs do change direction, the resulting organizations have been
greatly different from the way they were before. In the 1960s and 1970s,
for example, CEOs built conglomerates by siphoning cash out of mature
companies. Eventually, the mature companies were sold. This was especially true of railroads, which were having difficulty making money at that
time. Diversification away from railroading let companies get into steel,
soft drink bottling, land development and other enterprises. The railroads
were dumped. Few of the organizations succeeded in their new guise, however, because they faced operating challenges for which they were not prepared.

When a company chooses a prescriptive strategic message, it should ask
how the message fits products and services today. Chances are that prescriptive strategy will create dissonance. A company is not yet doing what
managers envision it should do. However, if a company communicates too
strenuously what it wants to do, it invites comparison with what it currently does. The proper communication of strategy, therefore, has an element of timing. A manager should ask for the possible. To know what is
possible and what is not is a question of observation, judgment and persistence. It is also a matter of luck. Winning strategies that come from hours

of observation in relentless detail followed by rigorous preparation fail in football on any given weekend. Companies are no different.

When a strategic message translates to action, its application will either support, neutralize or contradict the manager who devised the strategy. Implementation can even contradict a manager under the guise of support. This is not because bureaucracies are evil or naturally opposed to the leadership. Rather, actions have unintended consequences, and interpretations are often misinterpretations. Perceived conflict with self-interest can undermine a coherent strategy. It is only through a persistent weeding out of errant understandings and outcomes that a strategic message can be implemented.

A strategic message outlines what a company plans to do and serves as a benchmark of what it does. The swiftest way for a CEO to learn if strategy is succeeding is to visit the location where the work is done. The way in which employees interpret and carry out the strategic message *is* the message. Working directly with employees is often disappointing. Even if they can mouth strategy, application may be absent. Planning with in-depth objectives and tactics will only partly solve such difficulties.

Inevitably, plans that are correct in general will be wrong in detail. CEOs recognize the complexity of running large and diversified companies and respect the limits on their actions. As a former CEO of Motorola, George M. C. Fisher, once said: "The global nature of our business has made it so complex. . . . It's turned into a world where your biggest customers are often also your biggest competitors. You don't run a company like this. You cooperatively grow it."[9]

The marketplace can derail even well-defined plans. A manager may plan for the development of a high-efficiency, low-pollution car at the behest of the government, but having developed the car, may find that the public does not like its low power and limited travel distance. Physics and materials might prevent the manufacture of a high-efficiency, low-pollution auto with the same power and distance as gas-guzzling cars. Moreover, incremental innovations may take years to close the gap, just as the development of gas engines took decades to reach the power and durability we have today.

A strategic message also must fit societal and governmental expectations. If not, it can create dissonance. When society expects a company to act one way and it acts in another, the company may find that public opinion, regulation and the law are thrown against it. Strategic messages are, of necessity, bounded by public acceptability. CEOs who forget this truth have found themselves and their messages being attacked.

If a company chooses to communicate and coordinate strategy across units, it needs to assure the message's fit to:

- research and development
- financial goals
- individual and company action
- human relations and employment policies
- compensation
- customer policies
- distributor and supplier policies
- structure
- value judgments and emphasis
- information technology

Information technology transports the strategic message through the company and into the marketplace. A company is an information machine that processes, stores and transmits data, text, images and sound, internally and externally, to key participants in order to achieve strategic messages. The key to information technology is flexibility, or "maneuverability," as one author described it. The attributes of maneuverability are not that distant from the eight guidelines for corporate communication. They are: maintainability, modularity, scalability, adaptability, portability, openness/standards, autonomy, flexibility, data accessibility, interoperability and appliance connectivity.[10]

SUMMARY

The corporate communication of strategy is a judgmental decision made by managers who are responsible for the survival and success of an organization. Managers' decisions are bounded by the environment in which their companies exist, and by their own intentions. The communication of strategy should be:

- Simple: a strategic message encompasses an entire business unit.
- Timely: the goal or defined steps to the goal can be accomplished within an allotted time period.
- Open to all who must do the tasks leading to successful strategy.
- Defined: strategic messages turn into plans and objectives that specify actions.
- Flexible: the communication of strategic messages allows for opportunity and failure.
- Individual: the strategic message targets persons with responsibility for achieving the goals and implementing the processes.
- Meaningful: the strategic message has understandable and pertinent content for every person implementing the strategy.

Figure 5.3
The Strategic Message and Reputation

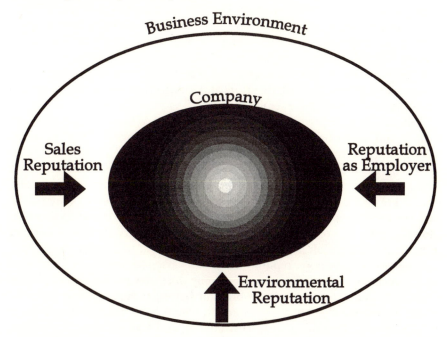

- Measurable: the strategic message has quantifiable outcomes to compare with specified goals.

THE STRATEGIC MESSAGE AND REPUTATION

A company does not have only one reputation, but many (Figure 5.3). The only reputations that count are those perceived by individuals who have the power to increase a company's economic transactions or put it out of business. A company's reputation as a supplier of top-quality meats might be counterbalanced by a poor reputation for environmental control because it flushes killing-floor waste directly into a town's sewer system. Restaurants in New York City might not know or care that the company's Kansas plant is overpowering a water treatment system. The town, on the other hand, might be ready to shut down the facility.

Because reputation can vary by location, culture, issue, interest and sociocultural group, a company can potentially divide and conquer. Its reputation as a good employer might outweigh its immediate threat as an aggressive monopolist. However, when reputation issues cross from one key audience to another, an organization must respond in an integrated fashion.

A company can have a poor reputation and yet survive because it has never reached a critical flash point. In other words, its economic value to society outweighs its perceived menace, giving it economic and marketplace leverage. This was true when, for example, the railroads had transportation monopolies and when American Telephone & Telegraph controlled all sectors of U.S. telecommunications. People complained about the companies yet dealt with them. It is noteworthy, however, that both monopolies eventually disintegrated. As with dictators and kings, when powerful companies show signs of weakness, enemies gather.

Tobacco companies have fought every lawsuit related to smoking and health and contributed heavily to political campaigns. They maintain strong support among tobacco farmers, employees and communities sustained by tobacco revenue. They have used legal and economic power to overwhelm the poor reputation of tobacco products. However, the companies know that the advent of the first sustainable lawsuit against them will trigger a cascade of similar suits. They cannot afford to look weak. Slowly, however, confidential reports from inside the companies and other damaging information is leaking out and beginning to sap their power.

Companies with poor reputations usually become the focus of societal and governmental investigations. The companies may act high-handedly for years but eventually they will be brought before authorities who have the power to revoke their business charters. There have been many instances in U.S. history, beginning with trust busting and then moving through the break-up of banking into investment and commercial practices and into the 1980s, when junk bond houses responsible for merger and acquisition financing were attacked.

Firms can operate in the shadows and keep their reputations sufficiently intact to continue in business. For example, migrant labor contractors have preyed on poor blacks and Hispanics on behalf of farmers. The labor contractors need only have a good reputation for delivering pickers to a farmer when the latter wants them. As long as labor inspectors do not show up, the contractor does not worry what the government thinks. As a young man, the author worked with migrant Mexican laborers. At the time, it was already illegal to hire Mexicans without "green cards," but every field had illegal laborers.

One day, the author witnessed a raid by U.S. immigration officers, who caught three Mexicans without cards. The owner of the farm watched calmly. When the immigration officers asked the farmer if he had any more "illegals" under employment, the owner denied that he ever had employed any. Had he admitted anything, he would have been fined. In California, this kind of charade went on for decades.

One might infer that a perfect communication strategy for a company wishing to remain hidden is to build small plant sites in dispersed geographic areas under different names. This is done, and the practice works.

The reputation of a firm is limited to the plant and company name in each area. The downside is that no one knows what the total company does, and its value and marketplace leverage may suffer accordingly. Each entity is left to its own devices, whereas a single name and marketplace presence might be more efficient and powerful. However, there are times and places when such a dispersed strategy works well because one wants to hide a company's real power in a market or because the products are so different that it makes no sense to unite them under a single strategic message.

A key role of corporate communication is to defend corporate reputation so that the company can operate. This has nothing to do with ethics or morality, and everything to do with a company's ability to survive. Reputation is as much a matter of perception as a reflection of reality. A company may appear to be a good citizen when it is not, or it may seem a villain when, in fact, it has the best interests of others in mind.

If there is moral conflict, it is up to the manager to resolve it. Resolution depends on the ethics of the manager and of those who have influence or power over him or her. Pragmatic managers can, and do, engage in unlawful and morally repugnant actions and still avoid damage to the reputation of an economic enterprise. Society attempts to influence what a person does, but if a manager is not caught or exposed for misdeeds, he or she may commit them throughout a career without retribution.

Managers may also be caught between owners and society in reputation crises. Owners may enjoy ill-gotten gain while society may wish to prosecute. The manager must serve both parties if the company is to survive. There are no easy answers for this conflict, and resignation may be an appropriate solution. Ruptures within family companies are particularly bitter and can set husband against wife and parents against children. When illegality is involved, a relative who blows the whistle has to have great courage or a strong self-interest. Few can emerge unscathed from such bitter fights, especially when they become public.

In general, whistle-blowers are rarely rewarded within companies or society. A whistle-blower who communicates publicly that a company has transgressed the law will be hounded. The company will consider that person a traitor, especially if exposure threatens economic livelihood. It is up to society to protect the whistle-blower. Whistle-blowing requires indisputable evidence for the whistle-blower to survive with reputation intact against the combined reputation of a company and the individuals in it who oppose him or her.

A manager ranks and tracks company reputation as it affects survival. The most important components of reputation reside with any group that can put the company out of business immediately. Among these, by definition, are customers, employees and owners.

With customers, one can track reputation partly through sales, but the long-term consequences of a poor reputation may not be immediately evident in sales figures. Individuals can be positive, negative or neutral about a company along several dimensions. Issues rise and fall in importance as time goes by. A company cannot excuse itself from the world. It must reckon with people's concerns when they threaten business, even if the issues prove to be passing fads.

There are several ways to track key reputation issues:

- reliance on industry trade associations;
- sounding out opinion leaders;
- secondary research in existing databases;
- primary research through panels, focus groups, surveys and polls.

Tracking can use charting methods from statistical quality control. For example, if one charted a company weekly by polling a statistically significant number of customers who rated it positively on cultural diversity, annual ratings would equal 52 data points. One would take the mean of these 52 points plus one standard deviation on either side to set up a tracking system with upper and lower control boundaries. Should one's rating exceed the upper limit, it means that the company's reputation for diversity has made a significant improvement. Similarly, should the rating fall below the lower boundary, it means that the company's reputation has deteriorated.

Such statistics are not absolute, however. A company's reputation for cultural diversity might rise meaningfully but so might the reputations of competitors and expectations of citizens whose perceptions are assessed. On the other hand, a company might do nothing different from what it has always done and yet watch its reputation decline because the environment around it has changed and expectations are higher than they used to be. Tracking is a warning gauge, and not an absolute. Unlike quality control techniques, where one can narrow the variance of materials over time, one cannot narrow public perceptions of reputation because they are not fixed. This is a crucial difference. Measurement can never escape relativity, but unless one tracks, there is no measure with which to work.

COMMUNICATING THE STRATEGIC MESSAGE

The communication of strategic messages focuses on implementation— on persuading an individual or groups of individuals to support a company's mission and goals. There are various theories of how this persuasion occurs, but all are based on:

- effective communication;
- bidirectional messages between sender and receiver;

• acceptance of the psychological state of the message receiver as a starting point;
• perception and fact.

One theory sees six linear steps to gaining and keeping support:

• awareness
• information
• evaluation
• trial
• adoption
• reinforcement

Each step links to the next in the series, and each describes a psychological state of an individual moving from ignorance to commitment (Figure 5.4).

A second theory sees an accumulation of information connected to other concepts in an individual's storehouse of knowledge. It is anything but linear, as the following passage indicates:

Often, the customer or prospect is not in the market for the promoted product. While the marketing communications message may be received or processed, it will not result in immediate action and there may not be any communication feedback. Instead the consumer may store the message for later use by attaching it to the concept or category in which the product is kept in the mind. Thus while the marketer has no direct measure that his or her marketing communication message had any impact, the message may well have been added to the concept of the brand, the product form, or the category for later use.[11]

The two views of effective communication are not necessarily opposed, although interpretations have conflicted. Some saw the six linear steps as involving one-way communication from message sender to message receiver, but this was never true because market research served as a response or market feedback from message receivers. It was also thought that a communicator replaced a concept in a receiver's mind with the communicator's own message, but this denied the role of memory. In the end, effective communication is seen as a "messy" process and linearity is an abstraction, but the six steps do describe states that individuals reach while accepting or rejecting messages.

The first state is awareness. One must be aware before one can learn. Awareness is recognition without information. If one were to ask an aware person whether he or she had heard the name of company or product, the person would say yes but would not be able to tell you anything about it.

The second state, information, requires effort. A person wants to find out something: the individual chooses to become informed. Studies of per-

Figure 5.4
Six Steps of Corporate Communication

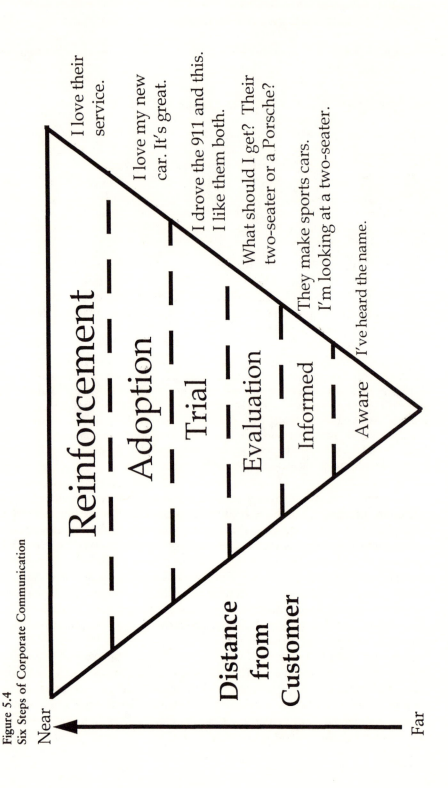

suasion and rhetoric have shown that if information appeals to the self-interest of an individual, the chances are higher that the individual will choose to learn about a product, service or concept. The strongest motivators are the same as those in the "needs hierarchy" for motivating work. The hierarchy, from lowest to highest, includes physiological needs, safety needs, belongingness, self-esteem and self-actualization.

During evaluation—the third state—a person weighs the pros and cons. Weighing alternatives may not be an active or compelling exercise, and a person may take time examining the issues. One might identify three makes of cars in one's price range and talk with owners of these cars, visit showrooms to look at the cars and collect brochures about them, show the brochures to family members for comment, research the cars in auto and independent testing magazines, look at the cars parked on the street, stop evaluating temporarily or permanently for other reasons (such as lack of money to buy a new car), continue evaluating and never make a decision or, instead, move to a trial or a decision to buy the car.

One may also skip evaluation when a product, service or idea is well understood. Habitual action does just that. Behavior is a short-hand method of living and acting that lets a person focus on other areas of interest. Once one has decided how to keep a boss happy and been confirmed in that decision by the boss, new behaviors become automatic with practice. Ideally, a company wants to persuade individuals to make its strategic message part of their life and work styles.

The trial is like a test drive. It allows one to view a product, service or concept and see if it works for him or her. Trial does not require commitment. Particularly with complex ideas or embedded behaviors, trial is a strong communication technique to help overcome resistance. Companies with a bad reputation for employee treatment may offer an independent figure, such as a journalist, an opportunity to work for a day or week at a company plant. The company hopes that the trial will show the journalist the company is not as bad as union critics say. Military services and armaments manufacturers use plane rides, ship tours, firepower demonstrations and other techniques to let the public experience the capabilities of war weapons. Similarly, in-store samplers introduce new foods and cosmetics.

The barriers to trial are economics and practicality. It might be too costly to allow trials of some ideas, products or services, and it is impossible to try some ideas without committing to irrevocable action. An idea requiring commitment without trial was the North American Free Trade Agreement, which reduces tariffs between the United States, Canada and Mexico. Expert witnesses took well-crafted positions on both sides of the issue. Even attentive listeners were confused whether the agreement would cost jobs or increase employment. Ultimately, President Bill Clinton put his prestige and political power on the line to gain the agreement's passage.

Such issues regularly occur in organizations. Should a company build a $100 million plant or sink $2 billion into new oil exploration? It depends on a forecast for market and product demand. There are always well-crafted arguments for and against market and product growth. Ultimately, a CEO makes a choice without a trial.

Adoption equals commitment. One lowers personal defenses or parts with wealth in trade in return for a new idea, product or service. Adoption may take minutes, months or years, or it may not occur at all. One can never persuade some individuals to adopt a different approach or view. Some habitual smokers, illegal drug users or heavy drinkers will not adopt the idea and behavior of sobriety, even when sobriety contributes to a longer life. Businesses that sell cigarettes, heroin and alcohol reap continuous wealth from such persons.

Adoption has psychological outcomes. Usually, there is a spurt of personal identification with the product or idea—a conversion reaction in which the effort of decision is replaced with the relief of action. For example:

• "Look at my new car. Isn't it a beauty? It runs like a dream."
• "Please don't smoke in my office. I stopped smoking six months ago and I hate cigarettes."
• "I'm celebrating my Alcoholics Anonymous anniversary. I stopped drinking a year ago."

After a period, the newness wears off and functionality takes over. Experience provides understanding, and at this stage, reinforcement begins.

Reinforcement might be essential, especially when there is a motivation to return to a former behavior or belief. It is easy to again start smoking, drinking or taking illegal drugs. Similarly, if one has a bad experience with a new car and a company does not appear to care, it can destroy one's commitment to a product and company. Auto companies have learned that the way in which recalls are implemented may actually increase customer loyalty.

The second theory, the accumulation model of persuasive communication, focuses on the role of memory and judgment in decisions to accept or reject messages:

The storage and retrieval system works on the basis of matching incoming information with what is already stored in memory. If the information matches or enhances what is already there, then the new information will likely be added to the existing concepts and categories. If it doesn't, the consumer has to make a choice, either the new information can replace what is already there or the new information can be rejected. In this case, the consumer would continue to use existing concepts and categories. We call this the "judgment system" in that consumers match or test new information against what they already have, then make a judgment to add to, adapt, or reject.[12]

The accumulation model defines three states—information exposure to the senses, information reception involving short-term memory and cognitive response involving long-term memory.[13] From there, information enters a network of concepts and assumes a place in the conceptual chain. Networks are not linear or rational. One concept will ally itself in peculiar ways to the others. Each network chain is unique to the individual. Decisions to accept or reject new concepts or new products and services come from individual decision processes occurring within these networked concepts.

No matter how one views the process of persuasive communication, implementation identifies where individuals are on a path from awareness through reinforcement and then sets quantifiable objectives for reaching acceptance or for the reinforcement of a message (Figure 5.5). Planning may be informal, but every company has targets for essential individuals. One must convince a certain number of customers to buy a product or service each year. One must gain willing commitment from employees to make, distribute and sell the product or service. One must keep owners happy to survive in a job or to avoid liquidation of the enterprise. It is always unsafe to assume that one has communicated a strategic message satisfactorily and the company's reputation is secure. To survive and succeed, an organization constantly assesses the effectiveness of its communication and its reputation.

Because a strategic message begins at the top yet is carried out at the bottom of a company, a manager makes the first consistency checks of a strategic message at the top. Because reputation begins outside the control of an organization and impacts on it, a manager starts reputation assessment outside a company and works toward its boundaries.

With a strategic message, if there is no consensus among the CEO and top officers, there will be no consensus below them. However, even when there is agreement at the top, a manager can never assume that there will be either awareness or consensus at the bottom. This might be due to communications failure, but not always. The reasons why employees do not know, understand or believe a company's strategy may not be apparent. There can be:

- differences between words and action: managers say one thing and do another;
- failures to communicate meaning: a subordinate believes that he or she is interpreting strategy correctly yet is doing the opposite of what is intended;
- disobedience: a subordinate disagrees with strategy and continues to do things his or her way;

Figure 5.5
Communicating the Strategic Message

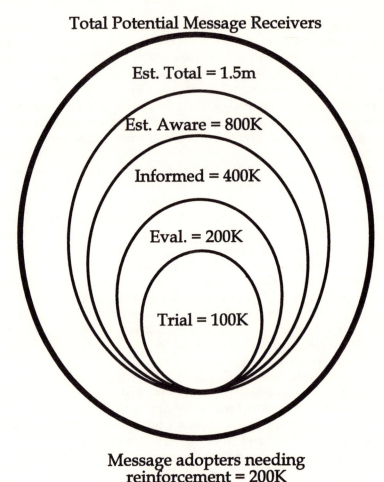

Total Potential Message Receivers

Est. Total = 1.5m

Est. Aware = 800K

Informed = 400K

Eval. = 200K

Trial = 100K

**Message adopters needing
reinforcement = 200K**

- credibility gaps: those who carry out strategy might not believe management intends it. For example, managers driven by bottom-line concerns are told to be customer oriented. The managers may not believe that the CEO means what he or she says;

- lack of persistence: management might believe in a strategy but become bored with the task of repeating the message and move onto something else.

The role of persistence and repetition was noted in an article profiling David Gergen, a master of political communication who supported several presidents. Gergen said that President Richard Nixon developed the rules of coordinated publicity at the White House.

[Gergen] learned the importance of saying the same thing, over and over and over: "Nixon taught us about the art of repetition. He used to tell me, 'About the time you are writing a line that you have written so often that you want to throw up, that is the first time the American People will hear it.' "[14]

It is too much to ask every employee to understand a strategic message or commit to it beyond work hours. Some want to do their jobs and go home: their interests lie elsewhere. Others are loyalists and do not ask questions: they willingly submit themselves to whatever they are told to do. Customers may not care whether a company has a strategic message as long as they can purchase products and services they want.

Concerning reputation, a company might not truly know how it is regarded. Companies have been trapped often by "unaccountable" changes of opinion and perception. A failure to understand a company's external reputation can have several possible causes:

• managers do not care to know as long as customers buy products and services;

• employees do not care to know as long as they are employed;

• individuals are not vocal: a journalist may refuse to answer questions about a company to avoid biasing entree to executives or giving a view that may change. This is a common position among regulators as well. On the other hand, some individuals may truly hold no opinion;

• individuals hide their true feelings;

• individuals use a company's reputation to their own ends. For example, a politician may bash a company to aid in a reelection campaign.

The author cannot recall any company in which he has consulted where the strategic message was clearly known and accepted throughout. Nor can he recall a company with a universally clear understanding of its reputation.

A manager examines key points for the effective communication of a strategic message and the preservation of corporate reputation and then discards the other points. A clerk without customer contact may not need to understand the larger scheme. It would be useful if the clerk were more involved, but the company will not fail if he or she is not. The clerk must only understand the task that he or she must get done to meet a particular objective. Strategy, for this person, is an immediate objective, and reputation involves whether a job is done according to rules. For example:

My job is to deliver inbound mail to all members of the department by 9:00 A.M. daily and to pick up outbound mail at 9:30 A.M., 12:00 noon and 3:00 P.M.

A clerk might execute such instructions perfectly and yet never understand the linkage of inbound and outbound mail to larger customer-service strategies. This does not necessarily mean that a clerk is kept in the dark. It may mean that he or she wants to know no more or is incapable of understanding more.

In this way, too, customers buy goods and services without the least idea of the reputation of the company that manufactures them. All the consumers know is that they can trust a product to work as it says it does. This is reputation enough. The product is a self-contained strategic message and reputation.

However, other products and services are so tied to a company that the organization is essential to the transaction. An automobile, washing machine, refrigerator or stove must be maintained over the life of the equipment. Consumers need to trust that the company behind the product will be there when they need it ten years from now.

A third category of product may have an association with an entirely different company. Manufacturers of foods, paper goods, household electronics and other consumer essentials often make private label products sold under a retailer's name. If there is a product problem, the retailer assumes the burden of healing its reputation, while the manufacturer remains invisible.

When a strategic message and reputation are important to the economic life of a company, managers must communicate them to every level. An example is Total Quality Management (TQM), which relies on employees to control variance in business processes. Employees standardize and improve processes, which they evaluate against larger customer service goals and the needs of the next process in the chain. If employees do not understand their roles, TQM fails. Maintaining "work-rule" habits when "work rules" are out of date will cause a company to fall behind its competition—an inherent problem with labor unions. Unions often rally behind outdated work-rule and manning provisions to avoid the exploitation of workers but end up by harming the companies and individuals they serve. Clint Golden, founder and vice president of the United Steelworkers of America and a self-educated worker, was spurned by his own union in 1950 when he called for a focus on cooperative labor-management productivity rather than conflict:

In what was perhaps his most important postwar speech, Golden stressed the need for productivity, pointing out that in the United States, "our greatest advances in productivity . . . have coincided with a phenomenal growth of the labor movement." Management has learned, or, is learning "that the workers in their factories hold many of the essential keys to increased productivity, and that treating them as partners in the production process can yield increased output, higher wages, and greater job satisfaction."[15]

Golden never lived to see the fruition of his ideas (nearly 35 years later) because the fierce opposition of labor and management, which was already decades old, prevented his message from being heard. Oddly enough, Golden's thoughts echoed those of Frederick Winslow Taylor, writing in 1916.

It would seem to be so self-evident that maximum prosperity for the employer, coupled with maximum prosperity for the employee, ought to be the two leading objectives of management, that even to state this fact should be unnecessary. And yet, there is no question that, throughout the industrial world, a large part of the organization of employers, as well as employees, is for war rather than for peace, and that perhaps the majority on either side do not believe that it is possible to arrange their mutual relations that their interests become identical.[16]

There is no correct way to apply a universal standard to decide what is successful communication of a strategic message or an appropriate reputation in the marketplace. A manager will apply the communication and reputation standards that a company has set for itself for as long as the company survives and is successful.

In companies that operate well and appear to carry out a stated strategy, the burden of proof of the need for change is on the manager, who may have to "create a crisis" to gain the attention of key individuals. In companies that are clearly not working well, a manager may not need proof as such companies are often looking for solutions. The ultimate decision maker concerning the effectiveness of the strategic message and a company's reputation is the CEO. Even if one has strong evidence that communication is failing and a company's reputation is negative, the CEO can avoid change unless he or she is forced to act by those with direct power over him or her.

Companies are groups of individuals with expectations, behavior and perceptions that are formed through experience and persuasion over time. A company might act better if its strategic message and reputation were understood better at all levels, yet this might make no difference if employees lack the capacity or desire to understand and carry out management's larger intentions, or if management has no desire for employees to know more than their assigned tasks. This is why employee publications have often been sops. Corporate editors who tried to make their publications relevant found themselves without support. Most were wise enough to put out a publication that management wanted rather than the communication that was needed.

External individuals are no different. One might expect customers to react positively to better service, but they may not. Customers may have had such a long history of bad service that they have adjusted to it. It may take a great deal of work by a company to build up credibility for a better approach.

However, customers may speak up if they have heavy investments in a company's equipment. Computer hardware and software manufacturers have users' groups who serve as loyal critics. Users groups help a company gauge its reputation, but they can also be a source of inertia. A company may have to move away from technology that it once espoused in order to remain competitive, yet its users may not want it to do so. The company thus finds itself trapped between a changing marketplace and users who want things to remain the same. This was especially true of the rapid change in computer hardware and software design during the 1980s. As proprietary architectures evolved into standardized open platforms, several computer hardware manufacturers found themselves trapped by customers who did not want to change. A company was thus faced with abandoning its loyal customers and repeat sources of revenue in return for an unknown future. Several companies elected not to abandon their users and were badly hurt.

There are formal and informal methods of performing audits on the effectiveness of strategic communication and appropriateness of company reputation. There are, as well, standardized and ad-hoc instruments to help one track communications more accurately over time. We will discuss these instruments later, but most follow survey research methods and include random sampling, questionnaire construction and interviewing. A manager should learn methods, techniques and their shortcomings without forgetting that:

An audit is merely a process of exploring, examining, monitoring, or evaluating something. Accountants audit our financial records, physicians audit our health, professors audit our learning process, and managers review, or audit, our level of performance. In other words, the auditing process is one with which all of us are familiar.[17]

SUMMARY

Reputation is a concept with economic implications that defines the trust expressed toward a company by customers, influentials and others who ensure its survival and success. A company has several reputations and need worry only about those that threaten business at the time. A company's reputation should be quantified and tracked regularly in key areas to provide a gauge of public opinion.

Corporate communication implements a strategic message through moving key audiences from ignorance to the adoption of company products, services and concepts. Audience reactions are measurable on a continuum from awareness to information, evaluation, trial and adoption, with the subsequent need for reinforcement.

Corporate communication of strategic messages should be:

- Simple: it focuses on a strategic message and reputation that directly affect corporate survival and success.
- Timely: it measures and reports the implementation of a strategic message and reputation in time to support a company's need to make continuous economic transactions.
- Open: it keeps managers and employees apprised of the state of a company's reputation among key participants.
- Defined: it measures the clarity of messages sent and the level of understanding of the messages received. It quantifies key reputation characteristics that affect a company's business today.
- Flexible: it allows for failure and opportunity in communicating and in guarding a company's reputation.
- Individual: it recognizes that individuals carry out tasks and hold opinions about companies.
- Meaningful: it emphasizes the clear communication of message content tied explicitly to a company's defined or informal strategic message. It focuses on reputation that directly impacts a company's ability to survive and succeed.
- Measurable: it establishes quantifiable metrics for both communications and reputation in order to track and report progress or setbacks.

NOTES

1. Carl Von Clausewitz, *On War,* ed. and trans., Michael Howard and Peter Paret (Princeton, NJ: Princeton University Press, 1976), p. 177.

2. Bernard M. Bass, *Bass and Stogdill's Handbook of Leadership: Theory, Research, and Managerial Applications,* 3d ed. (New York: The Free Press, 1990), p. 174.

3. Roger Rosenblatt, "How Do They Live with Themselves?" *New York Times Magazine,* March 20, 1994, Sec. 6, p. 36.

4. Bradley Johnson, "10 Years After '1984': The Commercial and the Product that Changed Advertising," *Advertising Age,* January 10, 1994, p. 12.

5. Ibid., p. 13.

6. Henry Scammell, "Life after Eastern," *Air & Space: Smithsonian* 8, no. 5 (December 1993–January 1994): 28–39.

7. Daniel Yergin, *The Prize: The Epic Quest for Oil, Money and Power* (New York: Simon & Schuster, 1991), pp. 35–110.

8. Kathleen Kerwin, with James B. Treece, David Woodruff, Kevin Kelly, and Michael Oneal, "Can Jack Smith Fix General Motors?" *Business Week,* no. 3343 (November 1, 1993): 126.

9. Barnaby J. Feder, "Motorola Will Be Just Fine, Thanks," *New York Times,* October 31, 1993, sect. 3, p. 6.

10. Bernard H. Boar, *The Art of Strategic Planning for Information Technology* (New York: John Wiley & Sons, 1993), p. 29.

11. Don E. Schultz, Stanley I. Tannenbaum, and Robert E. Lauterborn, *Integrated Marketing Communications* (Lincolnwood, IL: NTC Business Books, 1993), p. 31.

12. Ibid., pp. 31–32.

13. Ibid., p. 33.

14. Michael Kelly, "David Gergen, Master of the Game," *New York Times Magazine,* October 31, 1993, sect. 6, p. 68.

15. Thomas R. Brooks, *Clint: A Biography of a Labor Intellectual, Clinton S. Golden* (New York, Atheneum, 1978), p. 327.

16. Frederick Winslow Taylor, *The Principles of Scientific Management* (New York: Harper & Brothers Publishers, 1916), pp. 9–10.

17. Cal W. Downs, *Communication Audits* (Glenview, IL: Scott Foresman and Company, 1988), p. 3.

6

Corporate Communication and the Individual

It is unfortunate, but the reality is that many management teams have little credibility with the mass of workers. Each year, new programs are announced with tremendous fanfare and each year they die a slow death. The staff, understandingly jaded and cynical, reacts with a predictable maxim: "This too shall pass." They suspect that management believes deeply in little and is committed to less.

—Bernard H. Boar, *The Art of Strategic Planning for Information Technology*[1]

WHERE WE ARE

We started this book by explaining communication and then examining business as a function thereof. We looked at the business environment from a seller's point of view—as an unfriendly place where, through communication, a seller finds a buyer and receives wealth in return for goods and services. We discussed the strategic message as a driving force in economic transactions, reputation and links to credibility.

In this chapter we examine individuals—the message sender and message receiver. By understanding the person better, we can build a basis for more effective corporate communication.

THE PRIMACY OF THE INDIVIDUAL IN CORPORATE COMMUNICATION

In all effective communication, choice and action rest with the individual. Individual managers speak to individuals, who in turn carry out commands.

Individuals persuade other individuals to buy. Individuals fend off persons who threaten their ways of doing business. The weight of governmental regulation is built and administered by individuals.

It is hard for managers to remember individuals, and harder for them to deal with them, particularly in large organizations and mass markets. A manager is paid to get things done and not to understand a person's peculiarities. Indeed, understanding an individual is necessary only insofar as it helps complete the economic transaction.

Action depends on a person's willing acceptance of a message. The message receiver's free will can be either a wall blocking business goals or a lever through which a manager achieves unheard-of feats. A person is not a waiting vessel into which sight, sound, taste, touch and smell are poured to produce specific outcomes based on a mix of messages and appeals. Every human is possibility and probability, but never certainty. Each person carries a legacy of culture, upbringing, experience and belief that influences and fashions response. Any message to an individual carries as much implicit as explicit meaning (Figure 6.1).

Historians are well aware of how culture influences political, business and social behaviors. They call such culture *folkways*. "[A folkway] is defined here as the normative structure of values, customs and meanings that exist in every culture. . . . Folkways are constantly in process of creation, even in our own time."[2] Folkways are as important to corporate communication as they are to historians. They include:

- speech: pronunciation, vocabulary, syntax and grammar;
- building: forms of vernacular architecture;
- family: structures and functions of households;
- marriage: courtship, marriage and divorce;
- gender: social relations between men and women;
- sex: ideas about sexual convention and deviance;
- child rearing: child nature and nurture;
- naming: favored names given to people and things;
- age: attitudes toward age;
- death: attitudes toward death and mourning;
- religion: worship, theology and architecture of belief;
- magic: beliefs about the supernatural;
- learning: patterns of education, literacy and learning;
- food: diet, nutrition, cooking and eating;
- dress: dress, demeanor and personal adornment;
- sport: recreation and leisure;
- work: work ethics and experiences; attitudes toward work;

Figure 6.1
Corporate Communication and Individuality

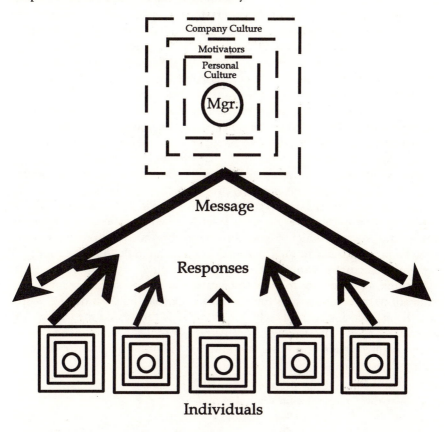

- time: use of time, methods of timekeeping;
- wealth: attitudes toward wealth and its distribution;
- rank: rules by which social rank is assigned; roles and relations between social ranks;
- social: migration, settlement, association and affiliation;
- order: ideas of order, institutions and forms of disorder;
- power: attitudes toward authority and power;
- freedom: ideas of liberty and restraint.[3]

Every organization has two sets of folkways—the folkways an individual brings to it and the folkways an organization imposes on the person. Add to folkways an individual's physiological needs, desire for material and personal security, wish for social acceptance and drive for self-fulfillment, and a manager has an infinite set of subtexts for any message.

When an organization trains employees to its culture, communication is easier because one accepts a shared understanding or is "washed out."[4] Companies as diverse as Arthur Andersen, IBM, Computer Associates and EDS built strong cultures that molded individuals in precise ways. Building a person's behavior according to a prescribed methodology is as well known a procedure in business as it is in the U.S. Marine Corps. In organizations that do not train employees rigorously, managers must continually negotiate and balance behavior and motivators.

Programmatic training, however, is not a simple solution for effective communication. An overreliance on method can lead to individuals being unable to respond to change except in programmed ways. Such persons either deny problems or attack them with formulas that are built on imperfect or inappropriate assumptions. Kurt Godel, the Czechoslovakian-American logician and philosopher, proved before World War II that "the consistency of a logical system cannot be proved within the system."[5] What Godel showed is that every logical system depends on assumptions from outside the system, which cannot be proved by the system of logic itself. Godel's proof applies to any logical system, including communication, because all structure encompasses only part of reality.

Unthinking obedience to communication can lead to self-destruction, organizational dissolution and societal harm. German Soldiers during World War II, in excusing their slaughter of noncombatants, said they were only following orders. This passage from Alfred, Lord Tennyson's "The Charge of the Light Brigade" notes the stupidity of the order behind the charge.

"Forward, the Light Brigade!"
Was there a man dismay'd?
Not tho' the soldier knew
    Some one had blunder'd.
Theirs not to make reply.
Theirs not to reason why.
Theirs but to do and die.
Into the valley of Death
    Rode the six hundred.[6]

Unthinking obedience cost the British army 20,000 casualties in 30 minutes at the battle of the Somme in World War I and thousands of Australian lives at Gallipoli. A strong emphasis on obedience to orders continues in the various armed forces today, partly because a questioning soldier might balk at going into a battle where his life and the lives of others are at great risk. Soldiers are taught to depend on commanders whose job it is to look out for their troops.

Outside the military, there are always individuals who believe one should give up everything for a cause, including one's right to choose anything other than what a manager dictates. Successful companies will always be built that way and can be immensely powerful, as long as they do not run amok in society, lose touch with the marketplace or subside in spirit.

CA [Computer Associates] salespeople quickly built a reputation for zealotry. Along with most of CA, you were either a zealot or out the door. In one bizarre instance, CA discovered that a star salesman so psyched himself up to come away with something tangible from his sales calls that he never left an office without slipping something into his pocket—a ballpoint pen, a sheet of paper, a paper clip, anything. He would not leave without something. His managers discovered it because he would do the same thing when visiting CA headquarters.[7]

Even in highly disciplined organizations, managers communicate a set of possible meanings that is bounded only by the number of individuals who get the message, whether or not they were targeted for the message. Managers who have risen through the ranks have a better chance of guessing outcomes among particular individuals than those who have not. However, even in small companies, it is impossible to know everyone equally well. Of necessity, communication to individuals contains assumptions and abstractions and, by definition, misunderstanding, based on the unique perspective of a message receiver.

To overcome misunderstanding, managers communicate the most intensively to those on whom they depend directly to get tasks done, whether clerks or managers. A manager's self-interest and the interest of the organization force the choices. Not every employee is equal in terms of communication, although every individual may be important to the survival and growth of an economic enterprise. The only equality in an organization is a person's choice to work for it. After that, a person can be, and often is, treated in unequal ways.

Ranking is a fact in communication, business and life. However, danger arises when a manager talks *only* to a favored few, as a narrow focus constricts communication lines and fosters politics. Moreover, a manager endangers the understanding of the business and environment because the favored few unavoidably interpret information selectively. Open communication aids survival as much as anything. Openness, however, does not mean an "open door." A manager's time is limited by tasks he or she must do. Sometimes the tasks are overwhelming and sometimes managers are seduced by their work and forget their other responsibilities.

A good rule of thumb is to communicate to those individuals who are key to the survival and success of a company at the present time. The more responsibility an individual has, the more a manager communicates directly to him or her to make sure the aims and objectives are reached. Store clerks serving customers have a fundamental task—the completion of economic transactions. Therefore, a store manager communicates directly to clerks to make sure that they treat customers well. However, if store clerks are ready to sell but no inventory is on hand, the manager's communication will shift from the clerks to the distributors. This kind of ranking follows no set system. Rather, it follows the marketplace and events. A manager goes to any dangerous situation at any time to ensure the company's survival and success, and each manager decides how far to extend personal communication to get the job done. This depends directly on the stamina of the manager and the subordinates to whom the former entrusts the responsibility for carrying out essential tasks.

With trusted subordinates, a manager knows from prior communication and experience how well an individual can grasp a message and carry on. With others, a manager may know little or nothing. Ideally for the sanity of a manager and success of a business, he or she will have subordinates to whom he or she need not communicate constantly. Practically speaking, this rarely happens because there are information gaps between the employee and manager, the business environment intrudes and changes expectations and normal communication lines break down or are overwhelmed with noise.

Breakdowns can be mechanical, such as telephone failure, or interpersonal. Interpersonal breakdown is more dangerous than mechanical breakdown. For example, one person stops trusting another. At that point, communication between the two becomes biased or slanted by perceptions. The tragedy of interpersonal failure has been the subject of drama for thousands of years—for example, Othello's homicidal jealousy toward his wife, Desdemona, in Shakespeare's play.

A manager checks message and media for effectiveness and remains aware of the factors that can harm effective message sending. Managers do not depend on any one message or medium. They use what works as long as they can satisfy themselves that it is working at least at a threshold level.

There are minimum and maximum levels of individual communication. The minimum is enough information to complete a task leading to an economic transaction. The maximum is any amount of communication beyond the minimum that supports economic transactions and does not harm understanding of specific message content or impede action directed by message content. Both have a place in business. The minimum insures the proper mechanical fulfillment of tasks; and the maximum, thoughtful involvement in company strategy. Beyond a minimum level, the amount of communication is independent of business survival and success. A manager may provide either a minimum or maximum level of communication but will succeed or fail because the message is either right or wrong. The level of communication depends on the behavior and preference of a manager, employees, customers and the business environment, among many variables. Each business is unique in the amount of communication required and the individuals to whom it communicates.

Companies are expressions of founders and of leaders who instill their views into individuals. These views can advance or retard a business at different times over its lifetime. A manager with practical economic insight into a marketplace and an ability to act can build a great business on instinct. On the other hand, a manager may fail miserably, even though he or she is well educated, because of an inability to persuade either customers or employees to follow a vision.

Even new and productive technologies fail when managers are unprepared for them. Work-group software that is used to coordinate departmental processes, for instance, has fostered unintended side effects, such as employees becoming unwilling to share work, officers who filter E-mail and subordinates who feel they are being watched. An article discussing groupware summarized the communication challenge nicely: "Everyone says groupware creates a flatter, more democratic organization. But that really only happens if the organization is ready for it."[8]

Understanding how to communicate to individuals is a multidimensional task. It is only by looking at a business environment in various ways that one can discover relevant facts. Using folkways, one might find:

- Building design: in R&D departments, openness in traffic flow is valued to encourage informal conversation.
- Family: some employees live to work while others live for home life.
- Marriage: among singles in a work environment, code words may express a desire for closeness that cannot be voiced openly.
- Gender: rough jesting among one sex may be inappropriate with the opposite sex.
- Speech: every profession or skill invents words, syntax and grammar.
- Sex: for years, business conventions allowed sexual propositions as long as they did not flare into the open. Today, that has become less possible but remains a factor.
- Child rearing: day care is an issue with working parents.
- Naming: the naming of products and services is a discipline in itself.
- Age: older workers protest being moved out of positions in which they believe they are still effective, as with mandatory retirement rules for airline pilots.
- Magic: in Hong Kong, geomancers site buildings. In Thailand, Buddhist priests drive demons from workplaces. In Hawaii, native priests get rid of evil spirits. Managers who do not believe in these practices have nonetheless bowed to them to keep employees in the workplace.

Sometimes, company culture can override or modify personal culture. Effective communication depends on sensitivity to the work environment and to influences from within and without. No manager has time to consider

ural and motivational options before communicating, but
consider a few and learn more through experience.

agers never assume that a message is understood by an
ead, they find out how it has been translated verbally and
key points. If a manager stresses customer service, he or she
on the sales floor. If a manager preaches quality manufacturing, he or she watches machines and assemblers. If a manager spotlights
selling, then he or she spends time with sales staff and potential customers.

Managers fail when:

- They focus on the wrong messages or individuals.
- They fail to follow up on communication to see if it has been effected.
- They fail to link company processes to a message.
- They are captives to culture and cannot speak objectively to colleagues or sub-
  ordinates.
- They are not perceived as powerful. Perception is of two kinds. The first involves
  how a manager sees what he or she is doing, while the second involves how
  others see the manager. CEOs have been removed from office because their esti-
  mate of personal power differed from that of the owners or owners' representatives or because employees refuse to take them seriously.
- Timing is bad; they communicate too early or too late to influence action.
- Communication skills are poor.
- They do not communicate. For example, a manager remains silent when something should be said.

A manager may use any verbal or nonverbal message or medium to communicate effectively to individuals. However, in cases where no message or
medium is effective, the message receiver may have elected to exclude him-
or herself from its intent. When the expectations are clear and reasonable,
individuals who choose not to follow orders in effect fire themselves.

One takes individuals as he or she finds them and uses methods that
work currently (Figure 6.2). A manager should know several tools for effective communication and be willing to use any or all of them. One author,
in summarizing techniques used by leaders to gain control of unfamiliar
companies, noted that leaders learn before they leap and co-opt the best
people.[9] They find out where the best managers are and get them on their
team quickly. Leaders learn shortcuts to an industry. Using Pareto's law,
which states that 80 percent of a company's problems comes from 20 percent of its procedures and methods, leaders look for the crucial 20 percent.
Leaders break the existing patterns. They find and communicate real and
symbolic ways to show that old ways have changed.

In communication to individuals, message content and presentation have
equal weight. If presentation is poor, a message will be vague. If a well-

Figure 6.2
The Communication Continuum

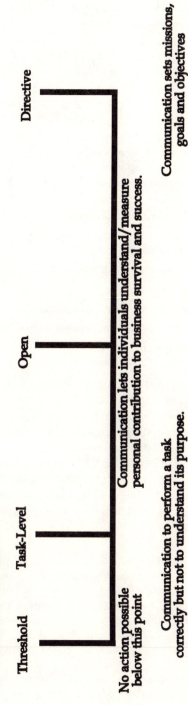

Threshold

Task-Level

Open

Directive

No action possible
below this point

Communication to perform a task
correctly but not to understand its purpose.

Communication lets individuals understand/measure
personal contribution to business survival and success.

Communication sets missions,
goals and objectives

presented message has inadequate or incorrect content, managers may drive a company off-course. A typical example is that some managers stress financial performance but not how one may achieve financial results. Such overemphasis on outcomes can rob a business of the investment and changes it needs to stay competitive.

Message receivers are not of equal value. A manager communicates first to persons with the most power to get things done, and not necessarily to the best-compensated or most highly placed individual. The powerful person is the one to whom most people listen and from whom most action comes. He or she might not be in a company at all or might be overlooked. For example, a chairperson's spouse might wield as much power as the chairperson. An administrative assistant might be at the center of economic activity.

To find the powerful individuals, a manager asks questions like:

- When a crisis occurs, whom do you call?
- When a project bogs down, who gets it restarted?
- Whom do you dare not cross?
- Who does the most important work in this company?
- Why do you believe some people are more effective than others in this company?
- How do effective people operate here?

Inevitably, such questions lead to a core group of individuals whose behavior or opinions must change in order for a process or company to work differently. In some companies, plant managers are the most powerful. Plant managers might rarely show up at headquarters, but they control the greatest number of people, assets and revenue-generation potential and they can form fiefdoms that are beyond a CEO's reach. It would be dangerous not to communicate to such individuals first and gain their support because their opposition can sink a message. This is what happened to an executive who was centralizing the operations of a nursing home chain, as related in the *Wall Street Journal*:

[It is essential to] build broad alliances with individuals inside and outside your department. The new president of one big nursing-home chain lost his job partly because he never did. Hired by the board of directors to centralize operations, "he went in there like a whirlwind," says Richard C. Grote, a Dallas career consultant and a friend of the executive's.

But the president's efforts drained power from the chain's 100 nursing-home administrators. To quell their complaints, the board dismissed him a few months later.

The man might have survived if he had sought support from some key nursing home managers during his early days, Mr. Grote suggests.[10]

The need to communicate to the most powerful actors first means that a manager may jump the chain of command when necessary but must also be careful not to create resistance when such jumping violates corporate culture. This is why a manager may sometimes be wiser not to approach individuals but rather have a surrogate ask—someone with no apparent political affiliation. A surrogate will often promise confidentiality so that employees, customers and others feel free to speak. This is good when a manager can receive a range of opinions that he or she would not otherwise get but bad when individuals do not tell the truth. Master game players can disguise self-interested intentions with convincing appearances. As a result, a manager should never trust any second-hand report completely (or even a first-hand report, for that matter) and can never be excused from using judgment and psychology in communication. With individuals, managers learn when to be tough and when to be warm. A sudden sharp remark may stop gamesmanship, and humor may relieve tension when an individual is tongue-tied.

Managers are usually better off maintaining open and clear communication lines, but they have been successful either way. Some great leaders have been secretive to a fault. Not the least among such leaders was Franklin Delano Roosevelt. Other managers never commit themselves. As a result, those around them engage in time-wasting speculation over what they intend. The former chairman and CEO of Philip Morris Cos., Michael A. Miles, was criticized for this:

Within the company, Mr. Miles' aloof, uncommunicative style is increasingly getting the blame for many of the company's problems. Particularly irksome is the fact that Philip Morris's stock-market value has fallen by more than $30 billion since 1992, although no one points a finger at Mr. Miles alone for that. . . . Mr. Miles has been virtually invisible, leaving many of Philip Morris's employees and customers wondering what the head of the nation's largest cigarette company thinks about the multitude of pressures facing the company.[11]

With aloof executives, communication becomes back-fence gossip and sign seeking, similar to Kremlin watching in the days of the Cold War, when Soviet experts learned to interpret abstruse actions as signals of intent. On the other hand, vagueness has merit when a business environment is hostile, and openness can foil efforts. With significant opposition, one may not wish to commit to an idea before a consensus forms. As was learned after the Cold War, vagueness in communicating at the Kremlin was partially due to the atmosphere in which its leaders worked.

A manager also may communicate too much in order to keep power, even to the point of injuring a company. This is persuasion being used to harmful ends. When self-interest overrides the owners' wishes or organizational welfare, a manager should be dismissed, but dismissal is not always easy or possible. First, there may be legitimate disagreement over what is best for a company. Second, owners may be clumsy communicators and fearful of removing a manager because greater harm might be done than by leaving the person in place. Third, managers build constituencies inside and outside of a company to preserve their personal power. The toppling of corporate executives during the late 1980s and early 1990s was historic because it was rare. Among those dismissed were James D. Robinson III, the head of American Express; Robert C. Stempel of General Motors; Kenneth H. Olsen, the founder of Digital Equipment Company; Joseph R. Canion, a founder of Compaq Computer; James L. Ketelsen, the CEO of Tenneco; Nicholas J. Nicholas, Jr., the co-CEO of Time Warner; Tom H. Barret, the CEO of Goodyear;[12] and John Akers, the chairman of IBM, among others. There had never been a period in U.S. business history when so many leaders were fired in such a short time, even when leaders were caught in scandal. Part of the reason why managers endured until the 1980s is that they had embedded themselves in their companies and used communication systems to protect their power.

When managers are embedded, individual communication is blocked because no one wants to see or hear the facts. A status-quo manager accepts a situation as it is, while a reform-minded manager becomes an unrelenting communicator until individuals either regain an appropriate view of the environment or leave.

For example, IBM owns and maintains an employee country club, which was a symbol of a healthy paternalism when IBM was successful. However, when the company hit rough times, the same country club became a symbol of wasteful ways. Closing the golf course might have been a symbolic way of expressing a need for change, and selling off a company jet is another.

On the other hand, symbolic message sending can backfire when actions become cliches, to which little attention is paid. Individuals come to expect ritual closing or cutting followed by eventual loosening. Sooner or later, they assume, everything will be back to where it was. Second, executives who attack symbols set themselves up for forced retreats. For example, a company jet might have an important economic purpose, while closing a popular employee perquisite like a golf course might cause such internal turmoil that a CEO has no chance to communicate an intended message. Managers use judgment and care to make sure that messages and media maintain their specified meanings and effective force with target individuals. Above all, a manager should not be afraid to use the most powerful medium a company has—its reward and compensation system. Few people object to individuals reaping wealth when success is evident. Dissent arises when the good times pass and rewards continue. This happens because compensation has become an embedded message. It is no longer a reward of success but a requirement of employment. A manager who attacks compensation, beginning with his or her own, usually gains credibility quickly among employees and owners.

Individual communication is directly affected as well by physical distance. Organizations with more than one place of operations have headquarters and field views of a strategic message. Individuals in the field often see headquarters as being out-of-touch with the business environment. An individual at headquarters, on the other hand, might consider the field to be ignorant about the company and the industry (Figure 6.3). A manager's message, such as, "We are all in this together," sounds as much like special pleading as fact to those in the field. Secondary corporate media, such as newsletters, magazines and videos, are rarely successful in balancing conflicting views. Those who produce the media often include assumptions in the content. Employees pick up differences or impute them.

The most powerful way in which a manager can level differences is by taking a message directly to individuals where they work. This can be done through personal presence or two-way audio and video conferencing that allows the manager and listeners to adjust to each other. Lou Gerstner, the chairman of IBM, met frequently with workers in his effort to turn the company around. Said Gerstner, "It's not something you do by writing memos. They've got to buy in with their hearts and their bellies, not just their minds."[13]

A manager also might ignore differences between the field and headquarters. When field units have self-defined missions in a diversified company, a headquarters view means little locally. A CEO might not wish to know or get involved in field businesses because the corporate role is one of financial regulator, banker and scorekeeper. Each unit manager defines a unit message and goals for individuals in the unit.

Danger comes when corporate headquarters thinks it can speak to the field about a business for which the field is responsible. This can happen when a unit fails to meet financial targets. The corporate message is, or implies that, only financial aspects have meaning—which is a simplistic view of business. One way to avoid this implication is to set a broader group of standards, without violating directness and clarity, in order to help individuals grasp connections. This is why communication in diversified companies is more difficult than in vertical businesses. A firm with one mission—producing steel—has a clear purpose that most persons can grasp. A firm with ten goals—producing steel, managing soft drink bottlers, buying and selling real estate, financing imports and exports, and so forth—rarely has an overriding focus other than the creation of wealth.

Organizations with an integrated message fail when their common purpose becomes divorced from the marketplace. For example, steel production has little economic result when there is a glut. Diversified organizations falter when they attempt to express unity beyond a name, logo and financial guidelines. The author once audited a medical instrument company that

Figure 6.3
Individual Communication and Distance

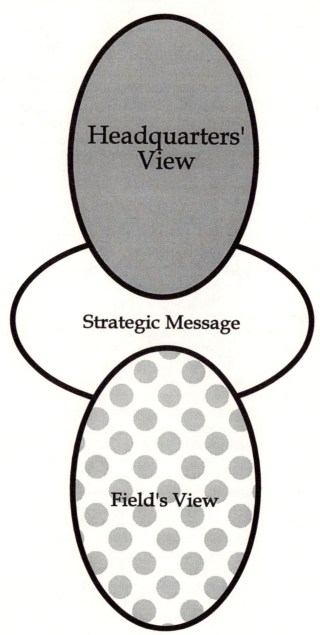

had several quality programs running simultaneously among self-contained units. The units were housed in common buildings and used the same hallway bulletin boards to send messages with different slogans and appeals. The result was cacophony. To attempt to unify the programs, the corporation devised a new symbol that was placed over all efforts. Unfortunately, the new symbol added to the confusion.

Flat organizations place an enormous burden on individual communication, while managers of horizontal companies delegate responsibility to the lowest levels. This calls for "loose-tight" communication, in which the organization sets a mission, essential controls and objectives but specific messages stay at the local level. Flat organizations depend on "process owners": these are self-managed teams requiring less supervision and involved in intense supplier and customer contact. They require each employee to have a clear sense of mission to participate in the process. However, getting to this point is a difficult task:

Indeed, simply defining the process of a given corporation may prove to be a mind-boggling and time-consuming exercise. . . . After that comes the challenge of persuading people to cast off their old marketing, finance, or manufacturing hats and think more broadly.[14]

The fluidity of a flat organization involves a perpetual tug-of-war between individual specialization and focus on business mission. Communication that is restricted to task execution, as a vertical organization might do, is not enough because specific tasks change. Flat companies rely on multidisciplinary and responsible employees to adapt. The overcommunication of simple messages is essential, and repetition is key. Competition, fear of failure, conflicting claims, efforts to win against tough odds, self-interest and perceptual distortion all inevitably get in the way. The manager of a flat company must communicate constantly to individuals because problems are omnipresent.

Service firms have difficulty expressing a common purpose because individual workers often provide a mix of offerings to different clients under a common roof. In brokerage, accounting, consulting and communication firms, some services complement one another while others compete for client dollars. It is difficult to have a single business goal beyond revenue enhancement. To counterbalance such diversity, service firms have used dress codes, relationship rules and career paths to build a common message around diversity. Sometimes rules are written, but just as often they are left for employees to learn through observation. McKinsey, the consulting company, places a premium on analytic ability, diversity of opinion and a ruthless weeding out of individual consultants who cannot submit to the collective nature of the firm.[15]

Managers focus on the nexus between customer and company and then

Figure 6.4
Individuals and Their Importance to Corporate Communication

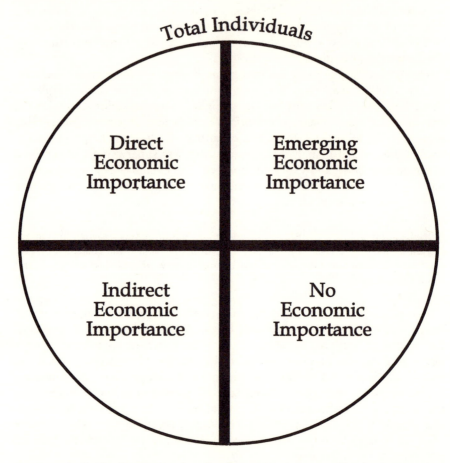

structure individual organizational communication accordingly. Structuring builds processes and lines of communication that tie person and task to economic transactions. However, it is never completely clear what will work. A manager's judgment frequently means the difference between success and failure. As Lou Gerstner, chairman of IBM, said about his efforts to reform the computer manufacturer, "There are no recipes. There are no certainties that what I'm doing is going to work. You've got to go on instinct."[16]

Only a few out of all the individuals connected to a company are important to its survival and success at any one time (Figure 6.4). Ideally, an efficient organization concentrates on these people exclusively, but no situation is ideal. Customers die, move away and stop doing whatever it was that required one's product. Interest groups come and go. Regulators rise and fall. Employees are hired, fired and retire, and they also quit. The job of communication is as much to find new supporters as it is to maintain relations with stalwarts.

A company can never know exactly who will side with or against it, but it can estimate where it stands. The estimate begins with ranking individuals in four ways:

- Direct economic importance: individuals with immediate impact on a company's economic success and survival.
- Emerging economic importance: individuals whose economic leverage is growing but is not yet critical.
- Indirect economic importance: individuals on whom a company relies but who are replaceable without undue threat to its survival and success.
- No economic importance: individuals to whom a company's products and services have no value.

A company communicates according to the four rankings. It concentrates on individuals with direct importance, it monitors individuals of emerging and indirect importance, and it ignores those without economic importance. No two companies have the same mixture of individuals and groups. For some, suppliers are as essential as customers, while for others, distributors are key. For most companies there are only a few individuals and groups out of a total potential audience who wield life-threatening power. Communication is essential only to individuals of direct economic importance; it is an elective for others. In extreme cases, when survival is an issue, a company must ask its core audience for permission to survive.

One way to estimate who is vital to survival is to use progressive ranking. Managers list individuals who are of potential direct economic importance and then:

- cut the communication budget by 10 percent and rerank them by direct economic importance;
- cut the communication budget by 25 percent and rerank;
- cut the communication budget by 50 percent and rank a third time;
- if necessary, cut the communication budget by 75 percent and rank a fourth time.

Using this method, a manager can usually arrive at a short list of individuals about whom there is agreement that they have direct economic importance to a firm. These are the *core* audience. There are usually less than ten core internal and external groups in any company. In the least complex firm, there are three—owners, customers and employees. Of course, under each of these three headings, individuals vary in importance.

The concept of core individuals is not always easy to apply because economic power may be diffuse, as in businesses that rely on many small purchases for sales (e.g., candy manufacturers, who depend on impulse buying) and transient businesses which may never see today's customers again.

In the first case, any one customer might not contribute even a fraction of a percentage of total sales. In the second case, a customer today has no importance to a customer tomorrow. Each sale is isolated from the next, as with an expensive, last-stop gas station in a desert. The station sells gas because it is the only one there. Drivers who have gone that way before know to fill up earlier, and it is only the unwary driver who stops.

However, even these companies have core individuals on whom they depend for survival and success. A candy manufacturer puts display racks at grocery store checkout counters where children can see the candy bars and urge their parents to buy. The transient business must maintain enough respectability with influentials to continue to operate because for a transient business, influentials are the core individuals.

An instance of this happened during a visit to Acoma—an ancient Indian town built on a mesa in New Mexico. The Indian guide warned the tourists about an old woman who used rancid cooking oil to make the traditional Indian flat bread. Most of the tourists would never tour Acoma again, but the guide took it upon herself to caution prospective buyers. Travel guide books and testing services also advise transient customers about products and services, such as the peril of the last-stop gas station. In some cases, as with restaurant reviewers, influential opinion is enough to make or break a business.

The openness required with individuals involves the communication of enough information to complete economic transactions and maintain societal permission to operate. A company can hide nearly all its activities and be successful, but it may be forced to throw open its doors to forestall a life-threatening event. In the Johnson & Johnson Tylenol incident, in which someone inserted cyanide-laced pills into bottles, the company opened its manufacturing facilities to outsiders to prove it used no cyanide in production. Similarly, Pepsi-Cola demonstrated its can-filling process to the world to prove it was unlikely that needles and other objects could fall into soda cans at the bottler.

A company in a business about which there is concern among core individuals may require openness as a condition of doing business. A utility with a nuclear generator may have to be open to individual regulators, politicians and citizens in order to keep a plant on line. Chemical makers have learned that health fears require openness to communities situated close to petrochemical plants. The Chemical Manufacturers Association spearheaded a drive to involve individuals from local communities with plant managers to neutralize community efforts to shut down the facilities. Publicly held companies must be open to the extent of regulatory compliance. They issue quarterly and annual reports, they have annual meetings, and they must perform other functions required by the government and exchanges on which their shares are listed. Beyond such basic compliance, however, they do not have to talk to owners, members of the public, financial analysts, interest groups or anyone else who does not have a direct economic impact.

If a company does not communicate and its stock consequently suffers, individual shareholders have the option of voting against management or leaving. They often sell, especially when the stock float is thin and management has control. In these cases, firms have remained nearly invisible. Entities listed on the NASDAQ exchange, "Pink Sheet" and as "penny stocks" are often closely held companies on which an outside investor has no influence because the majority of the company is held by management. There are more of these companies in the world than companies listed on the major stock exchanges.

The transition between open communication and the lack thereof is not simple. Closed companies usually build a psychological wall of silence that grows thicker as time passes and the ability to speak becomes dulled from lack of practice. Individual managers of closed companies frequently misjudge when and how to be open. The manager might understand that if a plant explodes, he or she must communicate. On the other hand, the same manager might not understand the need for openness as a part of combating unauthorized job actions or strikes. One tactic in labor negotiation is for workers to push for newspaper space and air time to voice grievances while company managers hew to a "no comment" policy. From the point of view of communication, this can be dangerous, especially when workers assemble political and economic power to back their demands.

Managers of closed companies also forget that openness may require symbolic messages and nonverbal communication to sway perception. A manager sitting behind a desk, acting nervous and fencing testily with reporters does not appear open, even if he or she is trying to be. A manager standing in a reception room to welcome and escort a reporter expresses openness, confidence and a willingness to speak, even if he or she then ducks the serious issues.

People read symbols well. Two examples of public management demonstrate the human skill in understanding nonverbal communication. Mayor Bilandic of Chicago lost his job in 1979 partly as a result of having stayed home while street crews dug the city out of a monster snowstorm. The mayor seemed distant: he reported to the media what was told to him by subordinates, but his managers were often wrong. The media picked up on mistakes and made the mayor look incompetent. On the other hand, Mayor Koch of New York City strolled the length of the Brooklyn Bridge during a transit strike and cheered on commuters walking to work. The mayor's physical presence won favor with the public.

Figure 6.5
The Individual and Corporate Communication Technology

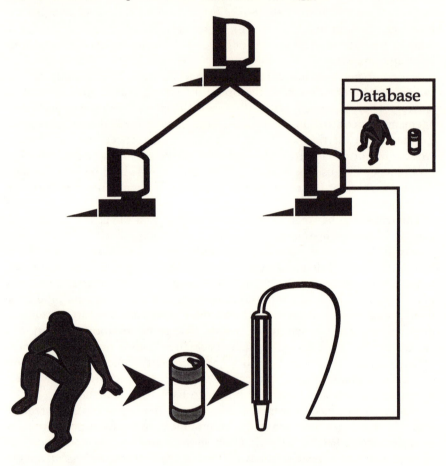

INDIVIDUALS AND CORPORATE COMMUNICATION TECHNOLOGY

Information technology has reached a point where even large companies can deal with core individuals as persons and not segments, groups or other abstract collections (Figure 6.5). It is practical now to identify consumers by name, address, stores visited and purchase behaviors. In supermarkets, software segments each customer by individual preferences and scanner data of actual purchases.[17] It has long been possible to identify interest groups, regulators, politicians and others with direct economic impact by name and political stance. The massive amounts of data produced by mass market identification require high-powered computing, but it is possible to tailor messages by individual perception, buying pattern and product use. Companies can speak to core customers as unique persons.

Gathering such detailed information is not a new phenomenon. An owner of a small shop knows the regular customers and predicts their wants and needs based on frequent involvement. Similarly, one business-woman had great success selling high-fashion clothing to men and women in Pittsburgh because of such detailed knowledge:

Ms. [Katherine] Barchetti knows about 500 of her customers on a first-name basis. Since she was a high-school graduate opening her first store with $1,000, Ms. Barchetti has meticulously recorded customers' sizes, styles and buying habits. . . . Then, she kept her records on index cards. Today, she keeps them in a database of about 28,000 clients.[18]

A grocer today does not need to know that Mrs. Jones buys steak on special. The grocer's scanners and computer find that fact and then generate a letter alerting Mrs. Jones to the steak special this weekend. The grocer's computer also knows that Mrs. Smith is on a fat-free diet and that a message about steak to her would be meaningless. However, Mrs. Smith's husband grills steak occasionally for barbecue. Since it is July, a tailored letter to Mr. Smith mentions the good deal on steak this weekend for backyard barbecuing.

Marketing studies have profiled groups down to zip-code and city block levels and by psychographic and demographic criteria. Technology has made the detailed observation of individuals a cost-effective process. Individual profiling helps a company predict purchases and perceptions within a reasonable range of accuracy. A specialty food wholesaler, called Frieda's Inc., has found markets throughout the United States for exotic fruits and vegetables through such database marketing:

"We've had prospective clients tell us, 'Sorry, your products don't sell in our area,'" says [Karen] Caplan [president of the company]. "Then we poll our database and show them how many strong customers we do have in that area, and what products they bought. It usually works."[19]

Companies have used direct communication to individuals for some time, both actively and passively. High-speed printers (especially the laser and inkjet varieties) allow mail to be sent to a home with a person's name inserted in several spots to make it more personal. One can see today six uses of a person's name on the outside of a direct-mail envelope and three more uses in the body copy, with printing quality so high that the unique name exactly matches text around it.

Marketers install toll-free 800-numbers to let customers report their difficulties with products or ask about using them better. Pillsbury Co.'s hotline handles an average of 2,000 calls a day, with 3,000 callers on the day before Thanksgiving. An estimated 66 percent of all manufacturers now offer 800-numbers.[20] Marketers place questionnaires on warranty cards. They use in-person, telephone and mail interviewing and they have invented new methods of interviewing that employ leading edge technology such as General Motor's computer-based "Information Accelerator":

It's called an information accelerator because in less than 2 hours a person using the system goes through the self-directed process of gathering information on whether to buy a product. The system measures the user's feeling about the product at regular intervals, providing a record of how certain positive or negative information affects the decision.[21]

Present methods of data capture allow a more accurate anticipation of customer needs and wants, and on a much larger scale. When one speaks of the "demassification of marketing" what is meant is the ability of marketers to target specific persons ever more closely, even though the "mass" in mass marketing remains. Large consumer brands still require large factories, huge databases and extensive sales and advertising budgets. The difference is in how these resources are now deployed. Edwin L. Artzt, chairman and CEO of Procter & Gamble Co., made the point in a speech to the advertising industry:

Barry Diller, at QVC [a cable television channel], told me he can sell 20,000 pairs of earrings in 5 minutes on his home shopping channel. That's terrific for a company that sells impulse items.

But Procter & Gamble, in a given year, has to sell 400 million boxes of Tide— and to do that, we have to reach our consumers over and over throughout the year.[22]

Today, businesses of all sizes can improve their ability to communicate proactively to individual customers and others. Data capture allows one to move more quickly to persuasion and commitment, using "rifle-shot" messages that hit close to the bulls-eye. (A message rarely hits dead center because individuals never precisely repeat their behavior.)

Some industries use individual communication tied to direct measurement, but here, too, variation is not completely eliminated. For example, demand-pull inventory methods communicate in real time so that parts can be supplied just in time to assemblers. If line speed is high, restocking messages are frequent. If line speed is low, restocking messages slow as well. However, neither the company nor the assembler can anticipate a change in part design or production methods from the inventory messages that are sent and received.

In other firms, individuals may not want to communicate with the firm as long as the company's product or service is available when the person needs it. Natural gas utilities provide an uninterrupted supply, but the lack of interruption makes them virtually invisible. Few know the company behind the pipeline except through an occasional meter reader or from news stories about pipeline explosions. One gas distribution utility in a major U.S. city faced a severe form of this dilemma. The company installed efficient metering systems that required simply that a truck drive past the meter and intercept a radio signal. The elimination of meter readers meant even less involvement with customers. If the company were a monopoly energy source, it might have welcomed anonymity but it was in a pitched and prolonged battle with three electric companies that were fighting to convert gas-fed households to electric heat. For this company, a part of communication had to be reminding individual customers of the value of gas and its delivery.

CORPORATE COMMUNICATION AND PROFILING OF CORE INDIVIDUALS

A company should know how core individuals have used its products and perceived its policies and how they are likely to accept its ongoing activities. Such detailing is often expensive because methods of reaching customers may be rudimentary and answers from individuals inaccurate. A customer may not have an opinion about a particular product or service or may not know how much of a product or service he or she uses, which is the case for most products, including common supplies such as screws, pins, paper clips and pencils.

Most companies have information about core audiences within the business processes, but information often lies in isolated operating units. Much of the effort behind information engineering and reengineering is to eliminate "islands of information" through the integration of communication technologies. Such efforts are subject to diminishing returns, but companies have profitably rebuilt the ways in which they do business through adding automated data capture. For example, the bar code scanner changed the nature of retailing. The universal product code is captured once and enters databases that describe exactly a person's buying habits. The captured data is available immediately to retailers, distributors and manufacturers for restocking, inventory management and marketing. Companies use automated data analysis as well. Computers have preset and flexible reporting formats that assemble buying profiles by individual, group patterns, regional patterns and other demographics and psychographics. Companies also use integrated databases, in which common data models join dispersed information, so one can access a complete picture of individuals anywhere at any time. Moreover, they integrate external databases into their internal databases to access information that expands their view of a business environment and individuals in it by orders of magnitude. However, achieving such integration is difficult. One estimate is that 66 percent of all reengineering projects involving information technology will falter.[23]

Data modeling is detailed and complex.[24] Computer-aided software engineering techniques were supposed to help, but their implementation was often flawed because business processes tend to be intuitive. Neither managers nor subordinates think about how they do what they do. They communicate in short-hand, which is part of a mutually understood context, while machine modeling requires an explicit process and messages. Second, humans vary process easily, but machines do not. Within the same skill set, humans perform endless combinations without giving any of them much thought. Over time, individual variations may add to definitive changes in process of which neither the individual nor the manager is aware.

Organizations change constantly without knowing that they do so. Stuffing envelopes has several steps, but few individuals ever think about envelope stuffing unless it is a major activity. Ten secretaries might stuff envelopes in ten different ways, with wide production variations among them. The only way to increase the total productivity capacity of the department is through communication to individual secretaries in order to change their unproductive habits. However, the actual productivity of any department is the sum total of many such overlooked processes. Reengineering requires effective communication, and not just information:

As difficult as it can be to create a vision for the organization and fully communicate it, you can't stop there. That's what managers learned at Direct Response Group (DRG), a unit of Capital Holding Corp. in Valley Forge, Pa. The company, which pioneered the sale of insurance products via direct mail and other mass-market approaches, delivered a clear message about its new directions to employees, but then didn't follow up. An independent consultant hired to survey employees found that even though they knew what the vision was, employees "were waiting for management to do something about it," says Direct Response senior VP of customer management Pam Godwin. "We were naive; we thought things would happen just by talking about this new vision. We may have lost as much as 18 months' worth of progress."[25]

Defining messages by the individual might require a substantial change in a manager's thinking. For example, a company is never a customer. A company is comprised of individuals who arrive at purchase decisions through multiple influences and opinions. One sells parts to a specifying engineer, a purchaser and an assembler, but not to a company. Profiling core customers in a company involves all the direct and indirect decision makers who influence a purchase.

Profiling core individuals is effective at the government and special interest level as well. In Washington, D.C., a public affairs professional or lobbyist identifies the Senate or House staffer working on an issue. The professional investigates the person's perception, attitudes and leanings, and then presents evidence to correct errors and clarify misinterpretations. The goal is to persuade a staffer to take a company's point of view on an issue. The staffer then can influence a representative or senator.

Variation complicates the lobbyist's task, because for every issue there are opposing views and external pressures that might have nothing to do with the case at hand. A persuaded staffer or representative might have a change of heart about an issue in light of new facts, pressure from another influential or the promise of a public works project for his or her district. Profiling is not a one-time process but rather involves the daily tracking of the external and internal forces and influences that are applied to core individuals. Interestingly, this collision and communication of interests is what James Madison envisioned in his pioneering design of the U.S. Constitution, which he saw as a way of protecting the weak from the strong.

The great desideratum in Government is such a modification of the sovereignty as will render it sufficiently neutral between the different interests and factions, to controul one part of society from invading the rights of another, and at the same time sufficiently controuled itself, from setting up an interest adverse to that of the whole Society.[26]

Much of business also engages in a collision of interests to prevent one department from invading the rights of another, and the CEO mediates among warring factions.

CORPORATE COMMUNICATION AND INDIVIDUAL MESSAGES

A company can tailor a core message in many ways, based on the particular individuals to whom it will be sent. Meaning can be forceful and direct or allusive and obscure. The only requirements are that the target individual understands the intent clearly and acts appropriately. For example:

- "Nobody will undersell [our store]. If you find a price lower than ours and we can't match it, you get the product free." This is a blatant hard sell.
- A picture shows a beautiful woman holding a jar of perfume over her head and pouring it out gracefully. The name of the perfume is on the bottle. This is an allusive, image sell.

The meaning of both invitations—to buy a product—is clear, yet the message presentations are opposed.

By focusing on individuals, it is possible for a company to use multiple

Figure 6.6
Corporate Communication and Individual Messages

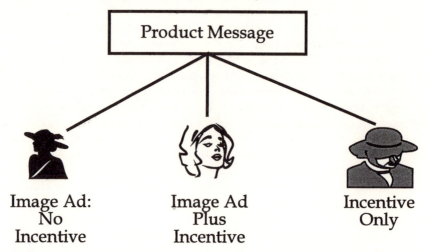

media and presentations without confusing the meaning (Figure 6.6). This technique is not new. Managers have intuitively understood the need to vary communication style by individual subordinate. General H. Norman Schwarzkopf, in reflecting on his own experience in the armed forces, wrote:

One of the first lessons I learned was that there was no *single* way for the leader of a small unit to command the soldier's respect: You had to address each person in terms he could understand. The college kids were persuaded by logical explanations, the farm boys by common sense, and what the dropouts understood was their leader's size and strength, and the fact that he could be one tough son of a bitch.[27]

The picture of the woman holding the jar of perfume might be sent as is to a customer who responds to the elegance of such an appeal. The same picture could be sent with a coupon to a second customer who buys fashion only on discount. A coupon alone could be sent to a person who cares little for elegance but a great deal for bargains. The businesses from which customers buy perfume are separated by enough distance to avoid message confusion. For example, the first woman might buy her perfume from department stores while the second buys from a direct-mail catalogue and the third from a home-shopping network.

However, no one can precisely measure individual behavior. A business can only measure aspects of behavior that are important to its survival and success, and can do so only within a probable range. Many individual behaviors are unimportant to a company. The brand of beer a person drinks has little meaning to a marketer of underarm deodorant, but the marketer should never forget the possibility of "spillover" in individuals. A person is a unified entity and not made up of discrete segments. To some person somewhere, there might be a relationship between deodorant and beer.

At the root of all measurement is uncertainty. This is true in both humans and materials. At the quantum level in physics is a fundamental uncertainty about where an electron or photon is in space. Physicists calculate probable, but not exact, locations.[28] Individual humans develop patterns of behavior that they usually—but not always—elect not to break. Measurement tracks patterns while expecting variations in them.

Neither the measurement nor the message is tailored for all individuals at all times because it is usually not economical to do so. However, there are exceptions, especially if a good or service is of high value or long duration. A company's economic interest in the long-term satisfaction of its customers might be essential to survival. It is a question of the data and communication cost versus the revenue generated—and of societal acceptance as well.

Privacy issues are already a major concern in data collection and will grow as databases expand and information on individuals becomes more detailed. It is possible, and probable, that large sections of individual activity will be put off-limits to preserve an individual's right to privacy. However, passive collection methods already open the possibility of building a detailed account of an individual's life. Documents from credit card records, bank activities, investment accounts, mortgage payments, publicly available property and tax records, insurance transactions and other sources reveal many personal activities.

One company responded to the societal disapproval of smoking to produce individual appeals to smokers. Philip Morris Cos. matched its database of 26 million smokers against Time Inc.'s subscriber list and then contracted with Time to place cigarette advertisements only in magazines going to smokers.[29] This avoided antagonizing individuals opposed to smoking while sending messages efficiently to those who did.

Individual messages are also limited by environmental change. When an industry shifts the way in which it operates, historical messages and measures may lose their meaning. For example, core customers may no longer be important. An example is the experience of typewriter manufacturers after dedicated word processors appeared. Typewriters were electromechanical machines of great complexity and minimal word-processing ability. Word processors were electronic machines of mechanical simplicity and robust word-processing ability. There still exist makers of typewriters, but most brands have disappeared. There are still makers of word processors, but most of them disappeared as well when personal computer software took over the word processing function.

A manager should never focus so closely on core individuals that he or she forgets the market environment. Some companies believe that if they focus tightly on customers, their products and services will change in concert with customers' needs. However, this is not always true. IBM stayed with mainframe customers much too long, and thus lost large and developing sectors of the computer market. Similarly, Digital Equipment Company[30] and Wang Laboratories stayed with their customers for their proprietary architectures for too long and fell into deep financial trouble.

A manager can accept ignorance about marginal individuals with no economic impact but must take care that these marginal individuals do not emerge to gain direct economic powers. To prevent this, a company should regularly measure all individuals with relationships to it. A manager's goal is to spot shifts suggesting a fundamental change before they impede the survival of the organization.

Information now moves faster and, as a result, changes in ideas and opinions can move faster as well. Today's hot product might be tomorrow's remainder. A high-flying company that is the victim of rumors can plunge in equity value in minutes. For example, traders can now watch court hearings on television and decide during the hearing—and before the decision—what the outcome will be. An example of this occurred when Courtroom Television Network broadcast two hours of live coverage of a merger battle between Paramount and QVC Network Inc. before the Delaware Supreme Court.

The red-haired Mr. Ostranger [Paramount's lawyer] looked scared, many traders concluded. They began bidding up Paramount's stock, convinced that the court was leaning toward killing Viacom Inc.'s takeover agreement with Paramount and allowing a more lucrative one from QVC Network Inc. to go forward. [After the market closed, that is exactly what happened.][31]

CORPORATE COMMUNICATION AND INDIVIDUAL OWNERS

Owners are internal or external. They are insiders when they manage their businesses. Formal communication lines lead to them, and they have, or should have, a total view of the economic processes. Owners are outsiders when they rely on surrogate managers. Most publicly owned companies have absentee owners, but not all absentee owners are the same. Managers focus on absentee owners in direct proportion to their size and power. Many absentee owners are ignored except for regulatory communication because their holdings are small and their political and economic leverage are weak.

Publicly owned companies report according to law and regulation. They must comply with reporting requirements, but even so, major holders usually have greater access because it is in the holders' economic interests to get it and in the managers' self-interest to give it. Major owners also have more access to managers because it is in their economic power to compel meetings even when managers do not consider those meetings to be in their own self-interest. Stock exchanges, law courts and regulatory authorities spell out to owners the content and frequency of the minimum level of communications. Even so, however, there are times when it is up to the judgment of a manager to inform an absentee owner of an event.[32]

Accounting conventions as well as recommendations and exchange rules from the U.S. Securities and Exchange Commission (SEC) and Financial Accounting Standards Board are designed to communicate fairly to an absentee owner the condition of the company as an economic enterprise. However, interpretations of economic events are fraught with disagreement over what is a fair representation. That is why proposals from regulatory authorities are often tied up for years in study and debate before a rule is promulgated.

Disagreements are more than economic: they can also be cultural. British accounting standards differ from those in the United States, while Swedish accounting standards differ from both. Communication according to each standard expresses economic activity with varying content and meaning, and one message about economic activity is not necessarily better than another. It is up to an individual owner to learn the differences among standards and the information that each reveals and conceals. There is no unified accounting language with exact messages and meanings applying to every business everywhere because individuals dispute the economic value of many business activities.

Arguments have raged over the meaning of a lease and whether it belongs on a balance sheet as an asset. Tempers have flared over the valuation of securities and whether they should be held at historical valuation or marked to market value. Rational individuals fight over the presentation of funds flows and cash flow statements and the interpretation of currency value.

As a result, an absentee owner cannot hope to understand the precise economic reality of a company because accounting language ultimately is a convention—a general agreement on usages and practices, but not necessarily a precise translation of economic activity. Convention comes from the interplay of interests, limited resources and human understanding. Individuals agree at a moment in time to see and communicate things in a certain way. Later, they may disagree or adjust their views based on new evidence or abilities to measure. To the owner, therefore, financial communication, for all its formal and regulatory stringencies, is as variable as the rest of human activity.

The fluid nature of public ownership also introduces uncertainties to a company, as ownership may change frequently. A company may never know its owners well at any point in time, even though it attempts to do so. Thus, communication to individuals, as mandated by law, might have little two-way communication or follow-up. By the time a company sends an annual report to a registered shareholder, the shareholder might have sold the equity.

Communication to owners varies by:

- Type of holdings: if a company is closely held, its needs for communication are different from one that is not.

- Intent: if the owner holds a stock strictly as an investment, that is a different situation than if the owner holds the stock for additional purposes, such as a merger.

- Locale: owners located near a corporation's place of activity can observe firsthand how it is doing better than those at a distance.

- Time: owners who hold stock for long periods may gain a greater understanding than those who buy and then sell a stock quickly.

- Behavior: actively involved owners receive more, and different, communication than passive ones.

- Knowledge: there are sophisticated owners with a deep understanding of operations or finance and accounting and unsophisticated owners who buy based on a tip delivered over a backyard fence or who never look at information about the companies whose shares they own.

Regulated financial communication suffers from the defect of every standardized message: some receivers understand it and some do not. The majority of individual shareholders cannot read a balance sheet, income statement or cash flow analysis with insight. That is why there are thousands of financial analysts who do so and report their findings to investors. Here again, however, the economically powerful person has more access to skilled analysis than other owners because the powerful owner can afford it, whereas the economically weak owner cannot.

It is left up to the individual company to adapt regulated communications to specific owners. A company may make extraordinary efforts to communicate its condition to its ownership, or it may make no effort at all beyond strict compliance. Usually, the determination to make the effort is directly dependent on the perceived power of the owner. A CEO might take the time to explain a balance sheet to a founder's grandson who inherited 20 percent of the company yet brush off a financial analyst asking about a footnote to the financial statements.

While regulated communications to individual owners have gone far toward explaining a business's activity, they by no means explain all of it, nor do they necessarily leave individual message receivers any more illumined than previously.

SUMMARY

A company constructs tailored communications to individuals based on each person's economic importance. Ranking individuals cannot be precisely done because there is too much variation. One can, however, develop estimates, while technology makes such profiles of individuals economically feasible. Individual corporate communication should be:

- Simple: managers concentrate communication on individuals on the basis of economic importance.

- Timely: managers convey information quickly enough to core individuals to continue economic transactions and maintain societal permission to operate.

- Open: managers communicate to core individuals the information necessary to accomplish economic transactions and maintain permission to operate. They are prepared to communicate to whatever extent necessary to ensure survival and success.

- Defined: managers isolate and analyze core individuals in detail to understand their needs, perceptions and preferences.

- Flexible: managers never tie a company completely to core individuals because audiences and markets change.

- Individual: as far as possible, managers communicate individually by need, perception and preference.

- Meaningful: managers concentrate on communicating messages that bear directly on company survival and success.

- Measurable: managers measure the effectiveness of messages to individuals against the survival and success of the enterprise.

NOTES

1. Bernard H. Boar, *The Art of Strategic Planning for Information Technology: Crafting Strategy for the 90s* (New York: John Wiley & Sons, Inc., 1993), p. 232.

2. David Hackett Fischer, *Albion's Seed: Four British Folkways in America* (New York: Oxford University Press, 1989), pp. 7–8.

3. Ibid., pp. 8–9.

4. Elizabeth Lesly, "Sticking It Out at Xerox by Sticking Together," *Business Week*, no. 3348 (November 29, 1993): 77. This is a brief examination of how ten black sales reps banded together to survive the culture at Xerox. Some succeeded; some failed and left the company.

5. James and James, *Mathematics Dictionary*, 4th ed. (New York: Van Nostrand Reinhold, 1976), p. 170.

6. Alfred, Lord Tennyson, *Poems of Tennyson* (Boston: Houghton Mifflin Company, 1958), pp. 274–75.

7. Hesh Kestin, *Twenty-First-Century Management: The Revolutionary Strategies That Have Made Computer Associates a Multibillion-Dollar Software Giant* (New York: Atlantic Monthly Press, 1992), pp. 10–11.

8. John R. Wilke, "Shop Talk: Computer Links Erode Hierarchical Nature of Workplace Culture," *Wall Street Journal* 222, no. 113 (December 9, 1993). The article quotes Esther Dyson, a noted technology analyst, on p. A7.

9. Brian Dumaine, "What's So Hot about Outsiders?" *Fortune Magazine* 128, no. 14 (November 29, 1993): 63–67.

10. Joann S. Lublin, "Managing Your Career: To Stay on Track, Maintain Your Balance in Job's First Days," *Wall Street Journal,* June 22, 1994, p. B1.

11. Eben Shapiro, "Who's News: Philip Morris's Embattled Chief Finds Unfriendly Faces on His Own Doorstep," *Wall Street Journal,* June 3, 1994, p. B1.

12. Thomas A. Stewart, "The King Is Dead," *Fortune* 127, no. 1 (January 11, 1993): 34–41.

13. Steve Lohr, "On the Road with Chairman Lou," *New York Times,* sect. 3, p. 1.

14. John A. Byrne, "The Horizontal Corporation," *Business Week,* no. 3351 (December 30, 1993): 78.

15. John Huey, "How McKinsey Does It," *Fortune* 128, no. 11 (November 1, 1993): 56–81.

16. Steve Lohr, "On the Road," p. 6.

17. *Progressive Grocer,* 72, no. 12 (December 1993): pt. 3.

18. Wendy Bounds, "Tenacity Sells High Fashion to Pittsburgh," *Wall Street Journal,* December 23, 1993, p. B1.

19. Clinton Wilder, "Who'd Eat a Blue Squash?" *Information Week,* no. 458 (January 10, 1994): 31.

20. Carl Quintanilla and Richard Gibson, " 'Do Call Us': More Companies Install 1–800 Phone Lines," *Wall Street Journal,* April 20, 1994, p. B1. See also Richard Gibson, "Pillsbury's Telephones Ring with Peeves, Praise," *Wall Street Journal,* April 20, 1994, p. B1.

21. Raymond Serafin, "The Information Accelerator and Me: Or, Scoping Out GM's Electric Car before It Hits the Showroom," *Advertising Age,* March 22, 1993, p. 47.

22. Edwin L. Artzt, [Speech on the future of TV advertising, delivered at the annual conference of the American Association of Advertising Agencies], *Advertising Age,* May 23, 1994, p. 24.

23. Bruce Caldwell, "Missteps, Miscues," *Information Week,* June 20, 1994, p. 50.

24. Robert Mylls, *Information Engineering: CASE Practices and Techniques* (New York: John Wiley & Sons, 1994).

25. Scott Leibs, "The Culture Trap," *Information Week,* November 2, 1992, p. 46.

26. Ralph Ketcham, *James Madison: A Biography* (Charlottesville: University Press of Virginia, 1990), p. 187.

27. General H. Norman Schwarzkopf, with Peter Petre, *The Autobiography: It Doesn't Take a Hero* (New York: Bantam Books, 1993), pp. 77–78, 88.

28. Richard P. Feynman, *QED: The Strange Theory of Light and Matter* (Princeton, NJ: Princeton University Press, 1985).

29. Eben Shapiro, "Cigarette Maker and Time Aim Ads at Smokers," *Wall Street Journal,* December 16, 1993, p. B1.

30. Scott Leibs and Marianne Kolbasuk McGee, "DEC's Last Chance," *InformationWeek,* July 4, 1994, pp. 12–13.

31. William Power, "Paramount-Takeover Hearing Glues Traders to TV Screens," *Wall Street Journal,* December 10, 1993, p. C1.

32. Wesley S. Walton, *Corporate Communications Handbook: A Guide for Managing Unstructured Disclosure in Today's Corporate Environment* (Deerfield, IL: Clark Boardman Callaghan, 1992), p. 323. See also Wesley S. Walton and Joseph M. Lesko, *Corporate Communications Handbook: A Guide to Press Releases and Other Informal Disclosure for Public Corporations* (Deerfield, IL: Clark Boardman Callaghan, 1993).

7

Corporate Communication and Messages

There is a very old saying among writers: "Difficulties with a sentence mean confused thinking. It is not the sentence that needs straightening out, it is the thought behind it." In writing we attempt, first, to communicate with ourselves. An "unclear sentence" is one that exceeds our own capacity for perception. Working on the sentence, that is, working on what is normally called communications, cannot solve the problem. We have to work on our own concepts first to be able to understand what we are trying to say—and only then can we write the sentence.[1]
—Peter F. Drucker, *Management: Tasks, Responsibilities, Practices*

WHERE WE ARE

Thus far we have discussed communication, its use by businesses, the environment from which communication arises and individual message receivers and message senders. Now it is time to discuss the message. This chapter will focus on the development of a message and its relationship to the message sender. As we have seen, meaning is never precise. Every statement has both explicit and implied content. Rules of grammar, punctuation and structure are useful only to convey clear ideas in mutually understood media.

Clarity comes from seeing the fundamental principles that drive the usual welter of detail, but a manager rarely has the time for ivory tower thinking. He or she usually learns clarity from hands-on action that either succeeds or fails in producing economic transactions. Clarity comes from doing—from the designing, testing, producing, assembling, distributing and selling that show whether a great idea had merit (Figure 7.1).

Figure 7.1
Steps Toward Clarity

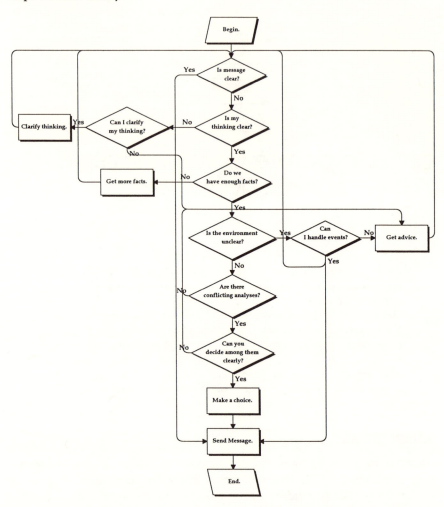

Managers are like surfers. Their job is to stay upright on a board and ride a business wave as far as possible. They concentrate on balance, foot positioning, wave speed, wind and other surfers competing for position. The only time they study the theory of surfing is on-shore, when they are off the board and out of the game.

WHAT CORPORATE MESSAGES ARE

In business, messages are not ends. Rather, they are instruments of or complements to action. They are tools to coordinate economically productive business transactions. Corporate communication is based on effective messages that ensure the completion of an economic transaction and lead to survival and success.

Often, corporate communication is taught as speech, presentation, media, grammar or writing skills, but even virtually inarticulate people send effective messages.[2] While proper discourse is preferable, in order to increase the chance of understanding, it is not essential as long as a message receiver can act according to the intended meaning. For example, the meaning of work songs, such as a sea chanteys, was not in the words but in the rhythm, which helped to coordinate physical action. Some work songs have no meaning beyond their cadence, but cadence in this instance is clarity. It expresses precisely what the message sender wants the message receiver to do.

One key to clear messages is clear thinking, as Drucker wrote in the opening quotation to this chapter. The message sender must know what he or she wants another person to do, and the action should have a probability of achievement. A message conveys a directive. However, clear thinking is difficult to maintain because so much changes, and so often. What is clear today might not be clear tomorrow, when the business environment changes under new internal or unforeseen forces. Clausewitz expressed the mental confusion that military managers face:

The general unreliability of all information presents a special problem in war: All action takes place, so to speak, in a kind of twilight, which, like a fog or moonlight, often tends to make things seem grotesque and larger than they really are. Whatever is hidden from full view in this feeble light has to be guessed at by talent, or simply left to chance. So once again for lack of objective knowledge one has to trust to talent or luck.[3]

A second key to clarity is confidence in one's ability to master events. A confident person might or might not know how events will evolve and how to handle them. Nonetheless, belief in one's ability is as powerful a persuasion as a message. Conviction is the message. Confidence becomes the motivator for those lost in argument or fear. The essence of charismatic leadership is just such self-confidence, which requires two attributes: "The leader must be a person of strong convictions, determined, self-confident, and emotionally expressive, and his or her followers must want to identify with the leader as a person, whether they are or [are] not in a crisis."[4]

There are many such examples of confident leadership. Joe Montana, who was called the ultimate turnaround quarterback in football, was a study in coolness and relaxation.[5] Douglas MacArthur's calmness and disregard for personal safety in the thick of World War I fighting was inspirational.[6] Colonel Aubrey S. Newman rose in the face of direct Japanese fire during World War II and told his pinned men, "Follow me!" After his troops swept the position, the colonel's words became the motto of the 24th Infantry Division.

Fear is as much at the root of confused messages as is lack of clear thinking. Fear has roots in one's personal psychology. Examinations of children show marked differences between those with high self-esteem and those without. High-esteem children "were confident about their own perceptions and judgments, expected to succeed at new tasks and to influence others, and readily express their opinions." By contrast, low-esteem children were "isolated, fearful, reluctant to join in, self-conscious, oversensitive to criticism, consistently underrated themselves, tended to underachieve in class and were pre-occupied with their own problems."[7]

A manager who displays excessive concern for the outcome of events cannot think clearly about them and will confuse individuals reporting to him. Matters loom larger than they are and proportion is lost. One imagines dangers upon dangers. General George McClellan was such a leader during the Civil War. He always overestimated enemy troop strength, supply shortages and other problems, which kept him from acting. He drove Abraham Lincoln nearly to despair.[8] Great leaders and managers reach a state of confidence in which they either master fears or mask them in order to keep their subordinates working at their tasks and thus to achieve a common purpose. General Ulysses S. Grant, on whom Lincoln finally rested command of the Army of the Potomac, was such a person.

Confidence is as much image as reality. Individuals create public selves and private selves. They put on either a best face, or a false one, that they wish those around them to see. They engage in *image management,* both verbally and nonverbally, and they cooperate with one another to maintain their respective images.

Especially in formal organizations, where being accepted depends on seeming to be cooperative and on appearing to know what is going on, there are pressures to help one another maintain images. . . . People establish working agreements to support one another's images. If any participants violate the implied agreement, they risk having others retaliate by undermining their images.[9]

Leaders come from anywhere, from the ranks of employees, from the outside, from the newly hired or the long retired. Their primary message is a willingness to act and to show the way. Thus, Stephen J. Frangos, who led a turnaround of Eastman Kodak's black-and-white film-making process, was a 34-year veteran engineer of the company who could have been dismissed as someone who had created the problem in the first place. Frangos described his opportunity to change Kodak's manufacturing flow:

Secretly, I was thrilled at the prospect of changing to [work] flow immediately, and later I learned that many others in the group felt the same way. Few things were as frustrating at the Park [Kodak's main manufacturing facility in Rochester, N.Y.] as trying to introduce change. The Kodak method was to study a project or proposal until it was rendered harmless, wait a bit longer to make sure it was neutered, and then wait some more just to be on the safe side.[10]

Primary messages do not have to be truthful or accurate. They need only be persuasive. Persuasion combines personal credibility with a veneer of evidence sufficient to make people believe and act. For example, "President Reagan was known as the 'Great Communicator' more for the perceived sincerity in his delivery than for its accuracy."[11]

Think of the relentless positivism of a salesperson: messages can be justifications, rationalizations or emotive statements built on nothing but the credibility of the message sender. Aristotle defined persuasive proofs as being of three kinds—based on the character of the speaker, based on disposing the listener in some way or based on argument that showed or seemed to show something.[12] In other words, "the construction of effective messages begins with a search for acceptable reasons."[13]

Unethical managers have misled people throughout history with a strength of conviction that their followers have found compelling. Followers want managers to keep an objective clearly in mind and to lead them to success through events that distract nearly everyone else from the mission. Managers are communication practitioners and not theorists. As Clausewitz wrote about war: "Knowledge in war *is very simple,* being concerned with so few subjects, and only with their final results at that. But this does not make its application easy."[14]

By contrast, a topic as simple as "concepts of leadership" have embroiled academics in discussion for decades. Leadership is defined as a focus of group processes, as personality, as an art of inducing compliance, as the exercise of influence, as an act or behavior, as a form of persuasion, as a power relation, as an instrument of goal achievement, as a combination of elements and more.[15] However, leaders do not debate leadership: they lead. Managers do not discuss theories of communication: they communicate. Leaders have the ability to "convey meaning and enhance retention."[16] In one firm, for example:

The messages were almost all single sentences and tended to be rules. The employees usually first heard the messages soon after they joined the firm and in private one-to-one conversation. . . .

These pithy memorable messages, usually from a sender of higher status to a recipient of lower status, provide sense-making structures and a guide to what behavior is appropriate in an organization. . . . Clearly, the manager who includes such memorable messages in his or her communications is likely to have a much greater impact on subsequent events in the organization.[17]

However, even repeated messages cannot entirely overcome multiple meanings: every employee who can repeat a single sentence will explain its functional and emotional meaning differently and, most often, within the context of personal experience and self-interest.

Unfortunately, some managers are unable to disengage themselves from the business environment in order to grasp a sense of mission or, having grasped it, to keep it clearly before them. They are overwhelmed. In enterprises where one can maintain direct influence on economic transactions on a minute-by-minute, day-to-day basis, this failing is not fatal because the message lies in the action and results. However, when an enterprise grows beyond the physical and psychological capacity of an individual, the failing can jeopardize a company's survival if actions and results become uncoordinated. This is why some entrepreneurs do not manage growth effectively and become enmeshed in minutiae. This is also why other entrepreneurs of extraordinary stamina have built great businesses only to see them wither or crumble when the founders lost their resilience.

CORPORATE COMMUNICATION AND THE STRATEGIC MESSAGE

Corporate communication is based on the strategic message. The strategic message is an idea that is communicated in depth to achieve fast, coordinated action leading to economic transactions (Figure 7.2). Speed is essential because a strategic message responds to, and shapes, the current business environment. All other business messages derive from the strategic message. Ford Motor Company's decisive response to a financial crisis that started in 1980 provided it with a strategic message and the credibility to urge its workforce toward lower cost production.

By far the most important and impressive factor in Ford's increased productivity involves increased cooperation by its work force. Over a period of years, Ford persuaded its employees, who historically had been suspicious of management, to work harder and smarter, and to help management find ways to cut costs.[18]

If individuals in a business cannot express the strategic message, there may be one of two outcomes. The first is the deterioration or death of a business. In the second, the strategic message is intuitive and the business muddles on. The economic purpose of the business is what the business does, although no one has formally written it down.

A strategic message pulls together, not one, but all disciplines in an organization and puts them to work toward a common end. A manager must translate a strategic message into the languages and assumptions of each discipline and gain acceptance for his or her views across disciplines. As Peter Drucker wrote:

Figure 7.2
Corporate Communication and the Strategic Message

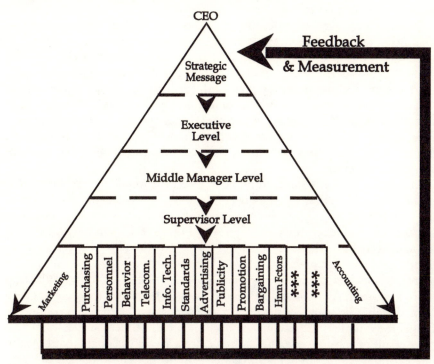

Nothing may seem simpler or more obvious than to know what a company's business is. . . . Actually, "What is our business?" is almost always a difficult question and the right answer is usually anything but obvious.

One of the earliest and most successful answers was worked out by Theodore N. Vail (1845–1920) for the American Telephone and Telegraph Company (also known as the Bell System) almost seventy years ago: "Our business is service."[19]

Vail later refined his message to "universal telephone service."

The organizational understanding of strategic messages only needs to extend to the successful and continuing completion of economic transactions. In fact, the strategic message may be simplicity itself—the completion of economic transactions. As Drucker wrote, "There is only one valid definition of business purpose: *to create a customer.*"[20] Most businesses have implicit strategic messages because the managers are too busy acting to spend time examining.

With an implicit message, a manager embodies strategy in action. Managers are thus *message models.* (A more common expression is *role model,* but that term does not stress the communication element of a manager's behavior.) A manager expresses action to subordinates, and subordinates pick up both verbal and nonverbal messages and emulate the manager.[21] Even if a manager's actions compromise business survival and success, employees are likely to follow.

Strategic messages, whether implicit or explicit, do not have fixed meanings because businesses are not fixed institutions. Meaning flexes in response to a business environment, though the words may not change. This in itself breeds controversy. In every organization (including governments), there are strict constructionists, who call for hewing to the original intent, and interpreters, who see words as guidelines. At any given moment, either side may be right or wrong, while sometimes the strategic message may become wrong because the business environment has changed. (Of course, if a strategic message is wrong and yet individuals follow it, the business will face extinction.)

Managers are sometimes left alone to effect the implicit or explicit intent of a business. The message may be, "We don't care how you sell the product, just get rid of it." This breeds variations that can sidetrack a business. On the other hand, companies may reward those who exemplify a strategic message and have them serve as guides to others. This also has built-in limitations, as companies may reward the wrong *message-model*. For example, a manager might be rewarded for achieving short-term results that harm long-term survival and success. However, because damage is not seen immediately, the manager may never discover what he or she has done. A frequent example of erroneous messages involves service businesses, where the pursuit of top-line revenue is often emphasized so strongly that bottom-line earnings—and, sometimes, legality—are forgotten. Managers are promoted on sales ability rather than their skill in managing resources, earnings and true wealth creation. On Wall Street, traders who make unauthorized or illicit trades in pursuit of commissions are common.

Time and again, seemingly successful CEOs have been succeeded by leaders who had to undo the damage left by predecessors, who had nonetheless retired with honor. This kind of scenario happened at General Motors, Philip Morris Cos., Citicorp and ITT. In some cases, a strategy pursued by the previous CEO had become stale and needed updating, while in other cases, a strategy kept by the previous CEO needed to be changed completely. At Citicorp:

The old culture, defined by Walter B. Wriston, the former chairman, emphasized autonomy, internal competition and risk taking and allowed Citicorp to become the most aggressive and innovative player in a stodgy industry.

But that culture also produced a strangling duplication of efforts, resulting, for example, in 11 different computer systems for checking accounts in the United States alone. And because the emphasis was on building revenue, and not assessing overall risks, Citicorp would end up with the biggest portfolio by far of bad real estate loans—not to mention the billions in bad loans to the third world racked up earlier in the 80's.[22]

There is no easy solution for mismatches between strategic messages and the business environment. Large organizations can run for years on inertia, maintaining appearances while their foundation crumbles. Chrysler once built autos for inventory. The firm ended up with thousands of unsold cars parked in lots all over Detroit. Philip Morris unloaded millions of Marlboro cigarettes on distributors who had no way of selling them at retail. General Motors' Cadillac division had a demographic profile so old it was the laughing stock of Detroit. Finally, Xerox Corporation gave away large chunks of a photocopier market it invented. A strategic message should have, but often lacks, a two-part focus on short-term economic success and long-term survival.

To effect a strategic message, a manager must first win the power to do so. This results in posturing and politicking that seem removed from corporate communication but are part of it. A strategic message cannot be divorced from people who communicate it, nor can its meaning be divorced from the cognitive and emotional meanings that message receivers take from it. However, posturing and politicking can breed cynicism among those who see managers as being out for their own gain. Every instance of seeming self-aggrandizement becomes evidence of, and a message model for, others to act in the same way. Self-interested managers who are out only for themselves make matters worse. They unabashedly accrue rewards and oppose any efforts to deny them perquisites and compensation. As a result, gathering power to effect a strategic message requires credibility and relationship building, during which one establishes concern for the success of the organization and not just for oneself.

Sometimes there is little that managers can do to effect a strategic message except to accomplish the tasks assigned to them and their subordinates. This might be enough to sustain economic transactions and business success for decades, but eventually, the business environment will change and managers will find themselves adrift. The 1980s were a decade when thousands of senior and middle managers were fired as businesses cut back. The managers discovered that strategic messages that had been given to them at the start of their careers had been replaced by different expectations, for which they were unprepared or no longer needed.

The reason is that a strategic message is more a synthesis of a business environment than a concept imposed on it. It is more a reactive than a proactive form of communication (Figure 7.3). In spite of a belief that leaders impose their wills on the world, the reality is that the world shapes leaders as much as they shape it. Leaders adapt to environments and move through them to achieve their own ends. Great leaders keep their strategic message in sight while proceeding in tangents. A classic example was William Cooper Procter, a third-generation heir to Procter & Gamble (P&G). He struggled for years to improve labor relations at the company through dividend sharing and stock purchase plans for employees. At the time when

Figure 7.3
The Strategic Message and Business Environment

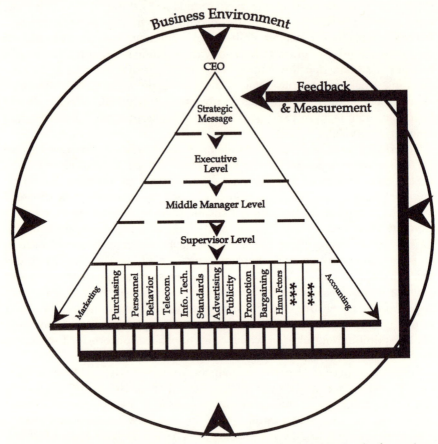

the first dividend-sharing plan was announced in 1887, both the unions and Procter's peers were aghast and opposed. When, later, a stock purchase plan was started, Procter again faced opposition from employees and peers. After 16 years of trying, Procter settled on binding profit sharing to the purchase of P&G common stock—a breakthrough in labor relations.[23]

Few managers proceed in a straight line to impose their ideas on resources, processes and people. Most tack and veer before they reach their objectives, even when they know what they want to do. *Message modeling* involves both intent and action. Managers either put an environment to work on their behalf or endure its burdens until they can act. English poet John Milton, who was prevented by blindness from serving in the seventeenth-century Puritan revolution, wrote a line that also expresses a manager's frustration with an inability to change things: "They also serve who only stand and wait."[24]

The ability to distill and effect a strategic message might not require study, but it does demand knowledge. One manager might draw from experience while another might go to a library, but success is not guaranteed by either approach. Some managers have no capacity to focus their experience or study into direction and action. Other managers' experience is too limited to help in the circumstances facing them. A manager who draws on personal experience and the experience of subordinates may fail to see that "wisdom of experience" sometimes is ineffective. This is especially true when new technologies change the rules of the marketplace.

Because strategic messages come from what is known or perceived, they fail when the facts are incomplete or in error or perceptions are inaccurate. They also fail when analysis confuses rather than clarifies issues, as when one analysis offsets another. Nor can a manager expect to be saved after communicating in error. Subordinates will act on the directives of an erroneous message if they see it as credible or if they perceive that action is in their best interests. A manager who rules out of fear might propose an absurd course that subordinates then follow to the letter out of a concern for job security. The subordinates' rationale is that a manager will have difficulty firing someone who has faithfully obeyed orders. The absurdity of this kind of miscommunication and response is that neither side has a reason to change its behavior until the business fails. There is no guarantee that either the managers or the subordinates will pay attention to emerging facts if it is not in their interest to do so. Companies have fallen in the past for losing sight of their economic reason for existence, and they will continue to fail in the future for the same reason.

DEFINING AN EXPLICIT STRATEGIC MESSAGE

A manager should first ask whether a company needs to define an explicit strategic message (Figure 7.4). If employees know what to do, if owners understand the company and if core customers are satisfied, it might be a waste of time to compose a formal statement.

Defining an explicit strategic message is not easy. Definition arouses expectations. The process can open stresses that are worse for an organization than if the message had been left alone. Managers must be confident that they can withstand the forces unleashed against them and the organization by insiders and outsiders who want to do either more or less than what is proposed.

If, in a manager's view, a company needs to make its strategic message explicit, then the manager should be sure that others see the need as well. A first effort in definition might be to convince colleagues that this is important to do. Composing an explicit strategic message is an empty exercise if the managers do not implement it. More than a few companies have

Figure 7.4
Defining an Explicit Strategic Message

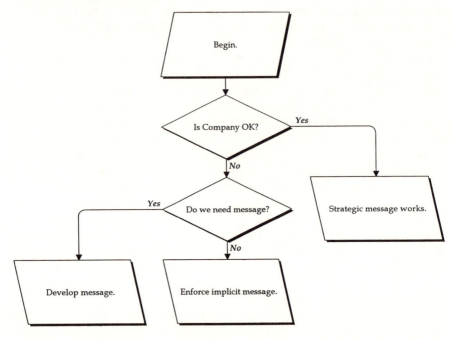

engaged in prolonged exercises to define who they are and how they fit into society without taking action.

Facing tougher competition and tighter budgets, more companies, cities, schools and even individuals are taking stock of who they are, what they do and how they plan to do it better. Then they're writing it all down. The result: a proliferation of "missions," "visions," "values," and the like, emblazoned on annual reports, factory walls and—companies hope—the psyches of their workers. It's the new groupthink: If we state our goals, we're more likely to meet them. . . .

Some management experts say that many organizations devote too much time to developing mission statements and not enough to meeting them.[25]

A strategic message should never state what a company should do or is going to do unless the company is ready to carry it out. It is wiser to summarize what was done, because such a message does not require a change in behavior. Such a summary can come from fact sheets, company reports, the testimony of managers or an analysis of company action.

To develop a strategic message, one should ask many questions before settling on a single statement. Questions might raise fear and will cause politicking and conflicts in points of view, but asking them can also help clarify thinking. For example:

- Do you thoroughly understand the company—its history, purpose, values, technology, capabilities, limitations, potential and place in the overall picture?
- How can you make sure the essence and facts about the company will be considered and communicated clearly, simply and effectively?
- What is not yet well understood?
- Why was the company established, and why is it in business today?
- What was the company's original vision, purpose or emphasis?
- How has the nature of the business evolved?
- Has the focus been maintained (with what important changes, and why)?
- How has the leadership changed and how has it stayed the same?
- What changes have occurred in the composition of the company and its style and attitude?
- How well has the company lived up to initial expectations?
- How do you account for the company's level of achievement?
- What have been the company's outstanding successes and how do you explain them, internally and externally?
- What have been the company's significant failures and how do you explain them, internally and externally?
- What do your products and services have in common?[26]

The result of the questioning should be one simple, declarative sentence, which should summarize and state what a company does to survive and succeed. The sentence might be a commonplace or it might be revelatory. Only after a manager summarizes what an organization does should he or she attempt to define what it *should* do. Whether it is a commonplace or not, an effective strategic message has large implications for organizations.

Theodore Vail's conclusion that AT&T's business was service spawned a massive investment to provide universal telephone service to all Americans. This investment took decades to complete and cost billions in resources, research and development and standards development. It accepted the pervasive regulation of the telephone business in order to achieve universal service. Universal service became a watchword that strung telephone lines to small farms in Idaho and under streets in New York City. Universal service drove managers into ice storms along with work crews to rehang fallen wire. Universal service spurred entire regional Bell operating companies working to get the central offices on-line after natural disasters.

After the breakup of AT&T on January 1, 1984, career employees were often derided, both internally and externally, as "bellheads," who did not understand customers and could not compete. This assessment seemed unfair because the "bellheads" had built a company that boasted service that was the best in the world at the time of its breakup. The author believes that what the jibe really meant was that career AT&T employees had great difficulties in accepting and implementing a new strategic message that was imposed by a business environment in which the company was thrust. AT&T still has one of the largest groups of scientists, engineers and managers in the world, and it is hard to believe that they all were too stupid to understand their customers and successfully compete.

Because a primary message gives direction to those who carry out its intent, it should be easily translatable into subsidiary messages and measurements that specify meaning and results by individual tasks. As one study concluded:

Managers seek information to give their efforts and activities direction. The information they seek is determined by their job responsibilities and their experiences. . . . The value of information is rarely determined on the basis of information content alone. Managers compare new information to expectations and benchmarks in order to determine whether action is needed.[27]

Effecting a strategic message takes time because simply defining measurements of success is time-consuming. The rule of thumb is, the larger or more complex the economic activity, the slower it is to effect a strategic message. A city street-corner vendor can change what he or she sells by the hour, and it is not unusual to see umbrellas appear instantly in vendors' hands at the beginning of a rainstorm. On the other hand, building an oil-drilling platform as high as the world's tallest building and then floating it to the edge of the continent in deep waters where hurricanes pass annually requires certitude about the oil one is likely to find and also about platform engineering, construction and placement.

It might seem contradictory that a strategic message must adapt to the business environment of today as well as the unknown environment of the future. However, a strategic message must indeed be sufficiently broad to encompass the present and future. A street-corner vendor's shift in inventory from watches on a clear day to umbrellas in a rain storm still comes under a strategic message of creating a customer and transferring wealth to the seller.

When AT&T's message of "universal service" was devised, the United States was still far from achieving it. The accomplishment of the task was understood by society and the company as a long-term goal that would require decades to achieve. However, after AT&T did achieve universal service, society changed the company's business environment from one of benign monopoly to one of open competition—which is how the telephone industry originally competed in the nineteenth century.

The most important attribute of a strategic message is its ability to be quantified. People must know what to do, where, when and to what extent. A strategic message must fragment into statements that impose measurable

Figure 7.5
The Primary Message and Translation

The Primary Message
("We are a Service Company.")

    ↘

    First Translation
    (Phone pickup in three rings.)

        ↘

        Second Translation
        (Customer hold < 20 seconds)

          ↘

          Third Translation
          (Service call completion <24 hrs.)

            ↘

            Fourth Translation
            (Phone call follow-up <28 hrs.)

              ↘

              Fifth Translation
              (Follow-up problem resolution <36 hrs.)

                ↘

                Sixth Translation
                ("We guarantee you
                service in 48 hrs. or less.")

limits on action so as to reach results. It is only after the quantitative translation of the message that one can speak about the qualitative aspects.

In Figure 7.5, the primary, or strategic, message is abstract and could apply to any company, anywhere. "We are a service company" means little from an economic point of view. The next five steps are quantitative and define specific aspects of a "service company" that set it apart from other companies that do not pick up phones in three rings, keep customers on hold less than 20 seconds, complete service calls in less than 24 hours, conduct phone call follow-up in less than 28 hours and perform follow-up problem resolution in less than 36 hours. Each specifies a limit on an action that leads to a concluding statement summarizing a guarantee that was specified in the previous five statements. The concluding statement also happens to be quantitative, but it need not be. One might have said, "We guarantee you fast service." Note that the statements do not specify the explicit service rendered, whether fixing washing machines or providing advice on software problems. That is another level of specificity that is essential to completing economic transactions. Offering problem resolution in "less than 48 hours" would be deadly for a firm that is totally dependent on a computer system. Problem resolution in less than eight hours would be more on target. However, problem resolution in less than 48 hours might be a highly competitive offer in appliance repair.

Quantitative translation results in specificity. One can only be specific if one is simple and clear. In turn, specificity defines relevance.[28] It says that in a given task, certain items, taken in a certain order and in specific steps, are important. Moreover, other possible steps are not important.

Specificity and relevance are, by definition, opposed to openness. While binding an organization to common action, they also limit its focus. A manager must struggle with this contradiction constantly. On the one hand, the manager sends precise, clear and measurable directions. On the other hand, the manager must remember that the business environment is rarely precise, clear or measurable because it changes constantly. At some point, offering 48 hours to problem resolution in an appliance service, for example, might no longer be competitive. Instead, it might be the standard. To set apart the company, a manager may have to move the organization to offering a shorter turnaround time.

A strategic message requires the right words in the right place and time. Words explain the who, what, where, when and why of a situation. A strategic message also eliminates the need for unproductive discussion which does not move an organization along its road to survival and success. "*More* communication is not always *better* communication. Communication takes time, and endless meetings and conferences designed to improve communication may simply result in reduced productivity."[29]

A good strategic message can be summarized in a headline. People speak and remember in headlines, not sentences. Thus, "Our business is service" became "Universal Service," while "Duty, Honor, Country," a strategic message from the U.S. Military Academy at West Point, has sustained careers.

Good headlines are short and carry the essence of a message clearly in the fewest words. An action-oriented strategic message encapsulated in a headline has a better chance of surviving transmission through the ranks. It is easier for a manager to interpret a mnemonic phrase than to remind people repeatedly. A short strategic message also enhances speed in accomplishment by focusing attention and resources on a common point of action.

One technique to maintain clarity and simplicity in the development of a strategic message is to make sure that each word is meaningful. This is done by *deconstructing* a message into individual words and explaining them separately. Explaining each word forces one to link it clearly and directly to action. Here is an example:

The strategic message: "The customer is right."

The: refers to the person on whom our business depends to survive and succeed.

Customer: anyone who enters our stores with the intent to purchase a good or service from us.

Is: there is never a time when a customer is not right.

Right: no matter how demanding a customer is, we serve that person to the best of our ability and strive to complete the economic transaction.

Each word is linked directly to the economic transaction and a policy that a manager directs subordinates to adapt. (The usual expression of this phrase, "The customer is always right," was not used as the word *always* is redundant with the active tense of the verb.) The message is short, memorable and clear. Even if a customer is high-handed and rude, a store employee will continue to work with him or her as long as there is the possibility of a sale. From a short explanation of each word in this strategic message springs clear action plans for how an organization will operate with the fully implemented message.

The strategic message is a directive and not a vision, an order and not a romantic description. This is something that managers often forget. Using the phrase, "The customer is right," a manager knows that to achieve the strategic message will require:

- training to help employees handle customers of all kinds;
- compensation and reward systems to make it worthwhile for employees;
- problem resolution and return systems for unsatisfied customers;
- store locations within easy reach of customers;
- choice of goods and quality levels that customers prefer;
- store layouts and checkout systems that simplify shopping;
- security systems to prevent persons who are not customers from stealing;
- standards of presentation and cleanliness that make the shopping experience desirable for customers;
- store management and information systems that feed back customer comments and requests;
- stock and inventory levels to satisfy customers needs within the patronage range of each store;
- communications and transport systems, to make sure that each store can be stocked efficiently, and warehouse systems within economic range of each store.

The list could be expanded along the same lines. One way for a manager to detail what is needed is to write a scenario of the future state. This is a description of how the strategic message works for customers when they enter, shop and leave a store. It is a way for the manager to put down how the business should operate so that he or she can check for accuracy, clarity, controls and information systems. It also allows an advance check on whether the manager's directives make a significant difference with the customers. No matter how detailed a scenario may be, if customers do not care, then the scenario and the message behind it have no economic validity. This is why advanced visualization techniques have been developed to help managers understand how to adapt a strategic message to the physical world of the economic transaction.

Here is an example of a strategic message and scenario from which a manager can begin testing or building an organization.

- *The strategic message: Harvey's House of Hats* fits customers with head coverings for adornment and essential needs: "Harvey's: The Hat Store."
- *Harvey's House of Hats:* Harvey's specializes in sales of head coverings and allied products and services.
- *Fits:* Harvey's sales staff works with customers to find correctly sized head coverings uniquely suited to an individual's taste and needs.
- *Customers:* Anyone who enters a Harvey's store with the intention of purchasing a head covering.
- *With head coverings:* Harvey's offers a full range of head coverings, from hats to scarves to caps and detachables with jackets or coats. Harvey's also offers head coverings for sports and special needs, such as football helmets, hard hats and baseball caps.
- *For adornment:* Harvey's trains staff to select and sell hats that will augment a customer's desired appearance.
- *And essential needs:* Harvey's trains staff to understand and sell the benefits of specific protective functions of hats.

The scenario—shopping at Harvey's House of Hats. A Harvey's customer starts with a need for a hat of some kind. The need might be personal, to achieve a certain look, or essential, in order to play a sport such as football.

A customer with an essential need is used to going to stores that provide a range of products for that need. A sporting goods store sells helmets, pads, footwear, clothing, and so forth. Harvey's knows that getting customers with essential needs to come to a Harvey's requires an offering of product and service that is difficult and, perhaps, uneconomic for competitors who sell full-range offerings. As a result, Harvey's will feature its patented head-shape analyzer as an essential benefit. Harvey's also will offer its proprietary hat-fitting service for both adornment and essential head coverings to ensure maximum comfort and utility to customers.

Customers with needs for hats will hear about Harvey's on local television and radio and see our ads in local printed media. We will use distinctive, in-your-face advertising to maximize awareness. We will give an

800-number (1–800-ALL-HATS) in every advertisement. The 800-number will let a person check the location of the nearest Harvey's store and availability of hat styles and order hats directly. Our 800-number will also be the premier hat information line in the market and will provide more information about hats than anyone else through an automatic voice-response system. We will adjust advertising to the preferred styles and essential needs of the moment. We will strive to get celebrities and others to wear our most popular hats on air, in our stores and elsewhere.

A customer who travels to Harvey's will find our store in a mall near mid-to-upscale retailers, a location intended to convey our seriousness about hats. Our stores will have two kinds of displays. The first will be high-fashion hats in well-presented windows, to show our skills in personal adornment. The second will be an informational display on the benefits of essential hats, such as helmets. When possible, the displays will be merged into a single presentation.

Harvey's storefronts are clean, well designed and inviting; the store entries are well-marked. The floor layouts will use a department system. The front floor of a Harvey's store will feature men and women's hats, displayed with matching outfits. Store personnel will also wear hats and matching outfits to show the latest styles. The rear floor of a Harvey's store will feature essential hats displayed with information that clearly details the protective benefits of each. There will be checkout counters in both store departments in easily visible, central locations requiring minimal walking. Checkout counters will use laser scanning and fast card readers to expedite processing. Harvey's patented head-shape analyzer and proprietary hat-fitting service will be prominently positioned in both the front and rear of the store.

A Harvey's store uses wall space and pillars for shelves to display hats by sizes, styles and colors, for mirrors so customers may check their appearance with ease and for store signs. Hat accessories will be in cases at the registers, where the sales staff may recommend them as the purchase is completed.

To emphasize service, the sales staff will be commissioned. Harvey's will have a liberal return policy to emphasize customer care and concern. Harvey's will sell hats at full margin because the hats that Harvey's carries are of good value, based on careful and mass purchasing. A Harvey's store will carry enough hat inventory to serve customers well without running out of stocks or overstocking. We will track hat sales on a daily basis to spot hot styles and fill orders quickly. Harvey's will provide hat blocking and repair services in each store and follow-up care for hat customers by capturing names, addresses, preferred styles and needs and then informing customers regularly when there are new hats that may interest them.

This incomplete scenario carries a wealth of information about how the business will operate and the messages it will send to customers. A manager and specialists can work through the scenario and identify both the verbal and nonverbal cues, information and message systems and accounting and budgeting needed to make Harvey's House of Hats a "category killer" that will dominate hat merchandising. From a scenario such as this, professionals can sketch advertising campaigns, storefront designs, floor plans, display cases and wall shelves in visual storyboards to test with prospective customers for credibility and appeal.

However, there is still a long distance from scenario to execution. On the whole, it is better to take a strategic message that works and scale it up than to invent a strategic message and try to make it work. Even a project based on extensive experience can fail. The troubled European Disneyland, in Paris, France, was tested in hundreds of ways and based on the experience of running three other successful Disneylands in America and Japan. The success of McDonald's hamburger restaurants was based originally on a store concept developed before Ray Kroc entered the picture. Pizza Hut started as a single store run by two brothers. Ford Motor Company started with a single mass-production design for an automobile. J.C. Penney started with a single dry goods store, and Wal-Mart, with a small chain of rural stores in Arkansas.

In these cases, the managers used personal experience to define and build systems to express a strategic message. They learned how to operate one store, then two, then 10, and 100 or more. As they grew, they solved the challenges of keeping a strategic message focused on the economic transaction. As problems escalated, they pushed for greater definition and system improvement. These managers understood that a manager's tasks progressively remove him or her from the point of sale and, if the manager is not careful, from the strategic message as well.

The founders of successful businesses worked hard to stay in touch with the base of their economic power. Sam Walton, of Wal-Mart, flew from store to store to check on progress; J.C. Penney personally served customers if he was visiting a store; and Ray Kroc ordered executives to get behind the counter of a McDonald's restaurant once a year to remind themselves what the company is made of. In Detroit, over the decades, auto executives were called either "auto men" or "money men" based on their concern for the product or financial side of the business. After years of money men, auto men took over the three major American car companies and began to recapture customers who had been lost to foreign competitors.

CREDIBILITY AND THE STRATEGIC MESSAGE

No matter how one crafts a strategic message, a manager must have credibility with subordinates, customers and others to effect it. One can be convinced of a position, state it succinctly and yet be removed for insanity, as was General William Tecumseh Sherman at the beginning of the Civil War when he said it would take at least 200,000 men to put down the rebellion in the Mississippi Valley alone. Only later was Sherman reinstalled when his superiors realized he was right.[30]

To be credible, a strategic message also has to fit the personalities of the sender and receiver. Intrinsically motivated people prefer general supervision that specifies broad goals and leaves the tasks to subordinates. Extrinsically motivated people prefer closer supervision and detailed instructions.[31] It is as important for a manager to know which kind of subordinate he or she has as it is to express a strategic message well. It is also important for the manager to express the source of power of his or her position in a credible way. Power might come from one's behavior or position. "The evidence to date suggests that prospective followers tend to consider the personal power of the highly esteemed expert more important than the legitimacy and power to reward and punish."[32] That is, subordinates tend to follow a person who knows more readily than one who was placed in charge.[33]

A manager enhances credibility partially by the way in which a strategic message is communicated. Some managers act insensitively and driven with their subordinates in order to present a coherent and appealing place of business to customers. Their temper transmits a seriousness of purpose about serving customers. Subordinates see such managers as the foremost practitioners of tasks and demands that they place on employees. Jeffrey Katzenberg, the former hands-on chairman of Disney studios, often used toughness to make a point:

Katzenberg has regularly waged battles over contract issues with such high-profile stars as *Sister Act*'s Whoopi Goldberg and *The Marrying Man*'s Kim Basinger. His run-ins with superagent Michael Ovitz are a Hollywood legend. In 1989, *Honey, I Shrunk the Kids* director Joe Johnson had the temerity to snub Katzenberg when the boss voiced some concern over the extended use of a $175,000-a-day set. Without warning, Katzenberg had the set ripped out, forcing Johnson to complete the film with existing footage.[34]

The chief financial officer (CFO) of IBM, Jerome York, used similar hard-driving methods to cut costs at the computer maker:

In a small conference room at IBM headquarters here [Armonk, N.Y.], Jerome B. York, the new finance chief, confronts two nervous executives from the disk-drive division and pummels them with questions.

Why, Mr. York demands, does the division split its development team between Rochester, N.Y. and San Jose, Calif.? Why does it ship parts to a plant in Mexico, only to reship partially assembled drives back to San Jose when transport costs are "eating us alive"? And where is the data the executives had promised to provide on competitors? . . .

At IBM, Mr. York has won early regard as a blunt, no-nonsense manager who spices his language with so many four-letter words that some subordinates have adopted his foul-mouthed lexicon. "If you don't deliver for Jerry," observes IBM chief strategist James Cannavino, "someone had better be preparing for your passage into the next life."[35]

Other managers will act in an opposite manner to achieve a strategic message. About June L. Rokoff, senior vice president for software development at Lotus Development Corporation, a newspaper wrote:

In the tempestuous, ego-driven industry that creates software for personal computers, she is a manager who combines technical savvy and an understanding of a programmer's mindset with intuitive people skills and a willingness to fight on others' behalf. Many people around her say she has saved more than one crucial product.[36]

Robert J. Eaton, Chrysler's chairman and CEO, stepped into the job over highly respected internal candidates who wanted the position. It was widely predicted that the outflow of executives from the company—nine in 30 months—would continue, but the opposite happened.

Arriving without his own secretary, let alone a cadre of deputies, Mr. Eaton, who is 54, has studiously promoted from within Chrysler's ranks, shared the limelight with Mr. Lutz [Robert A. Lutz, Chrysler's president and candidate for chairman] and others, and avoided trying to fix what he discovered was not broken after all. Since Mr. Eaton showed up in Highland Park [Michigan], Chrysler's sales, earnings and stock price have risen steadily.

"I don't take any credit for it," Mr. Eaton said in a recent interview. "I don't make hardly any decisions."[37]

In the end, a strategic message is an intricate web of understanding, resources and compliance that cannot be repeated precisely in the same way in every case. This is a daily challenge to managers. Business attempts to repeat actions, especially in manufacturing and service. Indeed, the reduction of variation in repetitious action is what statistical quality control is all about. However, manuals and memos cannot guarantee that reduction will come about, even with the mutual participation of subordinates and managers. Especially where humans are involved, variation is a major component in implementing a strategic message.

ASSUMPTION CHECKING AND THE STRATEGIC MESSAGE

Because every strategic message is built on assumptions about the business environment, a manager must regularly question all assumptions. If a strategic message is wrong, action stemming from the message will be wrong as well. If action is wrong, a company jeopardizes its success and, perhaps, its survival. Many a business has foundered on a great idea that did not work. Thousands of products enter and leave the market yearly without making a dent. The failure rate is so great that one may be tempted to say that the difference between successful and unsuccessful products is as much due to coincidence as to skill.

This is partially the reason why some companies start by making explicit a successful implicit strategic message. This helps a company understand the assumptions behind the message and any successful processes. It also prepares a firm for the day when it must define a new message and course of action. Many steps can go wrong during the analysis of a successful strategic message and the formulation of a new one: errors can be subtle—and fatal.

The most subtle error involves a manager's behavior and needs. A manager's strategic message can be an unconscious form of wish fulfillment. One ends up where one wants to be, even after analysis shows the manager to be in error. The manager's judgment may have been clouded by inexperience, an ignorance of probabilities or excessive self-confidence. Intellectualism alone cannot prevail over events, as Clausewitz noted when he wrote that an officer should possess a standard of judgment gained from knowledge of men and affairs and from common sense guided by laws of probability.[38]

The term *common sense* is an oxymoron. Common sense is not common. It comes from life experiences and observation which combine to provide an individual with insights into how the world works. The common sense of a leader is not the same as that of a subordinate because they have had different experiences and developed different ways of summarizing experiences into useful rules of thumb. One must learn to be either a leader or a follower. Both learn to be respectful of the position of the other without sacrificing personal judgment and responsibility. Studies of conformity and obedience show that achieving a balance between group pressure and individualism is difficult to do.[39] In fact, the studies have shown a marked tendency among individuals to conform to peer pressure and the opinion of a majority, even when another, possibly opposing, solution is obvious. Obedience, or compliance with the demands of an authority figure even to the point of abdicating moral responsibility, is pervasive. One is "just following orders."

While developing a strategic message, individuals and groups may err without ever knowing they have done so. Therefore, a manager should retain a sense of skepticism about outcomes, even when they are built on solid facts. Several techniques have been developed to combat this tendency toward group think, including:

- Small-group problem solving: isolated small groups study a problem and communicate conclusions separately to managers who weigh recommendations. (President Franklin Delano Roosevelt used this technique.)

- Large-group problem solving without management participation: the manager is present but says nothing or is absent to prevent unconscious conformity from setting in. (President John F. Kennedy used this approach with his cabinet members after the Bay of Pigs failure.)

- Anonymous solution generation: this is an extension of a suggestion box. In a modern version, participants type their thoughts into a personal computer. Ideas are visible to all without attribution to any one person. Individuals can be free to debate one another without pressure of conformity or obedience.

- Third-party checks: solutions are checked with outsiders.

- Distancing: one "sleeps on a problem" until he or she is far enough distanced from it to consider it objectively.

- Role playing: managers divide into teams to prove opposite sides of an issue, and the clash of ideas illuminates the core challenges.

- Mind flexing: managers are taught to look at a problem from different points of view.

The goal of all these techniques is to keep the mind flexible, to break through denial and to mute self-interest. A manager may use one or all techniques during the formulation of a strategic message.

There are other challenges of which a manager should be aware when checking assumptions behind strategic messages, and these are failures of reasoning. Managers are practical logicians in that they must be aware when arguments are in error. They should check their beliefs, knowledge and assumptions for accuracy. They should look in depth at facts supporting the arguments and test the facts against common sense, relevance and their understanding of the business environment. Facts and assumptions must be true or, as far as known, must correlate to the business environment from which they are drawn. Facts should link to arguments logically in the right way and be deductively valid. A manager needs to know that "An argument is *deductively valid* if and only if it's impossible for its premises all to be true while its conclusion is false."[40]

In addition managers should test propositions and messages for consistency and clarity and logical failures, such as:

- Tautology—statements that are true in every sense and tell one nothing about a business or its processes: *When you're good, you're good.*

- Contingency—statements that can be both true or false, depending on the choice of circumstances and facts: *Some competitors are ahead of us.* (Some competitors are behind us as well.)

- Contradiction—a statement that is false in every circumstance: *Nobody can do what we do.* (If we are doing it, then somebody does what we do.)

- Begging the question—the conclusion is the premise of the argument: *We have sufficient manufacturing capacity. Therefore, our manufacturing arm can make this item.* (The manager should ask, "Do we have sufficient manufacturing capacity to make this item?")

- Complex questions—these questions contain presuppositions: *How long have our customers been unhappy?* (This assumes that the customers are unhappy.)

- Personal attack—one discredits a position by attacking the person who holds it: *"If John made this suggestion, you know it isn't worth anything."*

- Confusing the issue—this is an irrelevant fact or issue that is introduced into an argument as if it were pertinent (a red herring): *Question: Won't this hurt customer service? Response: It is going to save us money.* (The issue of saving money has nothing to do with customer service.) A similar logical fallacy is to set up a weaker position and knock it down as a way of refuting another position: *We failed on the last attempt to export a product, and we're going to fail in this attempt as well.*

- Emotional Appeals—feelings are used as directional indicators: *I go with my gut,* or, *We make the finest, highest-quality chocolate in the world.* (Without factual backup, this is hype.)

- Appeals to common practice—*We need a quality program. Every other company has a quality program.*

- Appeals to force or fear—*Do this and you will be fired.*

- Appeals to pity—*If you shrink the company, thousands of workers will be laid off who can't afford it. Don't shrink the company.* (This ignores the possibility that shrinking a company might be the only way to save it and the jobs of those left.)

- Superficial appeals—Arguments based on ignorance, authority, false dilemmas and accidental characteristics. *No one says we cannot claim we are the best in this area.* (No one says we can either.) *I've been doing this for 30 years so I know I'm right.* (Thirty years of experience does not make one an authority on truth.) *This product will make us or break us.* (It might do neither and instead might be modestly successful.) *We provide all the services that the largest companies provide. There is no reason why we cannot serve you the way they do.* (This avoids the fact that your service department might consist of one person while everyone else has 10 persons—or 100. You might not have the resources to serve a customer in the same way large companies do.)

The number of ways in which a strategic message can go wrong is dismaying and a reason for taking great care in definition. Even when one attempts to make an implicit message explicit, the effort can go awry. A company might truly not know what makes it successful, and investigations into its success will tell it nothing about the wellsprings of revenues and profits.

A manager also should be aware that brilliance of mind does not stop one from making fallacious arguments. Many of our ways of thinking and speaking rely on false logic that we do not challenge, and applying false logic to business is a normal part of living. Superstition is a behavior that even highly educated people show. Some read horoscopes, others have their fortunes told and still others carry lucky charms. It makes no difference that nothing in objective observation of the environment leads one to believe that certain people or instruments can guarantee future outcomes. Nor does it help to tell people who buy lottery tickets that they have a greater chance of being struck by lightning than of winning.

It is up to the manager to make sure that investigations into the construction of an action-oriented strategic message are done with rigor. It is acceptable for a manager to be a poor writer and a faltering speaker, but he or she must have a clear idea of what to do and how to get it done.

SUMMARY

A strategic message should be:

- Simple, clear and easy to understand.
- Timely, so it can be acted upon at once even if its complete fulfillment takes time.
- Open, insofar that subordinates who perform its tasks and customers who complete economic transactions understand it, whether or not it is formally expressed.
- Defined: the message must break into specific messages to accomplish action.
- Flexible, to conform with the business environment of the moment.
- Individualized to those who must carry out its tasks.
- Meaningful with specific ideas and intentions for action based on solid logic and fact.
- Measurable: the intention of the message must be quantifiable.

NOTES

1. Peter Drucker, *Management: Tasks, Responsibilities, Practices* (New York: HarperBusiness, 1974), p. 484.

2. Norman B. Sigband and Arthur H. Bell, *Communication for Management and Business* (Glenview, IL: Scott, Foresman and Company, 1989).

3. Carl von Clausewitz, *On War*, ed. and trans., Michael Howard and Peter Paret (Princeton, NJ: Princeton University Press, 1976), p. 140.

4. Bernard M. Bass, *Bass & Stogdill's Handbook of Leadership: Theory, Research, and Managerial Applications*, 3d ed. (New York: Free Press, 1990), p. 220.

5. Doron P. Levin, "Joe Montana, a Study in Good Management," *New York Times*, January 23, 1994, sect. 3, p. 11.

6. William Manchester, *American Caesar: Douglas MacArthur, 1880–1964* (Boston: Little, Brown and Company, 1978), pp. 80–115.

7. LeRoy Gross, *The Art of Selling Intangibles* (New York: New York Institute of Finance, 1982), p. 613.

8. Shelby Foote, *The Civil War: A Narrative: Fort Sumter to Perryville,* Vol. 1 (New York: Vintage Books, 1986), p. 748.

9. Charles Conrad, *Strategic Organizational Communication: An Integrated Perspective* (Fort Worth, TX: Harcourt Brace Jovanovich College Publishers, 1990), pp. 78–79.

10. Stephen J. Frangos, with Steven J. Bennett, *Team Zebra: How 1,500 Partners Revitalized Eastman Kodak's Black and White Film-making Flow* (Essex Junction, VT: Oliver Wright Publications, 1993), pp. 42–43.

11. Bass, *Bass & Stogdill's Handbook,* p. 111.

12. Aristotle, *On Rhetoric: A Theory of Civic Discourse* (New York: Oxford University Press, 1991), p. 37.

13. Conrad, *Strategic Organizational Communication,* p. 83.

14. Clausewitz, *On War,* p. 146.

15. Bass, *Bass & Stogdill's Handbook,* pp. 11–20.

16. Ibid., p. 12.

17. Ibid., p. 12.

18. Neal Templin, "Team Spirit: A Decisive Response to Crisis Brought Ford Enhanced Productivity," *Wall Street Journal* 220, no. 118 (December 15, 1992): A1.

19. Drucker, *Management,* p. 77.

20. Ibid., p. 61.

21. Bass, *Bass & Stogdill's Handbook,* pp 341–44.

22. Saul Hansell, "Uniting the Feudal Lords at Citicorp," *New York Times,* Jan. 16, 1994, sect. 3, p. 6.

23. Oscar Schisgall, *Eyes on Tomorrow: The Evolution of Procter & Gamble* (Chicago: J. G. Ferguson Publishing, 1981), pp. 43–62.

24. John Milton, *The Complete English Poetry of John Milton* (Garden City, NY: Anchor Books, 1963), p. 216.

25. Gilbert Fuchsberg, " 'Visioning' Missions Becomes Its Own Mission," *Wall Street Journal,* January 7, 1994, pp. B1–B2.

26. These questions are from the IdeaFisher Strategic Planning Module, a software program from IdeaFisher Systems, 222 Martin St., no. 110, Irvine, CA 92715.

27. Sharon M. McKinnon and William J. Bruns, Jr., *The Information Mosaic* (Boston: Harvard Business School Press, 1992), pp. 19, 103.

28. Benjamin B. Tregoe, John W. Zimmerman, Ronald A. Smith, and Peter M. Tobia, *Vision in Action: Putting a Winning Strategy to Work* (New York: Simon & Schuster, 1989). These authors defined the five basic principles of effective strategic communication as a common strategic language, simplicity/specificity, testing for understanding, repetition and relevance.

29. Gary Johns, *Organizational Behavior: Understanding Life at Work* (New York: HarperCollins Publishers, 1988), p. 375.

30. Shelby Foote, *The Civil War,* pp. 62, 321.

31. Bass, *Bass & Stogdill's Handbook,* p. 359.

32. Ibid., p. 228.

33. Gross, *Art,* p. 561. Power has been parsed in many ways. A five-part distinction, originally proposed in 1960, defined legitimate power, reward power, co-

ercive power, expert power and referent power. The first is formal power invested in a role, the second refers to reward, the third to punishment, the fourth to special skills and knowledge and the fifth to personal behavior and qualities.

34. Ronald Grover, "Jeffrey Katzenberg: No More Mr. Tough Guy?" *Business Week,* no. 3356 (January 31, 1994): 79.

35. Laurie Hays, "Blue Blood: IBM's Finance Chief, Ax in Hand, Scours Empire for Costs to Cut," *Wall Street Journal* 223, no. 18 (January. 26, 1994): 1, A6.

36. Glenn Rifkin, "Profile: The 'Iron Lady' Keeping Lotus on Track," *New York Times,* January 23, 1994, p. 10.

37. James Bennet, "Outsider Smooths Chrysler's Ride," *New York Times,* May 16, 1994, p. D1.

38. Clausewitz, *On War,* p. x.

39. Gross, *Art,* pp. 560–86.

40. Daniel Bonevac, *The Art and Science of Logic* (Mountain View, CA: Mayfield Publishing Company, 1990), p. 21.

8

Corporate Communication and Media

The mass-marketing technique used with so much success by retail conglomerates such as Sears, JC Penney and Safeway gave way to a more
precise, sensitive philosophy referred to as micro-marketing. Micro
marketers found ways to locate smaller and smaller segments down to
the level of single individuals—segments whose profitability could be
assured and whose reachability was enhanced by novel channels of
distribution, promotional vehicles, and tailored messages made possible
by technology that was unavailable only a decade before.
—David J. Curry, *The New Marketing Research Systems*[1]

WHERE WE ARE

We have examined the business environment, message receivers, message
senders and messages. We discussed the twofold nature of message creation—information gathering and message development. We have emphasized why managers should understand the business environment and the
message receiver before communicating. Finally, we have stressed the need
for credibility.

This chapter focuses on media, the vehicles through which messages are
carried to target individuals, whether customers, interest groups, influentials, owners, employees or managers. A medium is any physical entity,
including one's own body, that carries information from one individual to
another. It uses sound or light waves, electricity, nerve endings and cellular
structures to transmit concepts.

All media are crafts requiring physical tools. Meaningful motion or gesture is as physical as producing eye blinks or sighs. Dancers and mimes

have raised physical motion and gesture to artful expression. Paralytics use eye blinks and puffs of air as their only means of communication in otherwise immobile bodies.

Managers rarely become skilled in more than one or two media, yet they are able to coordinate organizations and complete economic transactions with the few they use. Professional communicators sometimes assist in delivering messages persuasively, but even communicators know only a few media well.

WHAT MEDIA DO

Media deliver effective messages to support economic transactions and business survival and to receive information indicating whether a message was effective. Media are, by definition, bidirectional in their ability to carry messages. All media deal with presentation and with persuasion and human psychology. Even though media are physical, the messages they carry and their power of transmission may be conceptual or emotional.

Every medium has strengths and weaknesses and, as a result, most media are used in combination to increase their transmission power (Figure 8.1). Primary and secondary media vary by:

- flexibility
- cost
- presentation power
- reach
- skill required
- audience
- resources used
- time it takes to use the medium
- business environment
- managerial preference
- technology

No combination of media remains optimum for any length of time because a business environment changes constantly. For example, a medium that works effectively now may not work well later if your imitators take away its freshness and appeal. Today, it is fashionable to release information on CD-ROMs, sometimes because this is more effective but also because they provide a high-tech image. When almost all data is released on CD-ROM, however, the medium's image appeal will disappear.

All media carry messages in addition to the intended message, and how a medium is used also expresses meaning. For example, a handwritten note from a busy CEO saying thank-you for one's hard work has greater meaning than a call from a subordinate conveying the boss's pleasure. The message is the same in both cases, but the fact that the boss took the time to write a note lends its own force to the message. The clumsy use of media has as much destructive power as a negative message. In describing one company's botched attempt to communicate a decision to move the corporate headquarters, one author concluded; "Everything managers say—or don't say—delivers a message. Too many managers assume that communications is a staff function, something for human resources or public relations to take care of."[2]

A manager's choice of media is as important as the development of a message. Managers often avoid a new or unfamiliar medium because they do not understand it, an error that can impact business directly. The delay in marketing telephones for social use in the 1920s could just as easily apply to inertia in adapting personal computers and E-mail in the 1980s. "In promoting a technology, vendors are constrained not only by its technical and economic attributes but also by an interpretation of its uses that is shaped by its and their histories, a cultural constraint that can persist over many years."[3]

Before the 1920s, AT&T had concluded that telephones had strictly a business use, like telegraphy. It took outsiders who joined the phone company to convince the management that it was wrong.[4] The managerial attitudes that "you don't need a medium," "you have gotten along well without it until now," and "it isn't essential" still prevail. Similarly, in the late 1970s, when the personal computer (PC) first appeared, it was dismissed as a toy until the first electronic spreadsheet software went on the market. This ignited battles between line managers, who used PCs for analysis, and information technology executives, who felt that PCs threatened the viability of their mainframe reporting systems.

In fact, the explosion of electronic and digital media in the 1980s and 1990s has changed greatly how organizations communicate and, ultimately, will change how they are organized. Some of the new trends include:

- Substituting on-line information databases and CD-ROMs for sales forces. One commentator estimated that four customer accounts could be serviced 24 hours a day for less than the cost of a salesperson through "customer empowerment"— that is, providing customers with tools to obtain faster service without human intervention.[5]
- Installing work-group media to share information and speed customer response, such as the Nickelodeon/Nick at Nite television network's use of Lotus Notes software to distribute television program ratings[6] and real-time updating of organization information through the software's automatic data replication.[7]

Figure 8.1
Partial Characteristics of Some Media

Partial Media list	Verbal	Visual	Verbal and Visual	Sound	Touch	Other	Subjective Cost 1 = Low Actual & Opportunity	Persuasive Power 1 = Low Subjective Ranking
Releases	✓						3	2
Absenteeism/turnover reports	✓						1	3
Actual versus Planned Comparisons	✓						1	3
Budget decisions	✓						1	3
Customer satisfaction scales	✓						3	3
Definitions of Objectives	✓						3	3
Delivery performance measures	✓						3	3
E-mail	✓						3	3
Memo	✓						1	3
Naming	✓						3	3
Note	✓						1	3
Plan development	✓						3	3

Post -activity analyses	✓	3	3
Product specifications	✓	3	3
Projections/forecasts	✓	3	3
Proportions or percentages	✓	2	3
Sales effectiveness measures	✓	3	3
Statement of Strategy	✓	3	3
Status reports	✓	2	3
Suggestion systems	✓	2	3
Value/cost relationships	✓	2	3
Warranties/guarantees	✓	3	3
Work Rules	✓	3	3
Written Objectives	✓	2	3

Figure 8.1 Continued

Partial Media list	Verbal	Visual	Verbal and Visual	Sound	Touch	Other	Subjective Cost (Actual & Opportunity) 1 = Low	Persuasive Power (Subjective Ranking) 1 = Low
Personal Rating System	✓						3	4
Publicity	✓						3	4
Benefits	✓						3	5
Compensation	✓						3	5
Price	✓						3	5
Price variations	✓						3	5
Product improvements	✓						3	5
Expert opinion	✓						3	4
Advertising- television			✓	✓		✓	5	2
Events			✓	✓	✓		4	3
Public Affairs			✓	✓	✓		3	4
Ceremonies			✓	✓	✓	✓	3	3
Lobbying			✓	✓			3	3
Press Conferences			✓	✓	✓	✓	3	3
Proximity			✓	✓	✓	✓	1	3

212

Demonstration/exhibits	✓		✓	✓	3	4
Meetings/Large and small group	✓		✓	✓	3	4
Retreats/seminars	✓	✓	✓	✓	3	4
Conferences/conventions	✓		✓	✓	4	4
Videoconference	✓	✓	✓	✓	4	4
Face to face	✓	✓	✓	✓	3	5
Grapevine	✓	✓	✓		1	5
Open outcry	✓	✓	✓		1	5
Walk-through	✓	✓	✓	✓	3	5
Banners	✓				2	1
Brochures	✓				3	1
Bulletin boards	✓				1	1

Figure 8.1 Continued

Partial Media list	Verbal	Visual	Verbal and Visual	Sound	Touch	Other	Subjective Cost 1 = Low Actual & Opportunity	Persuasive Power 1 = Low Subjective Ranking
Letterhead/Business Cards			✓				1	1
Poster			✓				2	1
Advertising - print			✓				4	2
Press kits			✓				2	2
Awards			✓				3	3
Charts/graphs/tables			✓				1	3
Fax			✓				3	3
Giveaways			✓				2	3
Magazines			✓				4	3
Mail			✓				1	3
Manuals			✓				2	3
Newsletters			✓				2	3
Overnight Mail			✓				4	3
Promotional materials			✓				3	3
Work/Process Flow diagramming			✓				2	3

Product presentation	✓		3	3
Product packaging	✓		3	3
Product quality	✓		3	5
Advertising-radio		✓	3	2
Audioconference		✓	2	3
Radio		✓	3	3
Phone call		✓	1	4
Appearance-Office/plant	✓		3	2
Office size/look/furnishings	✓		3	3
Building design	✓		3	3
Appearance- personal	✓		3	3
Dress	✓		3	3

- Electronic rather than paper distribution of key financial data, such as prospectuses.[8]
- Using digital voice recognition for recording medical records, assisting plane inspectors and tracking parts in distribution.[9]
- Telecommuting by computer and modem to cut travel time and increase administrative productivity.[10]
- Creation of virtual offices where employees work in temporary spaces and remain connected to the organization when not at the place of employment.[11]
- Using virtual reality imaging for three-dimensional prototyping of parts, designing inner spaces and developing ergonomic machine controls.[12]
- Employment of local area networks for brainstorming.[13]
- Delivering real-time news directly by computer through electronic news services.[14]
- Integrating document production electronically through corporate publishing and document management systems combining text management, imaging, complex documents, multimedia, forms processing, work flow and hypertext to assemble documents dynamically.[15]

The change has been so rapid that inertia in adopting new media can harm an organization.

Every medium, including the new technology, is defined from two points of view—those of the message sender and the message receiver. The two-perspective definition of a medium stops short of action because a message receiver is free to act or not. In corporate communication, a message sender defines a medium as a way of sending a message to gain action for business survival and success and of observing whether the message was understood. To a message receiver, a medium is a way of receiving a message directing action for business survival and success and of showing understanding.

To unintended message receivers, a medium can have many meanings, based on their perceptions of the business environment, the message sender, message receiver and message. This can both help and harm a business. For example, aggressive arguing among colleagues may be one company's method of clarifying ideas, but to an outsider it may be oppressive and show a lack of civility. For example, Bill Gates, the chairman of Microsoft, uses a style of conversation that might seem normal to Microsoft employees and rude to anyone else:

To understand what it's like to work for Bill Gates, it helps to meet a woman we'll call Cynthia. Vice president of a leading computer company in Silicon Valley, she visited Microsoft for a job interview. With scarcely a hello, Gates began machine-gunning her with questions. Where do you see the business going? What are your competitors' strengths and weaknesses? Who's better than we are, and why? To this last, coupled with a request for numbers supporting her position, Cynthia replied, "I don't know. I need to do some research." "Forget that," Gates replied. "Why don't you have an answer? Are you stupid?"

This is the essence of Microsoft, something called the "Microsoft Way."[16]

A corporate communication medium is a two-way link between persons with self-interest in the outcome of an economic transaction. A medium transmits a desire, or lack thereof, to complete an exchange. The two-perspective definition of a medium also extends to media use. A manager can either push messages to message receivers or allow message receivers to pull messages to themselves:

Most employee communication programs are built around *push* strategies. They use traditional mass media to inform employees of important company activities, plans and events. . . .

Pull communication channels can deliver information to employees at the time they want it and in the amount they need.[17]

This author noted that with electronic media such as on-line databases, E-mail and bulletin boards, companies can let message receivers tailor media to their unique needs by combining push and pull media.

Any medium that involves more than one sense has greater transmission power, but not necessarily greater credibility. One can read about a plant strike in a newspaper. One can listen to a radio announcer in the center of strikers. One can even see and hear strikers shouting, "Scab!" on television. Nonetheless, the credibility of a strikers' message lies with the judgment and perception of a message receiver. If a message receiver is a stalwart member of management who believes in its view of the business environment, a strikers' chant has no credibility. The poor use of media may harm credibility, while a great presentation may help it, but neither will supplant it. Communicators and managers often forget that credibility precedes a medium. They use stylish presentations, assuming that the "fireworks" will seize people's interest and overwhelm their objections. Sometimes they work, but just as often, they do not. A company might spend millions on advertising that endorses the personal right to smoke and still be criticized for manufacturing cigarettes. An oil company might spend years defending its environmental record and still not overcome the loss of reputation from a major spill.

A medium's effectiveness is a function of:

• individuals to whom a message is targeted
• managerial credibility and skill
• the message it carries
• media type

- the business environment and culture

- the match between medium and message

A manager uses any medium that best serves his or her purposes at a moment in time and abandons any medium that does not work. Sometimes, high presentation value is appropriate, while at other times, a memo will suffice. For example, suppose a manager wants to motivate a sales force. The manager can visit each salesperson and urge the person on. The manager can write a memo saying, "Beat Allied!" The manager can anchor a ship's bell on the wall for successful salespersons to ring when they get an order or place a troll doll on a poor performer's desk to shame the person.[18] Any or all of these media may or may not work, depending on the individual to whom the message is targeted. A manager with experience will determine what works best for individual message receivers.

However, managers are not professional communicators. Their jobs are to complete economic transactions in order to guarantee the survival and success of the businesses they manage. That is why communicators often help select media. However, it is still a manager's responsibility to understand a medium's effectiveness. As a result, managers should try out new or unfamiliar media regularly. Experimentation increases knowledge, counterbalances false assumptions and offsets communicators' biases.

Communicators often let skills outweigh messages. Like other craftspeople, communicators learn a medium through persistent application. The process of acquiring a skill often results in one's becoming co-opted by the skill. A photographer looks at a sunset in f-stops; a painter, in terms of oils; and a musician in sounds. An advertising executive sells advertising. A public relations professional sells publicity campaigns.

A communicator's desire to create in a medium can take an upper hand. Frequently, one finds information and communication professionals competing to use one medium over another. This happens because each practitioner sees his or her personal economic welfare tied to practicing a craft and each believes that his or her medium can solve most of a manager's communications challenges. As a result, an inappropriate or overpowering medium may be used, which will call attention to itself rather than the message. This is a common failure. A communicator's justification is that a medium must gain attention first, but there is a line between excess and effective message transmission.

Corporate communication media are not arts to be appreciated in themselves. To judge business media on creativity and style is to miss the point. If a medium becomes a fine art in delivering an effective message, that is an added benefit. If it does not, and yet results in action, the medium is successful. The goal is not art but the economic transaction.

CHOOSING CORPORATE COMMUNICATION MEDIA

Managers choose media that best express a meaning to target individuals and persuade them to act in accordance with an explicit message content. In the process, the culture and behavior of both message senders and message receivers come into play, but the ultimate choice of a medium lies with the message receiver. Media is never *mass* to message receivers: it is mass only to message senders. Messages go to individuals, and not to units or departments or customer segments. Messages that are sent to groups inevitably miss individuals. Advertisers, by necessity, use mass media and generic messages to transmit appeals. They know that much of their media is noise and fails to hit home, but until recently, information technology did not allow precise targeting. Today, it is possible to address a million persons individually by their preferences and characteristics. Economically, this is not feasible, but database marketers have developed many techniques to target persons who fit characteristics that make them either probable or self-defined buyers of products and services. Direct marketers calculate lifetime value for customers, build formulas around recency, frequency and monetary values of purchases and use advanced statistics like artificial neural network analysis, logistic regression, factor analysis and clustering. From these tools, in conjunction with enormous computer resources, they have often mined profits through precision communication. As one expert wrote:

By communicating only to those who are interested, you will not only save money, you will begin to start a real dialogue. Several years ago, I was added to the mailing list of a large mainframe software company. After a week, I determined that this company could not do anything for me or my company. Since that time, they have written to me once a week. I must have received more than 200 letters from them to which I have never responded. . . .
The lesson: If you write to the right people with the right message, and if you respond properly and promptly when they write to you, you will create a dialogue that will result in better response to your promotional mailings.[19]

Ideally, managers choose media that will provide the most timely, persuasive and secure transmission of a message to an individual at the least cost. Managers can use models that explain and rank media to help them make choices more effectively. However, models do not excuse a manager from using good judgment. For example, the six stages of persuasive communication, beginning with awareness and ending with reinforcement, are useful in evaluating the status of target individuals and determining where one wants to move them. Media can be charted against these steps, but the business environment varies so greatly that the same combination of media will work differently at different times. The need to examine media effectiveness and delivery will never diminish.

Managers should be willing to change a medium when the economic potential of a new one becomes apparent. For example, Federal Express invented real-time tracking and reporting on packages in transit to make good its guarantee of overnight delivery. This computerized medium revolutionized the industry, and United Parcel Service of America Inc. was later forced to do the same to compete.[20] Similarly, when a soap manufacturer realized that many attendees at NASCAR races were women, it found an effective medium by decorating a race car with a giant logo of its laundry soap.

The medium of money is being replaced in some applications with "smart cards," electronic cards, which are more convenient and secure:

Physically similar to credit cards, smart cards are equipped with microprocessors capable of storing data such as bank account status and phone numbers and providing "electronic money." Users insert the cards in ATMs [automatic teller machines] to transfer funds from an account, in essence making an electronic withdrawal, then place the cards in POS [Point of Sale] readers to buy goods and services.[21]

College textbooks are being replaced by floppy disks and CD-ROMs that tailor courses to students, "but most college-textbook publishers aren't ready for this high-tech conversion. . . . They have a fortune sunk in the making and marketing of standard textbooks that are increasingly behind the times and technology."[22]

Even something as basic as truck repair benefits from a new medium to relay data to target individuals:

When a truck rolls into the maintenance bay at Ryder System Inc.'s New Brunswick [N.J.] facility, all Karen Reinecke has to do is push a button to learn instantly what's ailing the vehicle. Reinecke, a technician for the $4.2 billion transportation giant, simply touches the probe on the end of her handheld computer to a tiny coin-shaped disk on the truck's cab that has been gathering information on engine performance and fuel consumption from electronic sensors under the hood.[23]

Managers should remain objective about media effectiveness, but they often do not. They favor some media without examining why or for personal reasons, and they often do not understand differences among media. AT&T, in its early years, provided one example of managerial bias. AT&T helped launch modern publicity by hiring the Publicity Bureau of Boston in 1903 to place favorable newspaper articles about telephone use.

Over the next few years, the Bureau reported having successfully placed scores of unattributed stories in newspapers. . . . [Theodore] Vail [who took charge in 1907], however, preferred direct advertising and dispensed with the agency when he took over. By then one of the Bureau's officers, J. D. Ellsworth, had joined AT&T and was continuing publicity efforts in-house.[24]

AT&T's public relations arm was to later become the largest in the world and helped change the image of the company from a dangerous monopoly to one dedicated to "One Policy—One System—Universal Service."

Only if two media are judged equally effective should a manager choose the one he or she prefers. When it is not clear which medium is best, a manager should test them first. This is another reason why managers should understand message receivers better than do communication professionals. When practitioners argue over efficacy they create noise, which can make decisions harder, even with testing.

A final criterion in choosing corporate communication media is cost. Too often, cost is the first hurdle and not the last. Any medium requires an expenditure of assets or opportunities. Even a manager giving an off-the-cuff speech is engaged in an economic expenditure of time. He or she could have been visiting a customer, making policy decisions or any number of other activities that are important to the success of a business. Ideally, every message and use of a medium results in a proportionate increase in wealth, but they do not always do so, and moreover, this is impossible to measure. Organizations keep more media than they use to provide for security in delivery, and even well-targeted media may produce a cumulative rather than immediate result. The cost of a company's combined media distorts the cost of sending any one message. In accounting terms, media carry overhead. The cost of phone calls, computer networks, memos and clerks is often absorbed rather than attributed to the economic activities of each department or budgeted into the cost of each sale. The individual uses of each computer and telephone are often too difficult to calculate daily without automation. Some automated capture has been achieved, but not in every medium. There are phone-coding systems that automatically assign the cost to a client or department. Similarly, photocopier key systems charge costs to individuals or clients, and time clocks note when a person begins work and finishes. However, few firms actually calculate the cost of writing and sending a memo, as to do so would be prohibitively expensive.

The question a manager asks is, what media resources are needed to get individuals to understand what I want them to do? Economy dictates whether the proposed spending levels are feasible, but creativity and pragmatism also provide practical solutions. For example, perhaps network television advertising is the most effective way to reach a target audience but the company cannot afford television. Rather than giving up, managers look for affordable exposure, such as:

• Using an inexpensive but well-targeted cable channel.
• Buying spots in events that reach the largest number of targeted individuals. (For

example, Master Lock advertised during the Super Bowl football game using a compelling visual of a bullet punching through its lock, which stays closed, to gain awareness for the company in the coming year.)

- Buying ancillary advertising that uses a scene of a major event, as, for example, signs on the floors of boxing rings, the walls of soccer stadiums and baseball score boards. "The use of such ads at major-league arenas and stadiums increased 13% in 1993, according to a . . . study by Ernst & Young. The accounting firm counted an average of 77 signs in NHL [National Hockey League] arenas, 59 in National Basketball Association Arenas, 25 in baseball parks and 23 in National Football League stadiums."[25]

- Guerilla marketing, which uses an event for one's own purposes. Olympic games, for example, rely on high-priced sponsorships, but a nonsponsor may produce and run lower-cost advertisements that imply it is a sponsor.

Similar examples occur in other media. The publicity stunt has been used for decades to gain attention at less cost than advertising. This includes everything from registering performing fleas at a major hotel to hoisting cars on cranes. Direct mailers have used many inexpensive techniques to get people to open their mailings, from unmarked envelopes to imitating the look of official government correspondence. Promotion experts inexpensively stamp a company's name on caps, pencils, ties, jackets, helmets and more.

The least expensive media eliminate the human element and reduce message transmission to mechanics. For example:

In a race to cash checks, three helicopters land in rapid succession at the airport here. Workers scramble to unload hundreds of pounds of bundled checks, hurl them into carts and run them out to a waiting Learjet.

"Shake a leg, Louie," dispatcher Martin Evans shouts. He paces anxiously as shifting winds and incoming air traffic delay flight 401's scheduled 10:30 P.M. take-off by five minutes. On board are $600 million in checks that must get to banks in 46 cities by 8 A.M. or payment will be delayed a day—a costly proposition.

In contrast, Barbara Woollett, an accountant at Chevron U.S.A. Inc., has no doubt about the delivery time for an $11,637 payment she authorized that same day for parts used in one of the Chevron Corp unit's oil refineries. . . . Ms. Woollett zapped the payment electronically from Chevron's bank to the part's manufacturer's bank.[26]

Electronic payment eliminates helicopters, workers, Learjets and clerks writing checks and filing paper. One medium has helped companies boost the efficiency of accounting departments, reduce error and improve customer and supplier relations, but the process of getting to electronic data interchange (EDI) was not straightforward from an economic point of view. It took years of discussion and a change in attitude for companies to reach a point where they paid more than 35 million invoices electronically in 1993.[27]

It was not obvious at first that EDI was a better medium for payment transfer. Treasurers had been taught to delay payment to conserve cash, but cash management did not account for the cost of writing, transporting and tracking checks. Early adopters of EDI relied on their judgment of EDI's effectiveness against accepted business wisdom. This is another reason why basing media choices overwhelmingly on economics is risky.

A manager's job is to know the message, the individuals to whom a message is sent and the results to be achieved (Figure 8.2). He or she guides communicators. The manager forces them to think about what they do and prevents them from falling into easy solutions and settled habits, especially in noisy business environments. Therefore, a manager concentrates on clarity in the presentation of ideas and makes communicators focus in that way, too. For example:

- *Buy X soap. It makes you feel clean all over* (manager: "Ten other brands also 'make you feel clean all over.' Explain why X is different");
- *The needle shows the water temperature is too hot* (manager: "Is the gauge broken or is the water actually too hot?");
- *We are a quality company* (manager: "Does this mean we are implementing Total Quality Management?").

Ultimately, because a message receiver defines clarity, a manager must adopt the viewpoint of the message receiver. The only exception is when message receivers will not accept any message, no matter how clear, or are unable to understand the message. Hostile workers can buck a boss, and some workers cannot grasp a message because it requires skills that they do not have. For example, a manager may say clearly, "I want you to repair 10 channel banks in the central office at 1221 Hollister Avenue." However, the worker may have no idea what a channel bank is, much less how to repair one.

Media are most successful when they are integral to a message. For example, store layout and design are integral to expressing the shopping experience to a consumer. Integrated media do not take away a customer's choice of store: they simply make the choice clear to the consumer. Clothes jammed onto plain racks in open retail space signify a discounter. Wood paneling, elegantly designed cases and plush seating signify a better men's store. Similarly, a separate boutique for each designer's custom-designed clothes signifies an upscale department store.

Turning imagery on its head to present an opposite type of good or service deliberately plays against expectations but may still be integral to the message. For example, one might choose a discounter's look for retail diamonds and fine jewelry: the message is that customers get more for less.

Figure 8.2
Audience Stage in Communication

Partial Media list	1. Aware Most Useful Media - Indirect	2. Informed Most Useful Media - Indirect	3. Evaluating Most Useful Media - Direct	4. Trying out Most Useful Media - Direct	5. Adopting Most Useful Media - Direct	6. Staying Committed Most Useful Media - Indirect	1 = Low Subjective Cost Actual & Opportunity	1 = Low Persuasive Power Subjective Ranking
Banners	1	2				6	2	1
Brochures	1	2				6	3	1
Bulletin boards	1	2				6	1	1
Letterhead/Business Cards	1	2				6	1	1
Poster	1	2				6	2	1
Advertising - print	1	2				6	4	2
Advertising- television	1	2				6	5	2
Advertising-radio	1	2				6	3	2
Appearance-Office/plant	1	2				6	3	2
Press kits	1	2				6	2	2
Releases	1	2				6	3	2
Absenteeism/turnover reports	1	2				6	1	3
Actual versus Planned Comparisons	1	2				6	1	3
Audioconference	1	2				6	2	3
Awards	1	2				6	3	3
Budget decisions	1	2				6	1	3
Charts/graphs/tables	1	2				6	1	3
Customer satisfaction scales	1	2				6	3	3
Definitions of Objectives	1	2				6	3	3
Delivery performance measures	1	2				6	3	3
E-mail	1	2				6	3	3
Events	1	2				6	4	3
Fax	1	2				6	3	3
Giveaways	1	2				6	2	3

Magazines	1	2	6	4	3
Mail	1	2	6	1	3
Manuals	1	2	6	2	3
Memo	1	2	6	1	3
Naming	1	2	6	3	3
Newsletters	1	2	6	2	3
Note	1	2	6	1	3
Office size/look/furnishings	1	2	6	3	3
Building design	1	2	6	3	3
Overnight Mail	1	2	6	4	3
Plan development	1	2	6	3	3
Post -activity analyses	1	2	6	3	3
Product specifications	1	2	6	3	3
Projections/forecasts	1	2	6	3	3
Promotional materials	1	2	6	3	3
Proportions or percentages	1	2	6	2	3
Radio	1	2	6	3	3

Figure 8.2 Continued

| | | | | | | | 1 = Low | 1 = Low |
| | 1. Aware | 2. Informed | 3. Evaluating | 4. Trying out | 5. Adopting | 6. Staying Committed | Subjective Cost | Persuasive Power |
Partial Media list	Most Useful Media - Indirect	Most Useful Media - Indirect	Most Useful Media - Direct	Most Useful Media - Direct	Most Useful Media - Direct	Most Useful Media - Indirect	Actual & Opportunity	Subjective Ranking
Sales effectiveness measures	1	2				6	3	3
Statement of Strategy	1	2				6	3	3
Status reports	1	2				6	2	3
Suggestion systems	1	2				6	2	3
Value/cost relationships	1	2				6	2	3
Warranties/guarantees	1	2				6	3	3
Work Rules	1	2				6	3	3
Written Objectives	1	2				6	2	3
Work/Process Flow diagramming	1	2				6	2	3
Product presentation	1	2				6	3	3
Product packaging	1	2				6	3	3
Personal Rating System	1	2				6	3	4
Publicity	1	2				6	3	4
Public Affairs	1	2				6	3	4
Benefits	1	2				6	3	5
Compensation	1	2				6	3	5
Price	1	2				6	3	5
Price variations	1	2				6	3	5
Product improvements	1	2				6	3	5
Product quality	1	2				6	3	5
Appearance- personal			3	4	5		3	3
Ceremonies			3	4	5		3	3
Dress			3	4	5		3	3
Lobbying			3	4	5		3	3
Press Conferences			3	4	5		3	3

Proximity	3	5	1	3
Demonstration/exhibits	3	4	5	3	4
Expert opinion	3	4	5	3	4
Meetings/Large and small group	3	4	5	3	4
Phone call	3	4	5	1	4
Retreats/seminars	3	4	5	3	4
Conferences/conventions	3	4	5	4	4
Videoconference	3	4	5	4	4
Face to face	3	4	5	3	5
Grapevine	3	4	5	1	5
Open outcry	3	4	5	1	5
Walk-through	3	4	5	3	5

One might choose high-style appearance to merchandise paste jewels and zirconium rings: the message is that the products are as good as the real thing.

When a medium is used badly, effective communication is more difficult and managers must work harder. For example, a manager might preach quality, yet in the shop one finds high levels of heat and noise, filthy floors, grimy walls and dangerous conditions. Nonetheless, the manufacturer might, in fact, turn out quality goods through vigilance. In a second case, workers wear pressed uniforms, the floor is painted and clean, machines gleam, tools and parts are in their proper places and the shop is quiet and cool. A message of quality is supported by the medium, but again, appearance does not guarantee a quality product or service. The product or service may, in fact, be poor, and the appearance may be used to cover up its mediocrity.

Managers often blame media when it is the messages that cause the failure. This admission by the chairman, president and CEO of Mack Trucks Inc. highlights what happens when a message goes wrong:

Few traits can be as important to a company—or, under the wrong conditions, as dangerous as pride. When built on a foundation of excellent quality and service, pride can be the best of motivators. But if the foundation starts to deteriorate, the same pride can blind people to the need for radical change. . . .

A key to our reputation had always been the intense pride that Mack employees took in being part of the team that produced these quality vehicles, and their hard work paid off in a company that as recently as 1980 held more than 20 percent of the North America heavy-duty truck market and employed some 17,000 people.

But in the late 1980s, Mack's well-known slogans were beginning to ring hollow. Our quality was suffering, but we didn't know how badly because we weren't measuring it. Our pride had deteriorated into an arrogance that blinded us to the severity of our situation. By 1989, North American market penetration had dipped to 13% and employment had plummeted to 6,500. That same year, the company lost $185 million—the first of a string of nearly five years in the red.[28]

Happily, Mack rebuilt its quality and teamwork and regained market share and profits by 1993.

When a manager sends a tough message, he or she cannot expect a medium to persuade message receivers to accept it happily or do anything more than obey. A manager might personally explain a 25 percent workforce reduction, but one out of four workers will still suffer dismissal. The manager's objective is not to get a message accepted easily but to gain compliance in firing individuals. Media can make willing submission easier or harder, but it cannot guarantee acceptability.

Some messages are best told simply. There is never an easy way to tell workers that a plant is closing or for a manager to tell a spouse that his or her mate just died at the office. Messages receivers can perform even while resisting message senders. (They do the job but hate the boss.) The only person who prevents a manager from achieving a goal is one who does not act. This is why authoritarian managers often use fear as a medium. Fear helps overcome individual inertia through threats to personal security.

There are hundreds of media in every organization and new ones are invented daily, but a manager does not have the time to direct them all. Corporate communication is concerned only with media that directly support business survival and success. A cursory look around an office might reveal a phone; computer; letters and memos; posters and wall hangings; books; newspapers and magazines; pencils and pens with messages stamped on them; note cards and filing systems; floppy disk storage media; a modem; labels; office decor; desktop calendars; promotional items, such as a clock from a vendor; a calculator; photos and art; brochures; and company policy manuals.

Outside the organization, there are thousands more media that directly and subliminally appeal to people. In fact, were it not for the brain's ability to tune out messages, a person could barely concentrate when walking an average city street. Hundreds of media are in active use inside and outside the organization all of the time, and they compete for a message receiver's attention. A major challenge for a manager is to get the intended message receivers to attend to, and act on, his or her message amid all the noise.

Much corporate communication is information that may or may not have a bearing on economic transactions. There are messages and data about the business environment, the business and its customers and past results of business activities. The information, messages and media may be useful or useless to transactions now. Managers must choose from the information, messages and media available to them.

As a result, organizations cannot get rid of all "useless" media because managers never know when a medium might prove useful. What a manager can do is to regularly cut back excessive media to keep the purposes of an organization clear. Media that do not imperil an organization can survive as long as they do not absorb too many human and material resources. Some examples include:

- An employee newsletter that relates bowling scores, birthdays and retirements. Today, the newsletter carries no vital information about the business, but employees like it. A manager can let such a newsletter exist as long as it does not interfere, and he or she knows that at some point it could become a useful communication.

- Social conversation: managers and clerks gather daily to swap gossip. Some call friends and talk over issues that have nothing to do with work. This increases human contact but wastes productive time. A manager knows that he or she is not getting 100 percent productivity but lets some social conversation continue because it can be used to send key messages when needed and can reveal vital information that would otherwise stay hidden.

- Celebrations: some companies celebrate birthdays, new babies, holidays, weddings, work anniversaries and more. Pragmatic managers allow celebrations on the job as long as the work is finished and the celebrations boost teamwork.

It is up to managers to balance media and messages in any organization. Because organizations are subject to variation, some media are always out of control.

TYPES OF CORPORATE COMMUNICATION MEDIA

Primary, or *direct,* media are contained within the human body—in speech, facial and body movement, appearance, touch and smell. Humans use primary media more than any other, and many leaders rely on it, especially in managing by walking about. A manager presents his or her physical presence to message receivers to observe and communicate.

Secondary, or *indirect,* media are transmission vehicles that exist apart from the person. Secondary media are bounded only by the number of people who communicate to one another. Secondary media do not carry the full impact of all human senses, although they may come close, as in computerized virtual reality, which can combine sight, sound, touch and movement.

A primary medium involves multisensory communication among individuals with immediate feedback. Secondary media are limited sensory communication among individuals with either immediate or delayed feedback. Both primary and secondary media are neutral. It is how they are used that expresses the intent of the message sender. Managers choose media and presentation according to the personal behavior and meanings they intend to communicate.

Business is interested in effecting action now, and business communication exists in the present tense. Even the ledgers and prices in early Mesopotamian merchant accounts involved inventories of goods at the time the writing took place. There is nothing business can do today about inventories in 2112 B.C.E. This is not to say history has no bearing on present action, but the lessons of history are applied in the present.[29] Even policy-related messages and media have no meaning except in the present tense. "The customer is right," right now. The need for action means that business is better off using media with immediate response. This usually means primary media, but the need to coordinate large enterprises has also forced business to use secondary media heavily. Common forms of primary media are:

- Face-to-face communication: one watches the whole person, his or her body language and the surroundings, including other individuals. The manager can, for example, feel the firmness of a handshake and smell cigarette smoke or cologne. Both parties can directly examine the impact of communication on the other person directly.

- Speeches, lectures, seminars: one can watch individuals to see if they are interested, touch a person to make a point and hear the enthusiasm of applause. A manager can also feel the room temperature and determine if heat is affecting message transmission or smell the air to determine if it is stale.

- Walk-throughs: a manager absorbs the noise, vibration and activity employees, customers and influentials experience and thus can better understand their difficulties in absorbing messages. The manager can also elicit immediate feedback from individuals.

- Live exhibits or demonstrations: public demonstrations communicate through direct contact with individuals. A person sees, hears, touches, tastes and smells for him- or herself the product or service in action.

- Plays and simulations: role-playing can give one a feel for an experience—for example, being a minority in a workplace. A simulator can involve most senses in a recreation of real-life experience.

- Guided tasks: an experienced person coaches an inexperienced one in a new task. For example, an intern watches a surgery, then performs it under the guidance of a skilled surgeon and, finally, teaches it to another intern. Similarly, an older worker may teach a younger one through a "buddy system."

The power of primary media can also turn against the manager who fails to use them well. For example, a boring speaker can dissuade an audience quickly. Similarly, when a live demonstration fails, it can imperil a product or service. A public relations firm once introduced a new, "tasty" dog food at a press conference. The demonstrator spooned some food into a dish, and a dog was brought in to eat it. Unfortunately, the dog sniffed the product and walked away. Simulations can be either not real enough or too real. It was through overly realistic simulations that psychologists discovered how authority affects some individuals. They found that some individuals would seriously harm another person if told to do so. Guided tasks fail when coaches abuse authority. For example, craftspersons who put journeymen through inflexible apprenticeships can harm learning because students learn at different speeds. Inflexible apprenticeships are often a way for one person to communicate superiority over another in a way that is unrelated to the task at hand.

The technology of multimedia is rapidly moving toward personal, direct media. One can see, hear and interact with persons or machines that may be thousands of miles away or simply a creation of computer code. The progress in multisensory presentation, however, brings with it its own challenges. The risk of advanced information technology is a renewed effort to overcontrol, whereby managers are tempted to deny individuals latitude in getting tasks done. Insensitive practitioners try to force employees to perform tasks in one way without regard to an employee's view, abilities or perceptions. For example, information technology has transferred time and motion measurement into keystroke counting. Data-entry workers are watched from a distance on an administrator's console for the number of keystrokes they make, number of corrections and time without action and are called in if their actions fall below the norms.

Another factor challenging multimedia is noise. For every advance in sensory transmission, there is an equal and simultaneous advance in noise. The noise comes from the replication of messages themselves, media and a misunderstanding of the message-receiver. For example, software and hardware companies have learned that most failures come from inexperienced operators, so they set up customer service in a rigid, hierarchical manner. The first level focuses on easy solutions, the next on more difficult challenges and the highest is for situations rarely seen before. The difficulty is that skilled operators cannot bypass a hierarchical system to get to an expert because a company does not know who is skilled and who is not. Inevitably, an expert operator is forced to go through troubleshooting that he or she has already done, which wastes the operator's time and the technician's efforts.

Secondary, or indirect, media communicate to one or two senses, but not to all. The strength of indirect media lies in its reach and ease of use. The weakness of indirect media is its use of only a few senses. A message sender using an indirect medium can never be sure that it has conveyed a message accurately, nor can a message receiver be certain that a medium has not distorted a message. Since the invention of pictorial symbols, humans have transmitted ideas through secondary media over time and space using thought writing and sound writing. Thought writing transmits ideas directly through visualizing them, such as a picture of a tree to stand for *tree*. Phonetic or sound writing uses abstract symbols to convey meaning and information.[30]

However, message transmission can only imply the full, multisensory experience of another place or time. For example, archaeologists translate the writings of lost civilizations to gain a sense of how past societies operated. The writings cannot communicate the full experience of the society: they can only imply what life must have been like for some people, some of the time. The mores and manners of other individuals, while identical to one's own, may have a completely different source of motivation:

In many ways, . . . Quaker beliefs [about the family] seemed very close to that shimmering ideal of a "child-centered, fond-fostering, nuclear family" which would dominate thinking about familial relations in our own time. But it is important to recognize the vast distance that separated their values and purposes from those of secular American families three centuries later. The importance that Quakers gave to the ideal of familial love, the primacy of child rearing, and to the idea of the family as a spiritual sanctuary, all derived from a system of Christian belief that belonged to the seventeenth century and not to the twentieth.[31]

Perhaps the most powerful indirect medium in business is accounting, because it totals the wealth derived from economic activity. However, accounting communicates completed actions and not ongoing ones. Even with real-time data capture, accounting communicates only the process and completion of a sale. Accounting's strength as a medium is its ability to describe completed economic actions in a rational construct that can help managers project future outcomes. Accounting's weakness is that its description of business is only a pale representation. Numbers cannot define motivation, nor can they define what was said to whom in what order and with what force in order to make a sale.

INTEGRATING CORPORATE COMMUNICATION MEDIA

Managers coordinate and protect critical information pathways to core individuals. For example, the brain and spinal cord are key information storage and communication pathways of the body. They are protected by bone. From the spinal cord come 31 pairs of mixed nerves, or links, that provide two-way communication to parts of the body. These nerves are not protected by bone, but if one is cut, only part of the person is harmed rather than resulting in paralysis or coma, which follow spine or brain damage. At the end of the 31 pairs of mixed nerves are thousands of nerve endings, or terminals. Nerve endings are the principal receptors of positive and negative sensations from the outside world. If any one is harmed, only a small part of the body is affected, as with a pinch or pin prick.

As with the human nervous system, managers identify the principal information storage and communication pathways of organizational communication and encase them in security. Links branching from them to individual departments are more or less protected based on the part of the organization to which they go. Terminals, or receptors, at the extremities are open to the changes in the external business environment.

Ideal corporate communication is an integrated core of media and databases. Databases constitute the brain of a company, where results of economic transactions and business information are stored and from which messages are created. Media link core databases, such as marketing, accounting, manufacturing, purchasing, human resources, and public relations, to each other and to departments or subsidiaries. From departments and subsidiaries, integrated media form links to customers, owners, influentials, distributors, employees, and so forth.

In reality, core databases often do not share information because they are incompatible, employees carry vital data in their heads or links are informal and insecure. For example, a key executive may suddenly die, and with that person go the messages, information and relationships needed to maintain the organization. To survive, the organization must start over and rebuild what it has lost.

Media integration is an optimum and temporary mix of both personal and impersonal and verbal and nonverbal message delivery, which is adjusted for differences among message receivers, noise levels, transmission security and persuasive force. A manager judges the trade-off between cost and effectiveness in the mix. Ideally, one calculates the trade-off precisely. Practically, however, one cannot calculate it precisely because there are too many variables and experience teaches a manager to err toward overcommunication.

Ideally, managers integrate communication from the outset. In reality, however, inherent limits and interference from the business environment may make integration impractical. A classic example of media conflicts exists in auto retailing. Each manufacturer has its own computer system linked to the dealer and retailers with multiple franchises are forced to carry multiple and incompatible systems:

Megadealer Martin Swig is an admitted computer-phobe. Stacked in a room in his San Francisco dealership are seven or eight (maybe more—he's not sure) computers devoted to running his business and communicating with nine manufacturers.

His annual computer bill: about $100,000.

"It's wasteful," says Swig, owner of Autocenter. "We have a lot of factory communication devices, and they are costly."

Swig has a dream: Why not run the dealership with one computer system?

Like many multi-franchise dealers, Swig has separate computer systems for each of his franchises except Chrysler and Plymouth. One computer operates an electronic parts catalog. Each system does its job well—individually.[32]

There are at least 13 outside and non–manufacturer-related systems available to auto dealers, in addition to those from the factory. These come under names such as Auction Vision International, AucNet USA Inc., KarPower, EVA, Automotive Satellite Television Network, PowerView, NADA Guide 2000, AutoCareers Network Inc., Data Transmission Network Corp., Carfax, DialPolk, Bell & Howell and V-Crest Systems Inc.[33] Any one of these communication systems can be useful to a dealer, but the sum total of them are uneconomical and filled with noise.

Because a manager works within his or her knowledge of media, there is always a chance that an effective medium may be left out of integration due to ignorance. A manager is often not to blame for this failure because communication counselors also may be ignorant. For example, computer-based multimedia, at the time of this writing, were still developing. A counselor unfamiliar with computer-based multimedia might not know how to recommend them or produce effective results.

Knowing this, a manager should never depend on any one communicator or medium too heavily in building an integrated mix and should search continually for better solutions. A manager might search through reading, listening to vendors and attending briefings from inside and outside communicators while maintaining a healthy sense of skepticism about any one solution. For example, there have been many efforts to introduce interactive kiosks that look like automated teller machines as a way of informing people and selling to customers, but to date, kiosks have not proven popular in the United States.[34] Therefore, a "media-smart" manager would force an enthusiastic vendor to prove the demand for an interactive kiosk before using one.

A medium should fit the business function, and since the function of an effective message is to gain individual action, integrated media should fit both a targeted individual and the desired action. A manager's task is to use the least number of media to the greatest effect in getting individual action according to an organization's primary message. There are hundreds of media, but a manager only has time to integrate those that directly relate to survival and success.

Media ranging from office design to policy manuals may be critical in organizational communication. For example, Paul O'Neill, chairman of the Aluminum Co. of America, moved from his executive suite to a cluster of cubicle offices where he could lean over a makeshift wall to confer with any of nine other executives.[35] The U.S. Navy, when threatened by devastating publicity about sexual harassment in its ranks, published a sexual-harassment prevention handbook with precise descriptions of sexual harassment under three headings—"Green Zone," for safe; "Yellow Zone," for questionable; and "Red Zone," for behaviors that are always objectionable.[36]

Integrated media focus on ergonomics, human factors, personal skills, persuasion enhancement and the design of products and delivery of services that are easier to use correctly. For example:

- dress, neatness of appearance, proper use of scent, the sound of one's voice and attitude help bridge the distance between a salesperson and a prospect;
- the height of a table, the layout of assembly, feel of parts, loudness of machines and air quality can all help optimize the speed and quality of manufacturing;
- distances among persons, reduced ambient noise, and light and air levels can contribute to enhanced workplace communication;
- video and audio conferencing cut down on expensive and stressful travel;
- simple human-machine or human-task interfaces link up directly to the desired action—a media function about which one commentator wrote, "It is becoming

increasingly clear that the comfort of a good fit between man and machine is largely absent from the technology of the information age";[37]

• custom-tailored distribution of products and services makes restocking easier and purchases faster for consumers.

When software coding required punching rolls of paper tape, computing was slow and inefficient and only a few people could use the machines. Punch cards increased the speed, but not by much, and computers remained still the province of a few. On-line computer commands boosted speed dramatically, but only for those who knew computer language. Icons attached to computer instructions integrated the codes into a single command that boosted the speed of action and made computers accessible to everyone. The enormous productivity of computers in graphics, for example, comes from integrating hand-driven tasks into visual electronic instructions using a hand-held "mouse."

Every department and speciality in an organization contributes to the integration of corporate communication media. Business relies heavily on visuals to integrate messages because many actions are difficult to describe and coordinate in words. Some of the best visualizations of detailed and difficult business processes come from engineers who learned to integrate complex relationships symbolically with visual tools such as the following (see also Figure 8.3):

• The house of quality: a technique that helps engineers and others see trade-offs in product development. A house of quality is a two-dimensional graph of rows and columns topped by a peaked roof of rows and columns that tie the two dimensions into a third dimension.

• PERT charts: a way of visualizing mathematical network analysis. Each step in a project is placed in sequence as a node and joined by lines that show precedence. Through mathematical formulas, a critical path is drawn through the PERT chart to show steps that must occur on time for an entire project to meet its deadlines.

• Gantt charts: a visual method of showing multiple activities using time segments on a two-dimensional chart.

• Process and data diagrams: these show individual steps in organizational processes and the flow of data through them.

• Ishikawa diagrams: also called cause-and-effect or fish-bone diagrams, these show the relationships of the preceding processes to a present one.

• Statistical control charts: these place process control limits on an X-Y axis with upper and lower limits to help workers keep machine variations within tolerances.

Lawyers have contributed to precision in integrated communication through defining economic transactions and responsibilities in detail. Lawyers stipulate where the responsibility lies between buyers and sellers with

Figure 8.3
Engineering and Visualization of Process

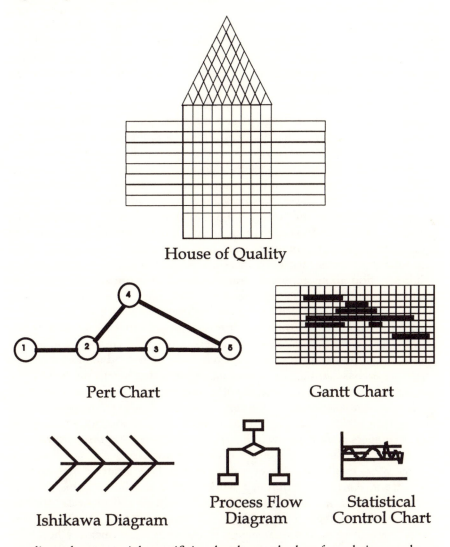

House of Quality

Pert Chart   Gantt Chart

Ishikawa Diagram   Process Flow   Statistical
                          Diagram   Control Chart

a tedious, but essential, specificity that keeps the law from being used as a competitive weapon against either party.

Marketers create paid advertising, promotions and direct mail. Public relations professionals develop and implement unpaid publicity and persuasive tactics. Human relations staff contribute benefits and compensation packages that define the importance of each person to a company. Public affairs experts build grass-roots campaigns and one-on-one relationships with legislators and interest groups.

Managers, however, ultimately must integrate all media because they are responsible for outcomes and because subordinates take cues about the importance of any medium from their superiors. If a CEO regularly looks at the customer satisfaction indexes, subordinates will watch these carefully. If a CEO looks at production uptime reports, subordinates will follow. Integration means that a manager chooses the type, amount, importance and relationship of any medium to another in the total collection of available media tools.

The manager's skill is to choose media that express the maximum amount of a strategic message at any moment. This skill comes from experience. Every business has its own internal—and external—measures of success. What this means, however, is that potentially valuable and useful media are often ignored because they do not have support at the moment. This is a frequent frustration for communicators who may sell the need for their media but find themselves prevented from using them. For example, a major Wall Street CEO rarely granted interviews except when he had a business purpose to do so. In the meantime, the job of his public relations executive was to parry requests from reporters.

A manager selects media for integration that carry the greatest amount of information about economic transactions. The more specific a message about an economic transaction, the more valuable the medium is that carries the message because it transmits multisensory information that is as close as possible to personal, or direct, communication. This is why bar coding, for example, has helped managers understand customers in greater detail. A computer can register each bar code by individual customer and recreate purchase and decision-making patterns that heretofore were invisible. In an ideal world, a manager witnesses every transaction as it happens, as does a shopkeeper at a register. In reality, however, managers must sample transactions because too many occur at any given moment. However, managers already can watch clerks at a cash register three states away and monitor totals of individual registers by store.

Integrating media also makes a difference in how strategic messages are carried out. An organization can work sequentially or in teams. In a sequential system, each department develops policies and processes to meet the goals of a strategic message. It then communicates its policies and processes through organizational media to the next department. When there is disagreement, the departments negotiate. With teams, however, departments integrate communication and resolve trade-offs simultaneously. Each method requires a manager who can maintain balance and motion. Team development is potentially faster because the communications lines are shorter. However, to achieve team development a manager has to break down the walls of self-interest that absorb specialists and then weld them to a common purpose.

Integrating media, whether internally or externally, requires an understanding of target individuals, which is not easy to achieve at the beginning of any economic cycle. For example, an entrepreneur may want to make and sell high-quality, custom-built tables and chairs. The first question the entrepreneur asks is where the customers are. It is likely that he or she will start by selling at craft fairs, which are frequented by people who purchase handmade items. After months or years of attending fairs, the entrepreneur might have developed a customer list that allows full-time work.

When one hires a new employee, there is always a period of adjustment as the impressions formed in interviews collide with reality. The person will not know the routines of the workplace and will fumble for awhile; moreover, the new employee may not be as adept in specific skills as he or she had led the manager to believe. Over time, a manager will learn whether to trust the employee.

The choice of media for integration begins with research. The same research tools can be used internally and externally to understand individuals. The only criteria are that the tools be used consistently and accurately and that their use results in action. For example, Charles Knight, chairman and CEO of Emerson Electric Co., used integrated planning media to build that firm. Among the planning tools were consistent assessments of employee opinion:

Rigorous planning is the heart of Chuck Knight's Emerson, and it involves every aspect of the business. For example, every two years, every one of its more than 70,000 salaried and hourly workers is asked to fill out lengthy opinion surveys, which ask questions such as: "Is the plant manager competent and doing a good job?" and "If you were starting over, would you go to work for this plant again?" The surveys are more than employee relations ploys. If more than a third of the responses to the above questions are negative, the division manager must come up with a proposal for correcting the defects. . . .

If the thoughts and feelings of the workers count heavily in Emerson's planning process, so do those of the executives. Knight goes to great lengths to get to know them and to plan their futures. He ushers a visitor into a locked unmarked room down the hall from his office. Covering the walls are passport-size photographs of Emerson's 650 top managers, each bearing a short resume of their current and past postings. Color-coded stickers indicate the managers' level of experience—and whether they are ready for promotion.[38]

Externally, one can use many data sources, though none may be as precise as one needs. There are enormous reservoirs of information in libraries and on-line information services. At times, however, a product, service or proposed action falls outside common experience. When this happens, research may be of little help and undifferentiated media techniques, such as mass advertising, may be more useful until one can identify potential customers and pitfalls. Indeed, the medium may be the research. For example, suppose a manufacturer of digital network access devices builds excellent products in a highly competitive marketplace. One major trade show a year draws together potential purchasers of these devices. The company sells exclusively through distributors who have no allegiance to its brand, and the firm has only a small marketing budget. Continuous advertising, even in trade media, is too expensive. Mass direct mail to the digital networking market is potentially more affordable, but not necessarily more effective. Mass direct mail, however, would allow the company to capture a list of potential customers directly—something it could not do through the distributors. The company may choose to test mass mailings until it can identify and build a database of likely customers.

A second example is a Fortune 500 diversified manufacturing company, formed from several mergers, that decided to adopt Total Quality Manufacturing. The company's wide offering of products and services and heterogeneous employee population, which was largely unknown at headquarters, posed a difficult challenge to adapting any approach. The CEO chose to write a statement of general principles for the company and then personally sold his view from plant to plant, where the media could be tailored by product line, service and business environment. The CEO's small, eight-page pamphlet provided a clear, five-step process with deadlines that every manufacturing facility was to undertake.

Other options include:

- Direct presence: open a business and let customers find it;
- Direct outreach: contact a potential customer group. This might involve door-to-door selling, participation in fairs or shows or other travel.
- Targeted direct outreach or presence: some locations are closer to desirable populations, and some fairs and shows have more of one kind of buyer than another.
- Mass advertising, mailing, promotion or publicity: this is the indiscriminate blanketing of a geographic area or segment of society to inform and identify potential prospects. For products that fit a broad demographic profile, mass media can generate awareness.
- Targeted mailings: targeted mailings go to zip codes, census tracts, city blocks, titles and demographics of persons who fit the profile of an inferred likely buyer. Mailing houses merge and purge lists to get rid of duplicates and identify desirable names, addresses, titles and occupations.
- Targeted advertising: one can target key media reaching likely buyers, such as trade publications or cable channels or promotions. In the cigarette industry, targeted promotions have proven safer than worrying about advertising bans.

Karen Daragan, Philip Morris's manager of media affairs, termed the [Marlboro Adventure Team] campaign "probably the largest and most successful consumer promotion ever launched by a packaged goods company."

More than 10 million smokers have clipped symbols and bar codes from their packs, and about half earned enough Marlboro Miles to order a total of 14 million sleeping bags, jackets, shorts, watches, lighters, caps and other gear.[39]

- Point-of-sale capture: for customers of mass merchandised products, managers use retail data capture systems such as InfoScan and SCANTRACK, from Information Resources, Inc., and A.C. Nielsen, respectively.[40]

Among indicators one can use to help make integrated media decisions are statistics from the federal government, including the Bureau of the Census, the Bureau of Labor Statistics, the Federal Reserve, the Department of Commerce, the Federal Trade Commission, the Federal Communications Commission, the Securities and Exchange Commission and others. There are private and commercial sources such as McGraw-Hill, Time-Life, Forbes, associations and universities and there are state, county and local governments.

If a company knows roughly where customers are located, it will often use integrated targeted.media to reach them precisely and with efficiency. There are hundreds of ways to break down even mass media into well-defined and coordinated segments. Managers in an industry usually are familiar with the media of the industry in which they work. However, they may not be familiar with the media that their customers use.

To isolate customers, media buyers use information services, such as Standard Rate and Data Service for magazines and newspapers and Arbitron and Nielsen for television and radio. They employ geodemographic systems like the Census Bureau's Topologically Integrated Geographic Encoding and Referencing system (TIGER), as well as ACORN from CACI-Federal, ClusterPLUS from Donnelley Marketing Information Services, PRIZM from Claritas and MicroVision from Equifax.[41]

When identifying individuals is beyond the budget, experience may be enough to choose corporate communication vehicles. For example, a simple expedient of cataloguing magazines in a purchaser's office can help detect what a purchaser reads. Looking at what a customer keeps in an office can provide clues. For example, some people save caps, T-shirts, desk accessories, wall plaques, pens, pencils, books, and so forth. A manager can imprint a name and message on items like these and use them as reminders.

Walking a plant or office floor is still one of the best methods of understanding how a workplace operates. Holding small-group meetings with employees, stopping by employee offices at random and swapping gossip around the coffee machine can achieve an integration that more expensive media fail to reach. Testing the knowledge of subordinates also reveals how one should use media to communicate messages.

Some ways of reaching individuals are counterintuitive. As one advertising person said about a make of luxury auto, "Television was the least efficient way to reach buyers of the auto, but the most effective." Similarly, one the most powerful media is not a brochure or advertisement, but a referral. Particularly in cases where credibility is an issue, referral may be the only useful medium. This is common in selling financial products, for example. One may not listen to a sales pitch, but a friend boasting about a broker may be enough to gain that broker a new customer. Finally, traditional hard-sell methods may remain useful even though an industry, such as auto manufacturing, is moving away from them:

Hundreds of what are known in the trade as "blow 'n' glow" dealerships still unapologetically sell cars the way they always have—with urgency, excitement, dickering, low-price teasers and more eye contact than you will find at a pickup bar. . . .

Why is Detroit down on "blow 'n' glow" antics, even when they move the metal? Excitement may generate sales, but high pressure salesmanship has given the car business a bad name. Surveys show that car salesmen are about as popular as Internal Revenue Service Agents.[42]

Cultural identification is another way of integrating media. For example, some population segments identify themselves by what they drive, the type of house in which they live, or their neighborhood and clubs. The process of gaining entry to this closed group is done through social examination. One gains entrance by being sponsored by an accepted member of the group. Once in, speaking to any member of the group is easy. (Edith Wharton's novels are useful in examining the ways of a closed society in which social acceptability was everything, and the opening of the film *Schindler's List* is a lesson in how to ingratiate oneself with a new group.) Particularly with tightly knit internal cultures, such as Wall Street traders, media integration comes from being accepted.

A medium may also be an antimedium. That is, one may hide a message enough to provoke interest. Allusions build interest in a message's content. Efforts to keep it "hidden" only provoke greater interest in exposing it or being a part of it. Secret societies or clubs are often built on this premise. Businesses have been built in the same way with products and services targeted at a "select" few who are "allowed" to learn the message.

In the end, the choice of integrated media comes from informed judgment supported by audits of effectiveness. A manager makes two estimates of effectiveness—the first, of the medium, and the second, of how the medium was used. Because effectiveness is decided by individuals for whom the message was intended, it is common to see a manager asking individuals whether they have seen an advertisement and what they thought of it, how they felt about a speech, and similar questions.

In well-understood business environments, it is possible to build mathematical models that balance the weight of media against potential sales or acceptance, assuming that a medium has been used correctly. Such models can be highly sophisticated in terms of defining population segments on the basis of demographic, psychographic and other characteristics. However, models also can mislead if a manager does not understand the assumptions on which they are based. For example, a model of mass advertising may ignore direct couponing. A model of promotional value through store positioning may ignore the value of advertising to build awareness of the positioning. A model of word of mouth for building sales may ignore the impact of advertising. (A typical example comes from the entertainment industry, where critics' comments are printed prominently in ads to enhance the referential sale.)

Before a manager accepts any model that explains the impacts of media on individuals, he or she should understand the model in detail. The unthinking use of models leads to conclusions that fail in action. Models are indicators. They do not take decisions away from a manager: they attempt to make decisions easier.

In every choice of media type and weight, a manager should start from a zero base. The first question that should be asked is, "What will happen if we eliminate the media?" For example, some products are so well established and dominate their niches so fully that media expenditures may waste money. This is the case with fresh fruits, vegetables and meats in a grocery store, for the most part, while internally, for example, a compensation system may be so longstanding and well understood that a manager need no longer explain it.

What a manager should look for in a zero-base consideration of media are the rationales and facts for using media in the first place. As often happens in business practices, activities take on a patina of customary behavior and go unchallenged. "We advertise because we have always done so." "We have always had an employee newsletter."

At the beginning of each economic cycle, good communications counselors present the basic reasons for using any medium. They review the business environment, expected challenges, individuals' behaviors and opportunities and analysis why a certain medium should be integrated with a corporation's communication. This leads to a recommendation of how to present a message in an integrated fashion, along with media types and weights.

It is the details, however, that a manager should probe to understand why a communications counselor has recommended an approach. What the manager should look for is objectivity rather than an overreliance on traditional patterns. For example, suppose a chemical that waterproofs wooden decks has been built into a major brand through television advertising directed toward men and broadcast during sports programming. Over the years of working with the brand, managers learn that a key component in the decision to waterproof a wooden deck is a wife's concern about weathered wood, which turns gray and splits and is unappealing to the eye and tough on unshod feet. The manager may work these themes into the original message and move the advertising to another segment of television programming to capture female heads of households. On the other hand, the primary message of waterproofing a deck—the high cost of replacing it—may be so effective to both male and female heads of households with wooden decks that one need not change the message. It is these subtle shifts that a manager tries to detect and exploit while integrating corporate communication.

SUMMARY

The media that a manager uses should be:

- Simple: use the least possible number of media to produce effective message transmission because: (1) media use assets; (2) it is easier to control fewer than more media; (3) a few media that integrate a primary message effectively are more persuasive than many media that carry pieces of a message ineffectively; and (4) fewer media mean less noise is generated by the media themselves.

- Timely: the best medium provides the right message at the moment the message is needed to complete economic transactions and assure survival and success.

- Open: a medium links senders and receivers in a two-way avenue of communication. If it does not, it is no longer a medium but has become noise.

- Defined: message senders and receivers both recognize a medium as the way in which a primary message is delivered.

- Flexible: managers choose robust media that can handle variations in the business environment without requiring major changes.

- Individual: messages are sent from one person to another.

- Meaningful: a medium transmits the greatest amount of the intent of a primary message with the least use of resources and interference from noise.

- Measurable: a medium measurably enhances the probability of action and can show that a message was understood.

NOTES

1. David J. Curry, *The New Marketing Research Systems: How to Use Strategic Database Information for Better Marketing Decisions* (New York: John Wiley & Sons, Inc., 1993), pp. 4, 5.

2. Jeanie Daniel Duck, "Managing Change: The Art of Balancing," *Harvard Business Review* 17, no. 6 (November–December, 1993): 111.

3. Claude S. Fischer, *America Calling: A Social History of the Telephone to 1940* (Berkeley: University of California Press, 1992), p. 85.

4. Ibid., p. 81.

5. Andy Kessler, "Multimedia at Work: Fire Your Sales Force—The Sequel," *Forbes ASAP: A Technology Supplement to Forbes Magazine,* April 11, 1994, p. 23.

6. Eric R. Chabrow, "Lotus Notes: Easy Client/Server?" *Client/Server '94: A Supplement to Information Week* (n.d.), p. 42.

7. Jamie Thain, "What's New with Notes?" *Data Based Advisor* 12, no. 6 (June 1994): 42–43.

8. Bruce Caldwell, "The Writing's on the Wall," *InformationWeek,* May 17, 1993, p. 25.

9. Mary E. Thyfault, "The Power of Voice," *InformationWeek,* May 9, 1994, pp. 44–45.

10. Bob Violino and Stephanie Stahl, "No Place like Home," *InformationWeek,* February 8, 1993, pp. 22–29.

11. Phil Patton, "The Virtual Office Becomes Reality," *New York Times,* October 28, 1993, pp. C1, C6. See also Kirk Johnson, "In New Jersey, I.B.M. Cuts Space, Frills and Private Desks," *New York Times,* March 24, 1994, pp. B1, B2.

12. John A. Adam, "Virtual Reality Is for Real," *IEEE Spectrum* 30, no. 10 (October, 1993): 22–29. See also Dennis Hancock, " 'Prototyping' the Hubble Fix," *IEEE Spectrum* 30, no. 10 (October 1993): 34–39.

13. Arielle Emmett, "Tech Briefing: Groupware Helps Feds Boost Productivity," *Federal Computer Week* 8, no. 16 (June 27, 1994): 32–33.

14. Thomas Hoffman, "News in Real Time," *Computerworld,* May 17, 1993, p. 66.

15. Robert M. Knight, "Publish Wisely or Perish," *Computerworld,* December 21, 1992, pp. 51–53.

16. Michael Meyer, "Culture Club," *Newsweek,* July 11, 1994, p. 40.

17. Brad Whitworth, "Strategies for the Electronic World: Putting the Pushmi-pullyu to Work," *IABC Communication World* 11, no. 5 (May 1994): 31.

18. Jaclyn Fierman, "The Death and Rebirth of the Salesman," *Fortune* 130, no. 2 (July 25, 1994): 86.

19. Arthur M. Hughes, *Strategic Database Marketing* (Chicago, IL: Probus Publishing Company, 1994), pp. 174–75. See also David Shephard Associates, *The New Direct Marketing,* 2d ed. (Burr Ridge, IL: Irwin Professional Publishing, 1995).

20. Linda Wilson, "Stand and Deliver," *Information Week,* November 23, 1992, pp. 32–36.

21. Bob Violino, "The Cashless Society," *Information Week,* October 11, 1993, pp. 31–32.

22. Meg Cox, "Electronic Campus: Technology Threatens to Shatter the World of College Textbooks," *Wall Street Journal* 221, no. 105 (June 1, 1993): A1.

23. Ira Sager, "The Great Equalizer," *Business Week, 1994 Special Bonus Issue, The Information Revolution,* p. 100

24. Fischer, *America Calling,* p. 63.

25. John Helyar, "Signs Sprout at Sports Arenas as a Way to Get Cheap TV Ads," *Wall Street Journal,* March 8, 1994, p. B1.

26. Fred R. Bleakley, "Fast Money: Electronic Payments Now Supplant Checks at More Large Firms," *Wall Street Journal* 223, no. 72 (April 13, 1994): A1.

27. Ibid., p. A1.

28. Elios Pascaul, "Manager's Journal: Mack Learns the Error of False Pride," *Wall Street Journal,* July 11, 1994, p. A12.

29. Daniel C. Snell, *Ledgers and Prices: Early Mesopotamian Merchant Accounts* (New Haven, CT: Yale University Press, 1982), p. 282.

30. Albertine Gaur, *A History of Writing* (New York: Cross River Press, 1992).

31. David Hackett Fischer, *Albion's Seed: Four British Folkways in America* (New York: Oxford University Press, 1989), pp. 484–85.

32. Charles M. Thomas, "Information Superhighway: No Entry," *Automotive News,* April 11, 1994, p. 22.

33. Ibid., p. 22.

34. Jeffrey A. Trachtenberg, "Interactive Kiosks May Be High-tech, but They Underwhelm U.S. Consumers," *Wall Street Journal,* March 14, 1994, p. B1.

35. Raju Narisetti, "Management: Executive Suites' Walls Come Tumbling Down," *Wall Street Journal,* June 29, 1994, p. B1.

36. Eric Schmitt, "Red Light/Green Light: Next Time the Navy Plans to Play by the Book," *New York Times,* April 17, 1994, p. E7.

37. John Sedgwick, "The Complexity Problem," *Atlantic Monthly,* March 1993, p. 96.

38. Seth Lubove, "It Ain't Broke, but Fix It Anyway," *Forbes* 154, no. 3 (August 1, 1994): 58.

39. Allen R. Myerson, "Selling Cigarettes: Who Needs Ads?" *New York Times,* March 3, 1994, p. D1.

40. See David J. Curry, *The New Marketing Research Systems: How to Use Strategic Database Information for Better Marketing Decisions* (New York: John Wiley and Sons, 1993).

41. For a complete listing of data sources and database software, contact: The Direct Marketing Association, New York, NY 212–768–7277; and Datapro Information Services Group, 1–800–DATAPRO. See also David Shepard Associates, Inc., The *New Direct Marketing,* 2d ed.

42. Douglas Lavin, "Youwannadeal?: Bucking Detroit Trend, Landmark Chevrolet Still Uses the Hard Sell," *Wall Street Journal* 224, no. 5 (July 8, 1994): p. A1.

9

Corporate Communication and Measurement

I once asked the training directors of three major airlines engaged in an expensive training program, "How do you know you're getting your money's worth? How do you know the training will do what it's supposed to do?" None of the three was able to provide an answer.
—Gerald M. Goldhaber, *Organizational Communication*[1]

WHERE WE ARE

We have discussed message senders, message receivers, media and the business environment and have emphasized that a manager's role is to get a job done using them all. The manager ensures that messages lead to action and that action leads to economic transactions and corporate survival. To achieve this, corporate communication is two-way. A manager sends messages and a message receiver replies, showing understanding and results, if any.

What we have not discussed is measurement. How does a manager know that economic results were sufficient? How does a manager know that a message, the understanding of the individual, the business environment or a combination of circumstances were in error? These questions are difficult to answer at any time and impossible to decide in the absence of measures.

Measures compare one thing to another: any finite thing can be measured in some way. The question is whether a measurement has relevance. In business, relevant measures tie to an increase in wealth and continued survival.

DEFINING MEASUREMENT IN CORPORATE COMMUNICATION

Measurement compares size, capacity, extent, volume, quantity, motion and time. Movement includes speed and direction, and time includes the present, past and expectation, or probability, of future events.

Business measurement compares:

- Wealth before an economic exchange to wealth afterwards. Measurement answers the question, "How much did I earn from this transaction?"
- Rate of growth in wealth over time. Measurement answers the question, "Is my wealth increasing or decreasing more quickly?"
- Probability or expectation of more economic exchanges in the period before an economic exchange to the probability or expectation afterwards. Measurement estimates an answer to the question, "Is there more business out there?"

Corporate communication measurement uses the same standards as business measurement, but communication measurement is not clear-cut because it is not isolated in an economic transaction (Figure 9.1). There must be a willing buyer and a willing seller, as well as goods or services and wealth. Without these elements, there is nothing about which to communicate. Based on the amount of each of these elements, the value of communication varies. With willing buyers and few sellers, communication's measurable impact may be simply that of awareness—letting individuals know where the seller is. With willing sellers and few buyers, communication's measurable impact may be persuasion—getting an individual to buy from me rather than someone else.

Communication's actual impact on any one economic transaction is probable and imprecise. The study of humans, especially, makes precision impossible since every person is unique, exercises choice and has a different set of circumstances motivating participation. A lack of precision, however, does not dispense with the need for measurement. Estimates can lead to action as much as precision. We know through measurement when something works, but we do not always know why. Because of variance in corporate communication measurement, it is a contentious subject among communication professionals.

Measurement involves a message, medium and noise. It tells those who communicate that they have specific responsibilities for wealth and survival and defines those responsibilities, but it also can become an end unto itself. A new manager of a computer operation that was subject to frequent and unacceptable failures discovered that each week, system operators completed a one-inch-thick book of system measures. The measures were impressive in communicating the blame for failures but said nothing about the effects on customers. The manager got rid of the book and rated em-

Figure 9.1
Corporate Communication Measurement and the Economic Transaction

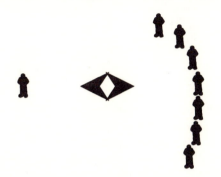

One Seller and Many Buyers.
Measurable communication = awareness.

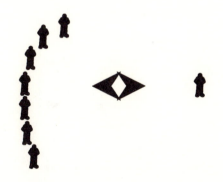

One Buyer and Many Sellers.
Measurable communication = persuasion.

ployees against a "Customer Pain Index" (CPI)—the number of minutes for which any customer did not receive proper service. The CPI measured the direct impact on the company's bottom line—the retention of customers. To achieve a satisfactory CPI, system operators measured many of the same variables in the one-inch-thick book, but the focus of their measurements shifted from avoiding blame to developing a diagnostic tool to support CPI.

Communication success is measured partly in terms of wealth. During

Figure 9.2
Measurable Components of Corporate Communication

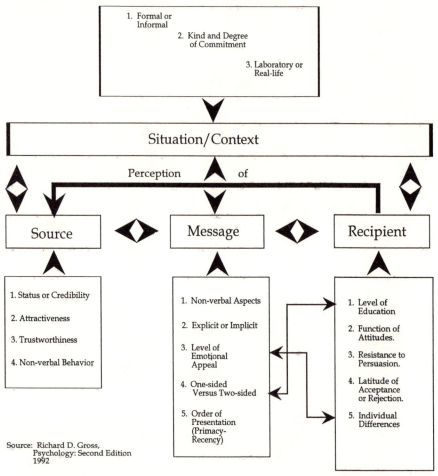

Source: Richard D. Gross,
       Psychology: Second Edition
       1992

an economic transaction, the prospect of increased wealth hangs in the balance. Neither the seller nor the buyer knows if an exchange will occur. Communication helps tip the balance toward an exchange, through awareness, information, evaluation and trial (Figure 9.2). Each of these four states is measurable but none guarantees that a transaction will occur. Individuals may fail or a transaction may be delayed, as in a long-term sale.

However, the completion of economic transactions is still the starting point for corporate communication measurement. What this means is that one traces the process backwards, from the results through the elements that led to it. In many ways, this is close to abductive inference. One projects "plausible hypotheses based on educated guesswork"[2] because communication variables are so intermingled that teasing them apart is difficult.

Communication measures six components. Each component has a primary gauge, and the measures are terms of economic transactions and survival.

Component	Primary Measurement
Message sender	Credibility
Message	Appropriate economic action
Medium	Persuasive impact on target individuals engaged in economic actions
Business environment	Extent of support for economic actions or noise interfering with them
Message receiver	Extent of voluntary action according to message intent
Action	Contribution to economic transactions and survival

Sometimes, measurements for these entities are clear and sometimes, they are not. For example:

- A chairman of a major accounting firm who lost credibility with his partners was asked to step down, even though he had helped the firm make needed changes.[3]
- Companies trying new management theories often give them up when they find that the messages behind the techniques are inappropriate for their organizations.[4]
- Two architects lost a commission because they used the medium of hand-drawn renderings while a competitor used a computer-generated, three-dimensional walk-through. The two architects realized that a drafting board was no longer acceptable equipment.[5]
- When the working environment became intolerable at a well-known New York law firm, 80 partners voted to close down the 200-lawyer practice. Said one partner, "It's not for any economic reason. There is no reason for this business to dissolve except that some partners could not live with others."[6]
- When there are too many messages, message-receivers can no longer use them effectively, as in this case:

    Electronic mail is a wonderful productivity tool, allowing users across the company and across the world to quickly share vital intelligence, memos, FYIs, research, queries, announcements and personal notes. But some folks get too much of a good thing. Consider Dick Adams, assistant director for fire operations at the U.S. Forest Service. He receives about 100 E-mail messages a day during the summer forest fire season. Some messages are really 20-page documents, some are mission-critical, and about one-third are useless, he said. . . .
    Experts . . . warn that unless users learn to effectively manage their E-mail—through better work habits and E-mail filtering technologies—the productivity gains possible from electronic messaging will be lost.[7]

- After 10 years and $1 trillion spent in new computer and information technology systems, companies learned that hardware and software were not contributing in a cost-effective way to the bottom line. "Companies are a long way from unleashing the real power of the technology they have spent so dearly to put into place. Technology spending soared in the 1980s, yet productivity grew well under 2% a year."[8]

Communication measurement in advance of outcomes is never precise. It measures probability, often with large variation. It sketches ranges for components and states of persuasion. The manager uses ranges to estimate the resources needed to increase the likelihood of success, reduce risk and estimate the total potential wealth. However, probabilities built on probabilities are open to dispute. A manager tests a message and medium about a new product with focus groups made up of targeted customers who provide an impressionistic baseline of how effective a message might be. Ideally, if a message is ineffective with the groups, the manager will reformulate it or abandon the campaign. In reality, however, managers often plunge ahead without testing because they are unwilling to wait.

The author had such an experience in a city where an unpopular mayor proposed selling the town's municipal telephone system. Citizens had to ratify the mayor's proposal with a 66 percent vote in favor. The company offering to buy the system was tarred as rapacious by the municipal unions. Focus groups showed that advertising was insufficient to lower citizen suspicion about the company. Company executives needed to show that they were human and to mollify city workers, but the company elected instead to mount an advertising campaign and keep the executives isolated. The firm never got close to the votes needed.

A second example happened at an advertising agency that served a client selling caulks and sealants. The client was determined to sell product kits on television, using an infomercial. The agency opposed the approach because research showed that it was unlikely to work. However, the client insisted and took charge of the campaign copy, visuals and media placement. The agency staff secretly set up an office pool on the number of caulk kits the company would sell. No bet exceeded 300 kits—far below the breakeven point of several thousand, and indeed, actual sales were less than 100 kits. (As is typical in a disaster like this, the client fired the agency for incompetence.)

Two kinds of measurement can be applied before, during and after communication:

- Subjective or impressionistic measures that cannot be independently verified.
- Objective, or fact-based measures, which can be independently verified.

Both kinds of communication are essential in business. A manager does not have time to measure everything. Much of what the manager relies on to

Figure 9.3
Feedback and Corporate Communication

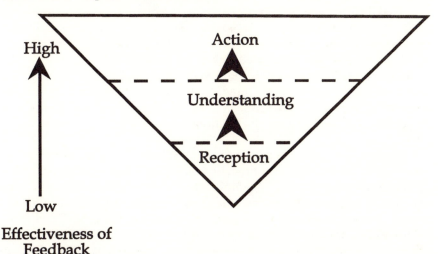

make decisions is judgmental data that is later either supported or modified by fact-based analyses.

CORPORATE COMMUNICATION AND FEEDBACK

Feedback is an essential, bidirectional measure used during communication. It is as measurable as the strength of message transmission. A message sender observes a message receiver for indications of understanding. The message receiver acknowledges reception and understanding through verbal and nonverbal expression.

Feedback has three parts. The first confirms reception of a message, the second confirms understanding, and the third part confirms the action. If a manager sees action, he or she can assume that a message has been received and understood (Figure 9.3). If a manager does not see action, the manager cannot confirm either reception or understanding. If a message was received and understood, feedback is positive even if a message receiver rejects the message. If the message was not received or understood, feedback is negative. With negative feedback, the manager sends the message again. It is like a radio operator on a crippled ship broadcasting SOS signals until someone acknowledges their receipt. A manager is always safer assuming that a message was not received until there is proof that it was. Direct communication is better than indirect for feedback because listening is multisensory and immediate. A manager can look at a subordinate, and the subordinate can look back. Even when individuals mask their reactions, the act of doing so is feedback.

Feedback need not come after a message is sent. Rather, it can be simultaneous with sending, as in a telephone conversation, or it can be established before message transmission. For example, one can instruct a person to call each day at a set hour to get orders. The act of calling at the appointed hour and the act of picking up the phone with an expectation of who is there is successful feedback.

Feedback verifies message reception but cannot measure the intent to act. A person can pretend to understand, feign interest or show loyalty without complying. In political circumstances, role-playing is frequent. A good role player can fool a manager before actions, or lack thereof, give him or her away.

Managers have different ways of using feedback. Some are proactive observers, and others, reactive. Proactive observers examine feedback. They are aware of variability and the probability of miscommunication. When a manager is uncertain how individuals are receiving a message, he or she should investigate reception and understanding. On the other hand, reactive observers assume reception and understanding unless the events prove otherwise. For example, a manager may give an individual a sales presentation and orders the person to learn it. The manager then finds out whether the presentation was learned during the first client meeting. Reactive observers use feedback only to indicate that messages have been received, and they deny or ignore variability. They consider feedback to be simplistic and mechanical when used in human relations. For example, suppose an employee repeats a command and then goes out in good faith and does the opposite. The employee responded mechanically but did not understand. A reactive observer does not accept such failures because he or she assumes that a message was understood and the person was capable of acting.

In noisy environments, feedback strengthens transmission through repetition. In the marketplace, repetition of a different kind is useful. Multiple message transmission helps pierce through the noise of competing claims. One repeats a message and hopes that target individuals hear it at least once. Feedback occurs when target individuals become aware of the message and can relate it through either unaided or aided recall.

Managers automate feedback when possible, especially with repetitive tasks, because mechanization is more productive and economical. Self-regulating mechanical systems have been understood since the development of steam engines, when the concept of the feedback loop was invented. Automated feedback is desirable because it removes human variability and the need for active listening. One need not keep a hand on the throttle of an engine that drives and stops itself. This is true with humans as well. A new worker might not understand the behaviors or crafts of a job as well as a seasoned worker. As a result, a manager may elect to keep seasoned workers in critical jobs because they regulate themselves and do not require as much active supervision.

Feedback is a matter of perception unless it is verified. It may be accurate but not factual. One assumes that feedback comes from the right message receiver, but it may not. Suppose one manager sends a memo to another via E-mail. The memo is intercepted and a response is sent in return. The response indicates receipt and understanding, but the target individual never saw it. In spying, this kind of dissembling lies at the core of a credibility conundrum. Only with a secure means of transmission can one have confidence that the right person has received a message, but one can never be sure that only the intended person received it. For example, some companies reserve the right to read every employee's E-mail.

Feedback may be a perceptual trap when individual response is substituted for that of a population. This, too, is a common mistake of managers. A manager may give an order and then talk with one or two employees to see how well it was understood. If the manager gets positive feedback from these employees, he or she may assume that others received the message in the same way. This is a false assumption. Feedback is by individual and not averages. The manager might have coincidentally talked to the only employees who understood the message. If a manager uses sampling, it should be randomized to give each individual in a message reception population an equal chance of verifying reception and understanding. However, mistakes occur even when care is taken to avoid them.

Feedback is limited. It may not tell one whether an action or message was successfully executed and how much a company's wealth was enhanced or harmed. Feedback provides only inferential measures of how well a message has been transmitted and received, but inferences may be enough. For example, a manager may speak before an assembly of workers and then chat with a randomly selected few. The workers say how excited they are to get started in the new venture and ask follow-up questions about it. The manager can feel fairly certain that someone was listening. On the other hand, if workers complain about the lack of resolution of their benefits package and the slowness of the human resource department, a manager has an indication that more message transmission may be needed.

There are commonsense guidelines about feedback that managers follow:

- Use one or two feedback methods regularly to get target individuals familiar and comfortable with them. Few people like or trust the unexpected, such as a remote boss who suddenly becomes friendly or a company that suddenly becomes oversolicitous of its customers.

- Vary the application of feedback methods to inject life into them and foil pretense. For example, one boss walks through the facility every day around 10 A.M. Everyone is ready for his daily visit until the day when the boss walks in at 9 A.M. unannounced. At 9 A.M., several people are missing from their posts.

- Informal feedback is better than formal feedback. If employees see the boss regularly, they are less likely to modify their behavior. However, if they see the boss only on special occasions, they are more likely to conform and to bury their personal opinions.

- Formal feedback is still effective communication, as it feeds back an elaborate version of an original message. This can be helpful in getting employees to assimilate the original message.

- Sending media without building feedback devices into them automatically limits the response. A message sender is, in effect, telling a message receiver that no reply is needed.

- Feedback is built on self-interest. An individual who does not want to do a job might feign misunderstanding. Another, who wants to impress a manager, might feign complete understanding but be ill-equipped to get the job done.

MEASUREMENT AND FACTS

Fact-based measurement is independently verifiable. It can be immediate but it usually is not because it takes time to develop facts (Figure 9.4). Fact-based measurement gauges communication before, during and after message sending, using instruments and standards with commonly accepted meanings, such as:

- conversion of leads to sales;
- media reach of target individuals;
- extent of awareness among target individuals;
- extent of product knowledge among target individuals;
- extent of trial among target individuals;
- number of key influentials recommending the product or service versus the competition's;
- percent of total market exposed to a message.

In critical situations, immediate, fact-based measurement is essential and multiple feedback instruments are economically justified. A nuclear power plant undergoing a reactor malfunction must shut down before a core meltdown can occur. The plant's warning system must alert operators, regulators and nearby citizens in case of a need to evacuate. During crises, managers use several forms of communication to make sure they stay in touch with one another even if one or two media fail.

Most measurement is not immediate because the elements of the process are not controlled as well as by a machine. In human communication, especially, measurement may be delayed. For example, suppose a manager

Figure 9.4
Fact-Based Measurement and Corporate Communication

Message

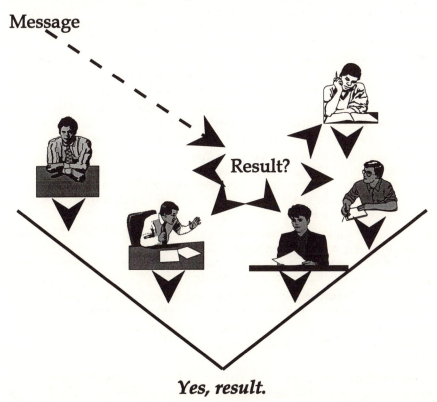

Result?

Yes, result.

mails 25,000 brochures offering a product or service. The manager esti-mates that, all else being equal, the 25,000 pieces will provide a 1.5 percent to 2 percent response—this is a rule of thumb for direct mail. The manager thus expects, and budgets for, 375 to 500 sales calls. If the manager gets 375 to 400 responses, the process has worked as expected. If the manager gets 250 replies, he or she must ask what went wrong. Initial feedback will tell a manager nothing about the elements of the direct mail process. To measure what happened, a manager might ask:

- Did the mailing reach target individuals? Direct mail lists can be inaccurate (the measurement of inaccurate addresses is based on returns, for which managers can set standards.)

- Was it the right audience? If a mailing did reach the target audience, the manager may have chosen the wrong target. For example, a company may market digital telecommunications access devices to local area network (LAN) managers, and the response is low. With closer inspection, the manager learns that the real audience is not LAN managers but supervisors of LAN managers, who understand the savings of dial-up digital transmission.

- Was it the right time for the communication? Mailing after corporate budgeting is finished or during the holidays will cause a lower response because monies have been committed elsewhere or external events get in the way.

- Was it the right appeal? If the LAN manager was the right target, perhaps the message was incorrect. The brochure may present a cogent message about savings, whereas the concern of the LAN manager is service.

- If it was the right audience and appeal, was it the right presentation? The message might have been presented too aggressively, too timidly or too technically. (The manager measures this through focus groups, interviews and surveys.)

- If you chose the right audience, appeal and presentation, was it the right offering? It might be that LAN managers are using a better connection device than the company offers. It also might be that perception of the company's product is undeservedly negative. LAN managers may think the product is too difficult to use (when actually it is not).

- If all else was equal to the competition, was the price right? Maybe LAN managers are buying a similar product for 20 percent less. Maybe the only way to get LAN managers to test a new and unfamiliar product is to offer a no-lose proposition—a two-for-one deal or guaranteed return?

- If all else was equal to the competition, was the right medium used? If LAN managers throw away such mail unopened, then direct mail may be inefficient.

- Finally, did responses produce the intended result? Did the company sell product or just send literature to tire-kickers?

The difficulty that a manager faces is that it is impossible to measure each variable for 25,000 individuals. A manager often estimates because formal testing is costly. Even with systematic testing, a manager may often be left in the dark. It is common in direct mail to conduct a split-run test. A split-run test changes one element—like a color band on an envelope—to see if that variable affects response. A split-run test might make 50 percent of color bands blue and 50 percent red. Through a statistically significant random sample, one can learn with a fair degree of certainty whether blue or red is more powerful in getting individuals to open an envelope. However, this split-run test will not reveal whether shocking pink or fluorescent orange are better than either red or blue.

The difficulty with fact-based measurement is due to the number of variables, the number of tests and time needed to examine them, the cost of producing and printing each test and the cost of logging and analyzing data. Companies can only afford a certain amount of fact-based measurement and still make a profit. In many industries where target individuals are few, a manager judges which variables to test, and such judgement is often difficult.

A second condition also hampers measurement: change in variables. Unlike with machines, where variables are controlled within narrow limits, communication variables can never be controlled for long. For example, a company may offer to donate to charity a portion of proceeds out of every sale. The promotion works well until competitors offer similar programs. The gain from the promotion is then lost in copycat campaigns that undermine the original effort.

In controlled environments, fact-based communication measurement can go to great lengths because testing is repetitive. A gambling casino is a manmade environment in which each element is constructed to part a customer from money. Casinos measure the effects upon customers of colors, odors, air-change frequency (to keep gamblers comfortable), bill and coin acceptor devices in slot machines, payout ratios in slot machines to encourage longer play, a gambler's movement through the casino and a gambler's revenue potential. They also measure the impact of free services, cheap meals and entertainment to encourage a stay in the casino; delivery of free rooms and other comps (complimentary services) to high-rollers based on an individual's previous gross; the impact of "starters" to get action rolling in high-stakes games like baccarat; the effect of large drinks; and the use of chips rather than cash to help gamblers lose touch with the amount of cash that they win or lose.[9]

A casino knows when it can gain 5 percent from a slight change in the pattern of play and the way in which dealers stand in pits. Where the casino's highly refined, fact-based measurement breaks down is in getting individuals into the casino in the first place. Outside of the controlled gambling environment, a casino must compete with other casinos for players.

Fact-based measurement is just as difficult when one has unexpected success. Returning to the direct mail example, if a manager gets 600 responses to 25,000 pieces of direct mail, the manager has the same challenge as when the response was too low. The manager wants to know what went right in order to replicate it, if possible.

With mass media, fact-based communication measurement is more difficult, especially since an appeal is placed before many individuals who have no interest in it. Many of the same questions apply:

• Did the ad reach the target individuals?
• Was it placed in the right magazine, including the right issue and in the right section of the magazine? Was it on the right part of the page to attract the eye?
• Was it sent to the right audience? Was it the right appeal, presentation, offering and price?
• Has it produced the desired economic result?

Fact-based measurement involves complex assessments of how much advertising influences sales—a topic that has never been proven to anyone's satisfaction. About the best one can establish with some communication campaigns is that sales either rose or did not. Sometimes, one cannot establish factually whether a rise had any link at all to specific communications. A product with strong word-of-mouth appeal may generate high sales even with weak promotion, while other products may generate high sales only with strong promotion. As one advertising industry consultant wrote:

The problem advertising faces, as a business, is that advertisers can't manage it in any meaningful way. It's like buying a multimillion dollar melon. You have to spend the money to find out if it's any good.

This uncertainty has pushed dollars to both promotion, where results are predictable, and to CPM [cost per thousand] buying, which is actually advertisers telling their agencies: "If you guys aren't sure either, buy me as much as you can for as little as possible."[10]

With all the uncertainties, it is no wonder that some managers do not use fact-based measurement in communication. However, failure to do so is a poor alternative. Communication thus becomes an exercise in the quixotic or self-referential. Success happens, but mistakes occur too, and one learns little from either. It is only through cumulative, fact-based measurement that one learns over time what works and what does not.

However, there is room for unmeasured messages and media that gain awareness for themselves and products. When it is unclear what motivates a customer, unbridled creativity may be as valuable as pretesting. Perfume, cosmetic and clothing makers often use campaigns that seem to have little to do with a product other than the statement of a name or creation of an image. A successful manager of radio stations who was known for his skill once said: "It's just a bunch of us moving on instinct, and that's unusual these days. We did this [turnaround] without any research or anyone doing it before us—we were going by the seat of our [pants]."[11]

One can understand a statement like this in two ways. If the manager succeeded turning around a dying rock-n-roll radio station in a major city through pure instinct, then he possesses a "magic gut," an ability to understand a target audience that translates into product and services. If other factors were at work, however, then it is likely that the manager's experience in turning around other stations guided this effort as well. That is, the manager learned what to do through prior, fact-based measurement.

Pure instinct depends on measurement beyond the scope of this book—and average managers. There are geniuses and "magicians" who operate in realms to which even bright humans cannot aspire. However, such persons have difficulty replicating themselves precisely because they cannot explain what they do. If other factors are at work, such as experience, they may be using feedback and fact-based measurement informally and heuristically. Over time, a manager may have observed what worked and what did not. Such informal measurement depends on cumulative events and repeated patterns. With one-time events, experience might be useless.

Much fact-based product pretesting attempts to measure economic potential and establish guidelines for communicating. Especially with product design, careful customer inquiry at the outset can define many details of what a product should do. An auto manufacturer might hold 20 focus groups, or "clinics," nationwide and interview as many as 4,000 consumers before deciding on a new car design that communicates the company's desire to sell to a particular customer.[12] In the process, clinics will test:

- power, fuel efficiency, drive trains and handling;
- car shape, colors and carrying capacity;
- steering wheel and dashboard designs;
- door handles and latches, locks and keys;
- instrumentation;
- seat designs and shapes;
- fabrics and interior colors;

The number of details that engineers and marketers measure in a typical auto are mind-boggling, and their job never ends because the public's tastes change. Fact-based measurement is the buyer's voice in the product and an expression of a company's desire to do business.

Fact-based media and message pretesting also is helpful, if artificial. Pretesting measures the extent to which an individual is attracted by the design of an advertisement and its message, although it cannot establish that a target individual will ever see them. One individual may skim a magazine and never look at the ads, whereas another may read a magazine from cover to cover and cross-check the ads for prices and features.

In the end, managers are not bound by fact-based measurement. They make decisions to help the company to survive and succeed. Even if measures show that a product is on the edge of success, a manager might cancel it if it is draining cash flow. If an award-winning communication campaign has no clear economic result, a manager may change or dispense with it. Justifying messages and media is often not a manager's task but the job of communicators and marketers. The manager's job is to make sure that the right, fact-based evidence is presented in the right way and that it ties to the economics and survival of the organization. What the manager needs to avoid is a rush to pass judgment. Many products and communication campaigns have been killed too early because they did not produce results immediately and the managers failed to understand the cumulative effects of communication. New products often face inertia—which involves a measurable delay in response to, or credibility in a message.

The author has launched products that generated virtually little response in their first year or two but then became established. Sometimes, it is the staying power of a company that forces a product into the market. This was true for Microsoft's Windows software. Microsoft created several models of Windows before the product caught on. Early versions of Windows were limited in use, badly designed and flawed. However, after the advent of Windows version 3.1, the program took off. In the intervening decade, the company sustained itself on sales of DOS operating systems and end-user applications such as the "Excel" spreadsheet and "Word" word processing software.

Internal communication measurement is similar to external measurement. It begins with results and works backward. It uses pretesting to set baselines for communication components and persuasive steps. It recognizes changes in internal environments and variations that affect media and messages. Perhaps, for example:

- employees do not trust first-line supervisors.
- first-line supervisors identify with the employees against management.
- The internal communication chain is weak. Middle managers (sometimes called "the frozen middle") stand against top management and are cynical about messages from the CEO. Newsletters and other media have little credibility.
- The CEO has lost credibility.
- The medium has no validity. A manager may talk to employees about business results but the employees do not know how to read a balance sheet or income statement.
- The target individuals are the wrong message receivers. A CEO may exhort employees to give better customer service yet managers push to get the job done without regard to customer feelings.

Few companies can afford to measure every internal message or medium all the time, so managers conduct periodic, fact-based measurement. A manager can get comparable results with a standardized approach such as the International Communication Association audit and questionnaire form, which has 122 items and 12 demographic questions.[13] A manager also may rely on different measures and questions to determine where to begin comparative fact-based measurement. The use of different vehicles is desirable when attempting to understand a communication process initially. A manager starts by using an undifferentiated collection of data until themes or patterns emerge and then periodically remeasures everything to find out if the themes or patterns still hold true. They may not if, for example, a generational change in employees affects the acceptance of messages and media. An older, unquestioning generation may have been replaced by a restless, younger group that is more difficult to lead. This might call for different fact-based measures or adjustments in existing scales.

There are assumptions that one can make about internal communication to aid in fact-based measurement. Among them are:

- Internal message-sending usually uses more than one medium. Therefore, there are opportunities to compare media effectiveness. For example, a CEO may speak to the employees. After the speech, the employees receive a copy of the CEO's remarks and then read about the presentation in a company publication. Three media thus enter the equation—one direct and two indirect. This presents an opportunity to test transmission by eliminating one medium at a time and checking for awareness and understanding.
- Internal audiences should be better defined, and so messages should be better targeted from the beginning. Human resource data can tell one a great deal before a message is ever created. One should know in advance of communication about the education of a workforce, its training, its longevity with the company, districts in which employees live and geodemographics.
- Internal media should flow first to key individuals who directly affect a company's survival and success, and fact-based communication measurement should start there as well;
- Fact-based measurement should stress clarity in relation to individuals who receive and act on messages and not in relation to senders who create and send them.
- Fact-based measurement should scale individuals for their propensity to accept or reject messages. An engineer or scientist is more apt to question orders than a clerk who is used to being told what to do.
- Too many measures are worse than too few. Too many measures create noise, while too few provide insufficient information to act.

Managers should not compare communication in one business location or department to that in another without adjusting for variations in people and tasks. A manager cannot expect a plant filled with high-school graduates to respond to messages and media in the same way as Ph.D.'s in a laboratory. Each unit should establish a benchmark for itself based on similar departments, even if they are outside the company. A company with one R&D laboratory might use as a communication standard a laboratory in a noncompeting industry.

Four events tell a manager when a fact-based communication measurement is insufficient. The first is that the actions according to messages are not replicated regularly. The second is that the actions according to messages are consistently done wrong or not carried out. The third is that the response to messages consistently exceeds expectations and one does not know why. Finally, the fourth is that the response to messages consistently meets expectations but one does not know how.

An example of the first case might occur in a situation where a manager tells an employee to be at work at 8:00 A.M. The fact-based measure of understanding is for the employee to arrive at or before 8:00 A.M. However, the employee arrives some days at 8:00 A.M. and other days at 8:15 A.M. or 8:30 A.M. Assuming that the employee does not listen or has a bad attitude might be wrong. Instead, the employee might have problems with day care or public transportation.

In the second case, a manager orders a plant to make a run of widgets but the plant makes a run of something else. The plant manager explains that this was due to an emergency. The manager again orders the plant to make a run of widgets, but the plant manager again makes something else and gives yet another reason for not filling the order. The manager's messages are clearly ineffective, and the reason might lie outside the message and medium. The plant manager might report to a third manager who countermands the first manager's requests. The real measure is the manager's leverage with the third manager, and not communication with the plant manager.

The third case is a sign that media and messages are targeted to individuals who are not well understood. For example, a manager might be dealing with a motivated or skilled individual who gets things done quickly. Similarly, the person might be underused and the manager may need to balance the work loads.

In the fourth case, a manager seeks to automate response and remove the burden of continuous direct observation but cannot do so. Suppose a manager of a successful fast-food restaurant seeks to franchise the concept, but each time he or she opens another branch, it runs into trouble. The only solution for this kind of failure is to observe again.

Conversely, a manager can tell there is too much communication measurement if employees spend more time reporting than acting, if there are too many measures to monitor and if it becomes clear that some measurements work just as well as, or better than, others. When this happens, it might be possible to dispense with other, less-useful measurements. In the early days of computers (and today in some organizations), managers received six-inch stacks of printouts monthly. Few managers read the printouts because too much data was presented.

Variation is the ultimate challenge to fact-based communication measurement. When people and events change so quickly that measurement cannot produce results, fact-based measurement is useless. A manager will opt for speed and less-accurate results rather than delay and precision. In fashion advertising, one knows the success of a fall dress design before the end of the fall sales period, but it makes no sense to go back and find out what did not work unless there are clues there as to what might work next fall. This is why buyers use intuition as they watch models parading down the runways. If a buyer is in tune with what the customers want, the buyer will be successful. If the buyer is out of touch, there is a chance for disaster. The rate of failure is such that retailers have moved to fast-reorder systems to hedge their bets. There is less stress on a buyer when initial orders are smaller and reorders are filled promptly during a sales season.

If a company can build trust in its name as a desirable provider of a commodity such as dry goods, fact-based communication measurement makes sense for the company's name but not necessarily for the items sold. Companies such as the Italian clothing manufacturer Benetton, Macy's Department Stores, Saks Fifth Avenue, Bloomingdale's, Marshall Field and Nordstrom have all been successful in this. Merchants know they will have failures, but they also bet on having more successes than failures. They do this by remaining in close touch with customers and applying that knowledge to purchasing, stocking and store presentation. The merchant is a medium between the manufacturers and the buyers. The company's name stands for retailing processes in dozens of departments, some of which will be more successful than others at any given period of time.

The shopping experience is as carefully engineered as a casino's gambling environment. A retail manager will ask many of the same questions that advertising and direct mail managers ask about why a product has sold or not, but the questions will include more about sensory experiences. A store is more than the sum of products sold. There is image, aesthetic presentation, the helpfulness and skill of the sales staff and the decision about which items to carry. Because so much of the outcome is intertwined with elements of presentation, location and service, it might be difficult to isolate specific fact-based measurements of success among elements.

COMMUNICATION MEASUREMENT TECHNIQUES

Measurement is communication that relies on understandable and comparable symbols. It can be direct or indirect, as well as continuous, structured or done by exception. Direct means that the content of a message can be measured against economic results. Indirect means that the content of a message is deduced from events. For example, a manager can measure awareness but cannot see the direct response of consumers to auto advertising. Indirectly, through shipments and dealership reports, a manager can get an approximation of actual customer behavior. Continuous measurement is like a dial or gauge charting variations in a process. A telephone company or electric utility watches traffic loads throughout the day and adjusts system routing or electrical generation, depending on demand. Each act of dialing a telephone or turning on an air conditioner enters the measurement stream. Structured measurement is based on systems design. The source, media and targets of messages are preplanned from the top down or the bottom up, and measures are assigned to each. Computer information systems are often built in this way, with standard reports targeted to each level of the organization. Reporting by exception sends an alert only when a measurement is outside a preset boundary.

Measurement may also be primary or secondary. Primary measurement is equivalent to direct measurement—going to the source and observing. Secondary measurement uses existing data.

Commercial and academic on-line libraries have grown in importance in business because of the immediacy and the depth of detail they carry in secondary data. Among these libraries are:

- Internet: a service that was started as an outgrowth of the U.S. Defense Department and has become an anarchic collection of information, bulletin boards and linkages among universities, businesses and individuals worldwide.
- CompuServe: a commercial service started in the early 1980s that has become a general resource in many areas, especially technology.
- Nexis: a commercial service that was begun as a lawyer's research resource and grew into a general information library. It combines law, federal government regulations and information from major newspapers, trade magazines and medical databases.
- Dow Jones: the premier U.S. resource for business information of many kinds.
- DataTimes: affiliated with Dow Jones, this commercial service carries many local U.S. newspapers and Dow Jones on-line databases. It is especially useful for detailed business information that may have been missed by larger news databases.
- Reuters: the premier worldwide resource for financial information of many kinds.
- Knight-Ridder: a news service that also provides financial information.
- Dialog: an on-line service for engineers, marketers and specialists started originally by Lockheed Corporation and now owned by Knight-Ridder. Dialog is an in-depth, worldwide technical resource covering thousands of subjects.
- Marketing information suppliers: vendors such as Nielsen Corporation, Arbitron/Sami and Information Resources.
- Specialized databases and bulletin boards: there are hundreds, covering thousands of topics.
- CD-ROMS with collected information, such as nationwide telephone books, business addresses and geodemographic maps.

On-line systems also are valuable in tracking competitors, particularly in poorly covered industries. Newswires like PR Newswire and Business Wire distribute companies' press releases and are valuable resources for finding out what is happening. Services, such as ZiffNet Information Service, which carries detailed descriptions of thousands of hardware and software products, make intelligence gathering easier for managers. A large part of a corporate library now is not in books but in on-line services and, in growing amounts, on CD-ROMS. The benefit of such secondary data collection is that it is updated constantly.

On-line databases and CD-ROMS have changed how managers create and send messages because assessing the environment and target individual has become easier and more economical. Some corporations provide access to on-line secondary databases directly to managers with software such as Lotus Notes, a database that stores unstructured data and replicates information throughout an organization. A manager now can learn more about target individuals and tailor communication more accurately than before.

It used to require laborious research or the recollection of a skilled professional to know where a journalist's interests might lie before an interview. Today, however, in ten minutes one can get a reporter's last ten stories, a bio and an indication of the person's range of interests. This helps managers tailor remarks to the individual's understanding, particularly for complex issues such as finance or technology, as well alerting them to questions that the reporter is likely to ask.

Secondary resources also let managers measure issues and information numerically. There are commercial systems that track newspapers, magazines and television, with scoring on intensity scales of concern and interest. They use methodologies such as:

- Number of mentions: a company counts the mentions of itself and competitors.

- Mentions plus positive and negative weights: a company counts mentions plus a positive or negative scaling of the context in which mentions occurred. For example, a mention of IBM is weighted as negative or positive if adjectives modifying the company are "troubled" or "resurgent," respectively. Weighting includes an analysis of story content. If the story is about IBM's problems, it is negative. If it is about IBM's successes, it is positive. If it is an even-handed report of successes and failures, it is neutral.

- Positive or negative product or service reviews: a reporter compares IBM's OS/2 operating system to Microsoft Windows, DOS and other operating systems. Positive and negative comments are tracked against OS/2.

- Omissions: a story covers operating systems but leaves out mention of IBM's OS/2.

- Weighting by media influence: a positive mention in an authoritative publication or television show is given more value than a similar mention in a little-known newsletter.

- Weighting by readership or viewership: a publication or television show that reaches and influences a precise target audience is scored more highly than mass distribution.

- Weighting by influence on other journalists: a story or medium that generates other stories is scored more highly than one that does not. For example, the Associated Press wire service will generate dozens of appearances in newspapers, radio and television. A story on Cable News Network (CNN) appears around the world and can be picked up by local media worldwide. A story in the *New York Times* often appears in major network news television broadcasts.

- Weighting by persuasive impact: a few media can change worldwide opinion simply because of their pervasiveness. One of these is CNN. When a dramatic story appears on CNN, such as a major political upheaval or a far-reaching disaster, world opinion can shift in minutes.

Scoring is often slow and difficult and requires judgment on the part of the coder. Even today, few companies weight all news stories and other information referring to them or their business environment. Rather, they weight instances applying to immediate tasks and store them separately by department or area of interest. A product department will track product or service reviews, while a public affairs department follows political issues and legal department torts. With integrated corporate communication, separate measurements are stored in such a way that everyone can draw on them, when needed, to shape messages and media. Work-group software is making general availability a reality.

Primary, or direct, research goes directly to the target individuals and investigates them. Primary research helps in fast-moving situations where individual opinion may shift quickly under the impact of events, such as disasters, mergers or allegations of wrongdoing. It is essential in controversial moves where public opinion can derail a company's business plans, such as building a waste incinerator in a community over citizen protests or constructing a theme park near a historical site against local opposition.

Basic primary research tools are passive observation, experiment, one-on-one interviews and group interviews, such as focus groups. Passive observation looks at behavior in an existing market or workplace and examines communication in relation to action. It involves a broad collection of data. Experiments focus on specific variables and how individuals react to them, such as a variation of color on the envelope (mentioned earlier in this chapter). One-on-one interviews assess the impact of communication on specific individuals, while group interviews assess the impact of communication on several persons at a time.

With all these tools, managers try to measure actual states of individual perception and avoid biasing outcomes. This is never easy to do because humans are not always forthcoming about what they think or feel and, moreover, may not know what to say or how to express it.

With passive observation, the observer is usually hidden or disguised to prevent biasing the action. For example, exposed cameras can cause an immediate behavior change. With experiments, a researcher will use a single- or double-blind format to avoid bias. In double-blind tests of pharmaceutical efficacy, neither the pill dispenser nor the pill taker knows whether the pill is medicine or a placebo. (In a single-blind test, the experimenter is informed.) Last, a neutral party usually conducts one-on-one and group interviews to avoid peer pressure.

Interviews are either open-ended or structured. In an open-ended interview, a person is simply asked to talk about a subject while an interviewer takes notes. In a structured interview, a person answers questions on a questionnaire. With well-educated and busy individuals, such as senior managers, an interviewer will often use an unstructured interview because such people are impatient with structured questions. With others, an interviewer will use questionnaires as long as an individual does not suffer burnout. The author once participated in answering a structured, 30-minute survey on brand preferences that became increasingly annoying. By the end of the survey, the interviewer was getting decreasing amounts of information because the author wanted the survey to end. This is frequently the experience with structured interviews.

Neither unstructured one-on-one or group interviews are quantifiable, although both can be important measurements of communication success or failure. Questionnaires are quantifiable because responses are recorded in a comparable format. As a rule of thumb, during the initial exploration of a topic, it is better to remain open and unspecific. An interviewer can never know precisely what he or she will find when first entering the field.

Some subjects are tight-lipped, others can be persuaded to open up and still others talk freely. An interviewer assesses the individual during the interview and adjusts the questioning accordingly. Good interviewers enter the session well prepared and learn to stick to the theme of an interview even when a subject goes far afield. They put subjects at ease unless they are trying to trap a person. Good interviewers allow a subject to digress when this is important to understanding and are alert for information that changes understanding. Interviews fail when key information is presented but the interviewer fails to recognize or follow up on it. A good interviewer listens actively and uses phrases such as: "I'm not sure I understood what you just said. Did you mean to say . . . ?" "Would you explain that in more detail?" Interviewers learn to make sure they have heard what they think was said by repeating the person's statements in order to advance their understanding.

Person: I'm unhappy with the way things are going around here.

Interviewer: You feel unhappy with the way things are going around here—why?

Person: This company is always saying one thing and doing another.

Interviewer: Give me an example of the company saying one thing and doing another.

Person: They promised bonuses this year but now they're deferred until the first quarter of next year.

Interviewer: Promising bonuses and then deferring them—is that what you meant when you said earlier that company morale was bad and going down?

Person: No, I meant more than that. Bonuses capped a miserable time for everyone.

An interviewer learns to talk in a subject's language to reduce distance between the person and interviewer and increase information flow.

Person: I'm not really happy with the way we held back on SIMM expansion in this product.

Interviewer: When you say you are unhappy about SIMM expansion, are you referring to the built-in limitations on the motherboard?

Person: Yeah. Do you know everyone else has seven slots and we went out with three? Can you believe that?

Guidelines for one-on-one interviews apply to group interviewing, but in group interviewing one also deals with peer pressure and individual characteristics that can bias measurement. Among the dangers are "talkers," who answer every question and do not allow anyone else to respond; "dominators," who attack opposite opinions; "mice," who listen but never speak; "storytellers," who get away from the subject; and "pleasers," who bury their personal feeling.

Interviewers use role-playing, questionnaires, congenial environments, affected ignorance about a topic or the appearance of knowing more than they do and other techniques to get individuals to express their true opinions. There is a good deal of manipulation in direct measurement that can bias interviews but can also get individuals to divulge information they otherwise would not reveal. An interviewer must be careful to avoid the easy trap of putting words into another person's mouth.

There are many techniques for eliciting information directly from individuals, including:

- surveys using binary (yes-no) answers or attitude scaling to show the strength of feedback;
- anonymous questions and answers;
- 800- or 900- telephone numbers allowing people to call in and register opinions;
- business reply cards;
- feedback columns;
- suggestion boxes;
- on-line discussions, in which a question or statement is posted on E-mail and respondents are encouraged to debate it;
- electronic voting, in which each individual in a group is equipped with controls to respond to questions with a yes-no answer or scale value to indicate the strength of opinion.

Getting rid of bias is difficult in communication measurement, and indeed, pollsters boast that they can come up with just about any desired result. However, biased measurement is not measurement: it is a form of persuasive communication. For example, a pollster may ask a random group of citizens if they favor the *president's* proposed health care program. Citizens strongly oppose the president's plan because the president is unpopular. Later, the pollster may ask a random group of citizens if they favor a health care program with a specific set of services. Citizens strongly favor the plan. However, it turns out that the first and second polls asked about the same program. Only the question differed.

Randomization is a first criterion of bias-free measurement, but it is not sufficient. A manager must understand that an average taken from a random sample does not stand for an individual. For example, a survey may ask a sales force about a new service. The average opinion is that the service is excellent and will sell. The star salesman, however, is against the service and refuses to sell it. In this case, randomization and average opinion do not help the sales manager, who has one employee whose opinion outweighs the majority because that person commands a large enough proportion of sales to singlehandedly stop a service.

Bias enters measurement in several ways, including who asks questions, how questions are asked, who is asked, how a survey goal is stated, use of self-fulfilling survey construction, survey exhaustion, lack of credibility when the sponsor of a survey is known, lack of confidentiality and rewarding participants to respond, some of whom might respond to get the reward when they really have no opinion about the topic.

Bias-free surveys usually require professional assistance from an independent researcher who is competent to construct and conduct a survey and who knows its limits. Surveys are good for assessing the state of groups and answering quantitative questions. Surveys are not good for understanding individuals and motivations.

Attitude scaling allows one to get a dimension of opinion about a topic, but again, group scaling does not reflect a particular individual's scale. There are several kinds of attitude scales, including:

- Thurstone: a method for devising attitude scales that uses judges to determine how much a series of statements implies a positive or negative attitude about an attitude or object.[14]

- Likert: a number of statements, for each of which subjects indicate whether they strongly agree, agree, are undecided, disagree or strongly disagree.[15]

- Semantic differential: a series of at least nine pairs of bipolar adjectives, representing valuative factors, potency factors and activity factors, for each of which there is a seven-point scale, from negative to positive.[16]

- Q Sort: a method of sorting cards containing statements that allow one to explore new ideas and concepts.[17]

A manager should expect surprises from bias-free measurement. Usually, the measurement turns up novel information about target individuals. Sometimes, it is key to message creation and delivery, while at other times, it can help one understand better and refine the messages and media accordingly.

Another method of getting measurable communication results is an audit. Audits are systematic checks of communication media against standards for communications. An audit requires standards and will make no sense without guidelines and objectives to which one can compare messages and media. Audits demand the collection of media and messages, but it is difficult to collect everything. There are usually many more media than a company is aware of, much of which is not effective. The author once counted 86 newsletters in a single company, which was unaware it had so many. Audits demand that media be catalogued by intent and actual use. An auditor reports the variance between what the message and medium were intended to achieve and their actual use and achievement. Audits also require a report on messages and media in terms of a company's key strategy. The report states whether a company's communications are doing what they are intended to do in order to enhance survival and success. Finally, audits should contain recommendations as appropriate. Managers use audits and documentation to set goals for future communication. This is no different from recording and tracking financial figures like income and sales.

One method of establishing communication standards is to establish a benchmark in order to compare communication results to the experience of others. Benchmarks are set, not against averages, but against leaders. A manager setting a benchmark for direct mail finds the best companies in the use of direct mail and examines their results as a guide to what his or her own company should do. Benchmarking usually requires a team effort, criteria selection and definition in relation to the fundamental goals of a company. It also involves data collection, both internally and externally. For example, the Malcolm Baldrige National Quality award focuses on communication standards throughout its examination criteria for senior executive leadership, translation of quality requirements, scope and management of quality and performance data and information, human resources management and employee involvement. Criteria also pertain to employee education and training, employee performance and recognition, customer relationship management, customer satisfaction determination and future requirements and expectations of customers.[18] By tracing an organization's messages and media through these elements, one can develop a sophisticated and measurable process map of how communication works in a firm.

Most companies have hundreds of media and messages in use. The automatic tracking of major media can provide detailed insight into usage, such as numbers of loads on company phone switches, packets through company computer circuits, calls to 800 numbers and calls by division, department and worker. For example, phone records can reveal call patterns. In companies where customer contact is important, such as outbound telemarketing, the number, type and length of calls can tell a great deal about how a telemarketer is doing on the job. A manager can check calls to personal numbers rather than businesses. A manager can track completed calls versus attempts and can examine the length of call to see if a full script was delivered before a call ended. Physical measurements do not tell one how effective a message is but rather who is communicating where, when, with whom and how much.

Physical measurement and human factors are important in measuring the ability of communication to reach target individuals effectively. The quantity of light, contrast, color and emotional tones, reflectivity, physical dimensions of an object, viewing distance and time permitted for seeing all have direct influence on whether a visual message is received and understood.[19] Other measurable physical factors include:

- noise: unwanted sounds that interfere with communication;
- vibration through a whole or portion of the human body, which may distract workers from messages and media;
- thermal conditions and temperatures that prevent a person from acting on a message;
- memory: the ability, or lack thereof, of an individual to remember messages and meaning;
- physiological fatigue: the worn-down condition of message recipients;
- the work regimen;
- the presentation of information, such as indicator lights, acoustic signals and shape and size coding of objects.

Although there are many ways to measure the effectiveness of corporate communication, the final measure is still in the results. A communication program may win awards, but if the product did not sell, something has failed. However, when results occur regularly and within expectations, a smart manager seeks to improve communication through measuring what it does and enhancing it.

SUMMARY

Measurement of corporate communication is:

- Simple: managers focus on critical messages and media.
- Timely: feedback and measurement directly support organizational survival and success.
- Open: measurements go to those who can do something about them.
- Defined: measurement ties directly to the organization's objective.
- Flexible: a manager chooses any feedback and measurement method that can help determine whether messages and media are effective.

- Individual: measurement is by individuals, and not groups.
- Meaningful: managers use measures that focus most directly on survival and success.
- Measurable: the process of measurement is made measurable itself to avoid bias, failures and irrelevance.

NOTES

1. Gerard M. Goldhaber, *Organizational Communication*, 4th ed. (Dubuque, IA: Wm. C. Brown Publishers, 1986), p. 354.

2. David A. Schum, *The Evidential Foundations of Probabilistic Reasoning* (New York: John Wiley and Sons, 1994), p. 462.

3. Alison Leigh Cowan, "Unmourned Departure at Coopers," *New York Times*, January 17, 1994, p. D1.

4. Fred R. Bleakley, "The Best Laid Plans: Many Companies Try Management Fads, Only to See Them Flop," *Wall Street Journal* 222, no. 3 (July 6, 1993): A1.

5. Philip W. Yetton, Kim D. Johnston, and Jane F. Craig, "Computer-Aided Architects: A Case Study of IT and Strategic Change," *Sloan Management Review* 35, no. 4 (Summer 1994): 57–67.

6. James Barron, "Shea & Gould Partners Vote to Close Law Firm," *New York Times*, January 29, 1994, p. 35.

7. Mitch Betts, "Coping with the Deluge," *Computerworld*, May 17, 1993, p. 53.

8. Dennis Kneale, "Unleashing the Power: Companies Have Spent Vast Sums on Technology. Now They Have to Figure Out What to Do with It All," *Wall Street Journal Reports: Technology*, June 27, 1994, pp. R1, R6.

9. James Popkin, "Tricks of the Trade," *U.S. News and World Report* 116, no. 10 (March 14, 1994): 48–52.

10. Erwin Ephron, "How Advertising Lost Its Way," *Inside Media*, August 3–16, 1994, p. 46.

11. Michael Wilke, "WXXX: Designing a radio format for Generation X," *Inside Media*, August 3–16, 1994, p. 30.

12. Kathleen Kerwin, "GM's Aurora," *Business Week*, no. 3363 (March 21, 1994): 90.

13. Gerard M. Goldhaber, *Organizational Communication*, p. 411.

14. LeRoy Gross, *The Art of Selling Intangibles* (New York: New York Institute of Finance, 1982), p. 518.

15. Ibid., p. 518.

16. Ibid.

17. Fred N. Kerlinger, *Foundations of Behavioral Research*, 2d ed. (New York: Holt, Rinehart and Winston, 1973), p. 594.

18. Stephen George, *The Baldrige Quality System: The Do-It-Yourself Way to Transform Your Business* (New York: John Wiley & Sons, 1992).

19. Benjamin W. Niebel, *Motion and Time Study*, 9th ed., (Homewood, IL: Irwin, 1993), p. 259.

10

Corporate Communication Structure

> System was indeed to be one of their watchwords as they transformed
> the stodgy old DuPont Company into a modern corporation. . . . To
> achieve this transformation, they created a new communication system.
> First, they developed new patterns of communication at the executive
> level, establishing themes that would also penetrate lower levels.
> —JoAnne Yates (on the rebuilding of the DuPont Company),
> *Control through Communication: The Rise of System*
> *in American Management*[1]

WHERE WE ARE

So far, we have discussed the components of corporate communication. In
this chapter, we focus on structure: on how parts relate to the organization.
Communication structure evolves from the business environment, from the
buyer, the seller and the product or service and from key influentials who
may support or hinder a company. It is driven by the need to complete
economic transactions and maintain survival, and it is integral to the fabric
of organization.

There are no fixed rules of how to communicate as long as economic
transactions are completed. Nor are there fixed rules for structuring communication as long as an organization is successful. Some companies communicate little and others vigorously, yet both may be successful. For other
companies, however, the success may be elusive. Structuring communication for the greatest probability of successful economic outcomes requires
judgment and flexibility. Managers who view communication and communication structure as formulae limit their usefulness.

Pragmatic managers honor traditional corporate communication structure only if it works. A hierarchical company may stay top-heavy if that proves successful, or it may turn into a flat organization if that promises to work better. A company with brand managers might get rid of them, while another, which has never had brand managers, might develop them. Communication structure blurs as business environments change. Managers help departments evolve or find new communication solutions. Sometimes, this calls for tinkering, while at other times, it requires smashing a system and replacing it.

For example, VeriFone Inc., a manufacturer of point-of-sale terminals, configured itself to operate no matter what the location of its executives and managers. Moreover, these individuals are everywhere because the company believes in "forward deployment"—placing employees and plants close to customers worldwide. VeriFone says that one-third of its employees are on the road all the time. Every manager at the company has a laptop personal computer and taps into VeriFone's network to coordinate activities. Even though the company is headquartered in Redwood City, California, its chief information officer lives and works in Santa Fe, New Mexico.[2]

Communication structure is embodied in individuals; it is also dependent on, and limited by, them. People carry out strategy. If there are too many changes in structure, individuals become confused. If there are too few, they become ineffective. Moreover, managers can move employees only part of the time. There are human limits to action and communication structure. Managers face choices about individuals through whom they build an organization. Managers may be forced to make do with the individuals they have or find talent by letting go those who cannot adapt.

Corporate communication structure is not static, nor is it an assemblage of diagrams, policies and assignments that run by themselves. Parts of corporate communication structure develop, or are reassembled, daily. However, the friction built into communication structure also challenges a manager's skills. Investments in some communication technologies are so great that they cannot be replaced if a manager has made a poor decision, especially with computer and telecommunication webs.

The challenge of corporate communication structure is to identify, track and communicate with core audiences constantly and with potentially important audiences when necessary. This ties directly to our discussions of proactive and reactive observation, hard and soft information, audience ranking and methods of data capture.

CORPORATE COMMUNICATION AND SIMPLE STRUCTURE

A "perfect" communication structure would place the right information, message sender, message, medium and message receiver in the right place at the right time so as to maximize economic transactions and maintain corporate survival. However, a perfect communication structure is impossible to achieve: there are too many variables internally and externally. Instead, a manager must develop a simple, efficient and controllable communication structure that enhances the chance of completing transactions and survival within the constraints of economics, human resources, assets and the business environment. A manager should choose a communication structure that is good enough for business today and flexible enough to adapt to business tomorrow.

An example helps to explain the manager's challenge. Assume that a simple public company has a CEO and departments of accounting, purchasing, human relations, manufacturing, distribution and sales. Each function communicates to every other but to only one external audience. How many ways can this simple company communicate internally and externally? A matrix shows the combinations (Figure 10.1).

This simple business has 66 obvious ways of communicating to internal and external individuals and other, less obvious ones. Were we to add governmental relationships, relationships to competitors and other possible linkages, the matrix would grow quickly. A shareholder might also be a vendor, a regulator or a member of an interest group.

A manager can envision many corporate communication links that must exist, but he or she cannot envision them all. Corporate communication is messy. Each function has its own constituency, messages and, often, media. Functions often devolve into competing processes that compete for resources to accomplish their jobs, but not necessarily the task of a business. Managers coordinate the functions so that they can produce and sell goods and services, collect wealth and ensure survival. Through communication, managers fight the entropy that splits functions into factions.

Classical organization structure studied "*activities* that needed to be undertaken to achieve objectives."[3] Systems structure focused on "*decisions* that need to be made to achieve objectives."[4] The human relations approach looked at individuals, groups, motivation and dynamics.

All these approaches, however, are limited. Function-driven structure buries individual personality in tasks. Decision-based structure assumes that with the right information, an individual will make the correct decision, but this ignores free will, self-interest, unique intellect and behavior. Human relations focuses on individual and group dynamics but can ignore the functions and information needed for a group to perform. Corporate communication's focus on the message sender, message, medium, message receiver, business environment and economic action encompasses classical, systems and human relations approaches to structure. This is why corporate communication structure is complex, imperfect and evolutionary.

Managers develop simple communication structures in two ways—from outside an organization to inside and from inside to outside. These direc-

Figure 10.1
Internal and External Corporate Communication Matrix

	CEO	Accounting	Purchasing	Human Relations	Manufacturing	Distribution	Sales	Owners	Vendors	Employee	Supplier	Wholesaler	Customer
CEO		x	x	x	x	x	x	x	x	x	x	x	x
Accounting	x		x	x	x	x	x	x	x	x	x	x	x
Purchasing	x			x	x	x	x		x		x		
Human Relations	x	x			x	x	x			x			
Manufacturing	x	x	x	x		x	x		x	x	x	x	x
Distribution	x	x	x	x			x					x	x
Sales	x	x	x	x	x					x	x	x	x

tions are not exclusive; they represent a continuum of motion, like a pendulum. The beginning of the swing, however, always lies outside with economic transactions.

Working from outside to inside starts at the boundary of a company where hundreds of messages and media clash for attention and then moves inward to greater levels of abstraction. Corporate communication structure forges clear, simple and common links from an economic transaction or influential to each organization activity. It does not encompass all messages and media at the boundary, because it cannot.

Corporate communication structure is process-based, like systems analysis, but it involves more than information flows. Communication structure defines interactions between individuals within business functions and externally. However, even when the lines are clearly drawn and the processes defined, communication structure is blurred because human interaction does not work the same way each time. Corporate communication structure exists where rationality mixes with emotion, where information is never sufficient and individuals may not be persuaded to act. Corporate communication structure seeks to reduce variation in order to enhance the probability of economic transactions, but it can never eliminate variation entirely.

Information technology and work flow analysis are two paths companies use to develop corporate communication structure in the late 20th century. Both have made enormous contributions to simplifying communication structure.

Information technology in its broadest definition includes computers, telephones (which are becoming computers), software, databases and networks. Work-flow analysis, or work process, analyzes each step in the accomplishment of a task and determines how it fits with economic transactions and survival. Work flow encompasses data collection, graphical tools, auditing and setting benchmarks, decision making, preventive measures and creativity techniques, input-output analysis, statistics and data dictionaries.[5]

Applications of information technology and work process have grown so rapidly that it is not clear how whole industries will look in a few years. Companies are finding, developing and implementing communication solutions that let businesses restructure or reengineer. Such solutions include:

- virtual offices and managers;[6]
- video, multimedia and document conferencing;[7]
- electronic publishing, document imaging and indexing;[8]
- efficient customer response systems and electronic shelf labeling in retailing;[9]
- electronic badges that unlock doors and transfer phone calls;

Figure 10.2
Communication Structure Before the 1980s: A Paper-Based Configuration

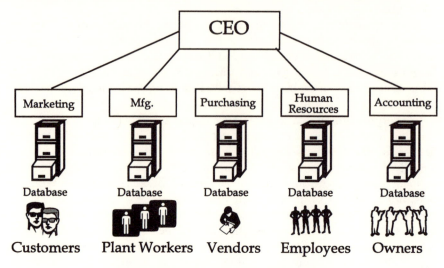

Each Department Maintains Own
Information, Messages and Media.

- *whiteboards,* which transmit writing from one site to another;
- group scheduling, voice mail and voice recognition.

Until the 1980s, business functions largely retained their own communication structures. They were islands of information and were often held together by manual systems of coordination (Figure 10.2). Each had messages, media and languages. Each defined target audiences uniquely, with little concern for overlap. Accounting was about the only common language across all functions.

As information technology was innovated, managers became aware of opportunities to synthesize information, messages and media, but in most cases, technology outstripped understanding. Biases favoring longstanding ways of operating, along with the cost of new technologies, often slowed the infusion of advanced communication structures. Where economic advantages were evident, managers often were eager to change. For example, accounting systems were computerized first, eliminating dozens of clerks and adding machines. On the other hand, the economic advantages were frequently unclear. Technologists did not always understand the subtleties of a marketplace and the individuals in it and, as a result, their poorly developed solutions hurt their credibility. Apple Computer's bumbled introduction of its Newton hand-held personal digital assistant was one of

Figure 10.3
Communication Structure Before the 1980s: A Computer-Based Configuration

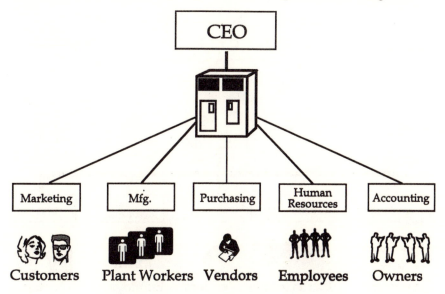

Each Department Maintains Own
Information, Messages and Media
in Separate Files in a Common Computer.

many instances of immature technology chasing an uncertain market. Although Newton's slow introduction was better than AT&T's failure with its similar product (EO), Apple's CEO, John Sculley, stepped down and was replaced by a less visionary cost cutter, Michael Spindler.[10]

The growth of information technology from the middle of the twentieth century to the present has followed a path toward information integration, if not integrated communication structure. However, the possibility of developing integrated corporate communication rose with technology advances. As machines and software grew in power, functions such as human relations, materials requirement planning, customer files and vendor data were placed on computer as separate files or databases linked only peripherally (Figure 10.3). Relational databases in the late 1970s and through the 1980s offered new opportunities for placing separate files in the same file structure and integrating information, messages and media (Figure 10.4). The application of relational technology was slow because designing and implementing an integrated database takes years, and corporate communication structure was held back by the same difficulties. For example, a function diagram with a "CRUD" (for create, read, update, delete) matrix,

Figure 10.4
Communication Structure in the 1980s

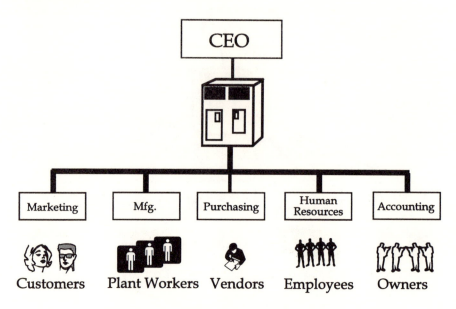

Departments Store Information
in Common Database.

a key component for information architecture, could include 3,332 cells and 13,328 possible entries.[11]

Information technologists also learned early that their challenge was not just storing data but also delivering it in ways people need to see it, where they need to see it and as they need to use it to develop and send effective messages. Information technologists understood before managers that corporate communication structure does not depend on a workplace in which one communicates to employees. Rather, it relies on accepted rules, interfaces and policies that individuals incorporate into behavior anywhere in the world. This requires extraordinary efforts in interface design, flexibility and robustness.

Network development has supported the technologists. Networking has progressed from having all functions communicate to a single entity in one location—a mainframe computer—to having all functions communicate to one another, anywhere in the world. In the latter half of the twentieth century, networks began transmitting analog voice and data, such as television pictures, and then analog and digital data. Today, networks transport data, voice, images and text (primarily in digital ones and zeros), at speeds and carrying capacities that are made possible by fiber optic cable, compression, fast switching and routing, as well as layered transmission protocols and advanced storage media from hard disks to CD-ROM and WORM (write once read many times) formats. The ability to see and talk to an employee halfway around the world at any time, day or night, is now a reality.

As a result, corporate communication structure in business has dispensed with chronometric time and replaced it with event-driven time. In financial services, traders buy and sell the same financial instrument 24 hours a day. A trading day begins in London, moves to New York and Chicago, shifts to Tokyo and Hong Kong and then returns to London. Books are closed for accounting purposes daily at 6 P.M. New York time and trades are registered against dates and times, but trading decisions are made against events. If the Japanese yen falls against the U.S. dollar or the British pound rises against the German deutschmark, traders react simultaneously around the world. Lags due to the time of day have largely disappeared.

With high-speed networking have come distributed databases built on integrated information architecture. Not only can any function communicate with any other anywhere in the world, but information captured by each function enters a local database with a format common to every other database anywhere in an organization. One person at a computer terminal can pull information seamlessly from all databases at the same time and in a common format.

Such panoptic power to integrate information, however, does not eliminate the need for a message sender to develop an effective message and deliver it in a timely manner. It does, however, measurably advance the consistency of information entering messages, and it allows individuals to pull from a system the information they need, how and as they need it. Simplifying access to information—a first step in simplifying corporate communication structure—is well underway.

Media and message receivers, however, are open issues in simple corporate communication structure. There are two extremes, and both are dependent on message receivers. One is a single medium that provides sole contact between the company, customer and influentials. For example, a pay cable channel might sign up viewers through television and bill them directly by credit card account. The pay cable channel also might rely on television for advertising. That is, each time one turns on the television, as happens in hotels, there is a listing of available movies. Outside the television, the pay cable channel may not exist for customers or influentials.

The other extreme involves many media personalized to each individual. In this case, one customer might get a letter, another a phone call, a third a videotape, a fourth a personal sales call, and so forth. Companies use media on a continuum between unity and diversity due to economic restraints and the multiple requirements of individuals to whom they communicate. Visualizing this process in a simple corporate communication structure is not easy. One method is to place key audiences in the center and core databases and functions around them. This is an audience-centric model (see Figure 10.5). Another method is to draw circles around a company core. The core is where information resides, and around it are the functions (see Figure 10.6). Around functions are customers and key audiences. Messages radiate from the core to internal and external audiences. Communications from audiences and the environment simultaneously radiate into the organization at one or more points and are reflected into the core's database. One variation involves eliminating the core and locating databases within each function around a virtual core made up of cross-linked databases from which one extracts views of individuals and functions as needed.

In a "perfect" corporate communication structure, messages radiate evenly in all directions on a single medium like a wave from a single stone dropped in a pond (Figure 10.6). In actuality, corporate communication is like several pebbles dropped at various times, with multiple waves and interference patterns canceling out or, sometimes, amplifying a message. Each wave might be a separate medium or the same one used at different times or frequencies (Figure 10.7).

The reason for complexity lies in the variation in the business environment. The circles around an organization are not concentric because some audiences are important all the time and others, only some of the time. Moreover, information technology and corporate communication structure, even at their most advanced, only partially capture records of messages, media, individuals and economic results.

The technical and economic challenges of building a database to store data, text, voice and image are beyond most organizations. Such a database might include demographic data in relational storage matrixes, recordings of phone orders in object-based storage, records of store transactions on videotape in object-based storage, records of past transactions in archival relational storage and secondary data, such as news stories, in text form and key-word searchable storage. The utility of, and applications for, such an integrated multimedia database are still largely unknown. Moreover, estimating economic results from multiple phone conversations with customers is difficult to achieve without using techniques to extract data. This risks a loss of the information needed for effective message sending. For example, service representatives type records of complaints into computers that generate reports on numbers of auto defects per 100 deliveries, but records cannot communicate the vocal anger of a customer who complains that a new car has a rattle in the engine compartment. On the other hand, it is feasible to build an audio report on customer telephoned complaints by stringing separate conversations together into a single transmission. However, it is not clear whether it is always economically practical to do so.

Figure 10.5
An Audience-centric Data Model

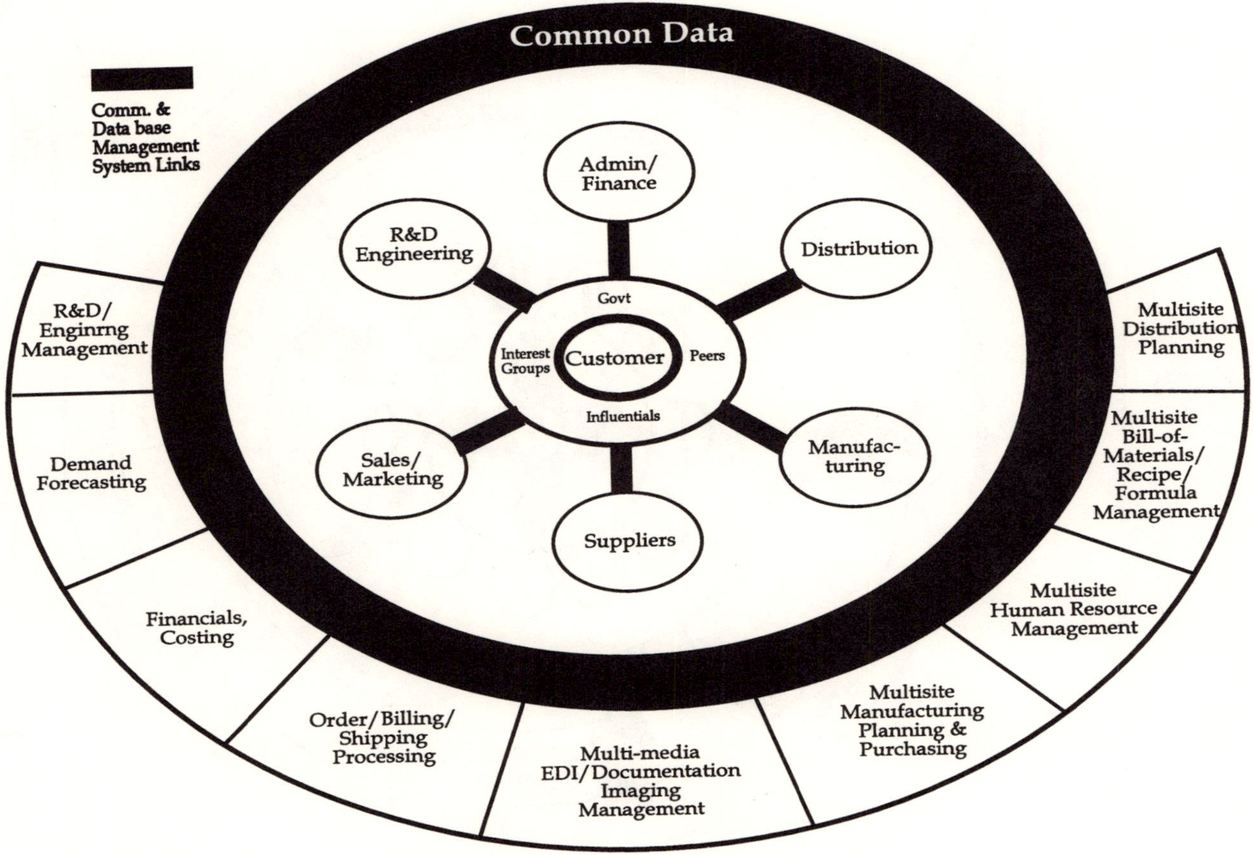

Common Data

■ Comm. &
Data base
Management
System Links

Multisite Distribution Planning

Multisite Bill-of-Materials/Recipe/Formula Management

Multisite Human Resource Management

Multisite Manufacturing Planning & Purchasing

Multi-media EDI/Documentation Imaging Management

Order/Billing/Shipping Processing

Financials, Costing

Demand Forecasting

R&D/Enginnrng Management

Distribution

Manufac-turing

Admin/Finance

R&D Engineering

Sales/Marketing

Suppliers

Customer

Peers

Influentials

Govt

Interest Groups

Figure 10.6
Corporate Communication: A "Perfect" Structure

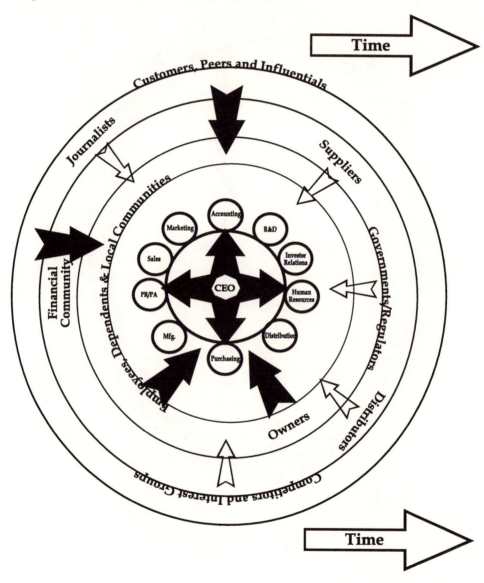

Figure 10.7
Corporate Communications: Actual Structure (Confused Messaging)

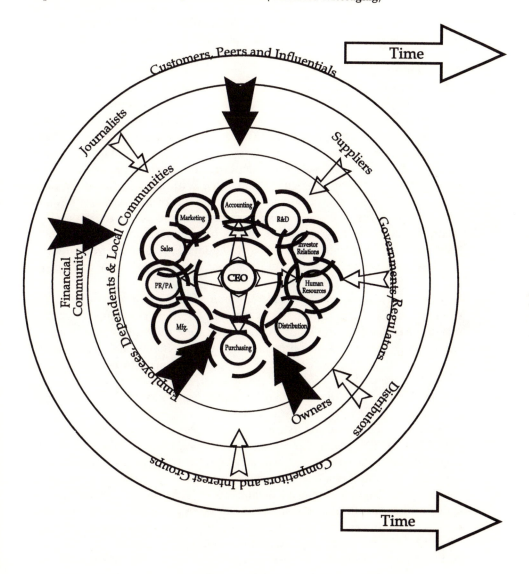

The present corporate communication structure relies heavily on databases to communicate effectively to customers and influentials. Today's databases can tell an individual's frequency in purchase of a new car, multiple relationships with a dealer or auto company, membership in auto clubs, number and type of service calls, insurance carrier, vehicle financing, credit cards held and so forth. This becomes a resource for personalizing standard media in an approach called "data mining."[12] A similar approach has been used in public affairs through recording votes of senators and representatives, along with their speeches and campaign promises, to determine how they are likely to stand on various issues.

In a simple corporate communication structure, a manager looks for the most effective and least costly medium to deliver information. It is vital to identify commonalities that let one medium be used equally well in place of two. Such a standard vehicle then becomes part of an organization's communication backbone. E-mail started as a way to coordinate and brainstorm in research and development departments. Then, it became a way to brainstorm and coordinate within functions. With its subsequent development, it was used to move information in and out of databases within and between functions, thus dispensing with paper forms. With more development, E-mail, with newswires fed into it, helped whole organizations stay abreast of external marketplace events. Today, E-mail sends voice messages, written words and video and document images worldwide to employees, customers and influentials.

As each new use is placed on the communication backbone, other media should be displaced and the costs of maintaining them eliminated. A robust medium handling several kinds of communication moves toward structural simplicity because it transports information effectively at a lower cost. However, the economics of unifying around one medium are not always clear. The "paperless" office has not arrived, and in some organizations, new media are overlaid on the old, creating complexity but not necessarily greater communication effectiveness.

For every medium added to a business, simple corporate communication structure calls for getting rid of another unless there is a strong economic reason to keep it. The purchase of work-group software for coordinating departments should result in fewer face-to-face meetings, phone calls about routine matters, photocopies of documents (which can be routed electronically) and forms. In offices that have adapted to work-group software, this has occurred, but in offices where work-group software is only an overlay, it has not. On the other hand, where communication has been insufficient, adding a medium should increase the number of economic transactions and enhance corporate success. A manager often uses judgment to determine whether to keep a medium. In the author's experience, cutting away media often does less damage than is feared. One way to determine a medium's value is to get rid of it and then see how many individuals complain and what their complaints are.

It is more difficult in external communication to identify and implement a robust medium that handles several kinds of communication, rather than one. The effort depends on individuals to whom one communicates. The delivery of financial trading information by computer worldwide is accepted in financial services. On the other hand, the delivery of the same financial information by computer to the home was not generally accepted at the time of this writing. There, financial information is largely paper-based. In financial trading, the robust electronic pipeline rose out of a need for speed in buying and selling stocks, bonds and other financial instruments. Users drove the conversion as much, or more, than the companies behind them. Nonetheless, brokerages still use paper to send end-of-month statements and solicitations. They use voice mail for service calls and television and newspaper and magazine advertising to keep their names in front of present and potential customers. They also use visitation and telephone soliciting to find and sell to new customers.

A brokerage firm may want to tie present and potential customers to it through computer-based terminals, but the company knows it will not achieve that goal right away, if ever. Therefore, it retains a communication structure with multiple media. The communication structure cannot be simplified externally if a company wants to compete in the broad market. On the other hand, a company could restrict its business to those who use computer terminals. Such a niche strategy has worked for many firms.

In other instances, it is questionable whether multiple media might not be replaced by one medium that performs the same communication task less expensively. The author's word-processing software came with four manuals—a guide, a comprehensive reference, a tutorial and a listing of templates. The author can send away for a videotape to learn how to use the software or sign up for on-site training. He can follow a tutorial built into the program, consult a built-in "help" screen, dial a computer bulletin board or call an 800-number.

No doubt the software company made a structural communication decision to use multiple media in order to increase customer satisfaction and provide affordable service. Customer satisfaction comes from presenting data as individuals prefer to see it, while affordability comes from charging for expensive forms of assistance. However, it might be less expensive for the company to virtually give away a CD-ROM, a CD-ROM reader and a modem with autodial to a bulletin board. The cost of producing manuals, videotapes, on-line tutorials and training programs amounts to overhead that does not necessarily make communication more effective than presenting all the elements on-screen while a person works.

For a firm with an opportunity to use a common external medium, it is up to the manager to merge the existing media into one form. This is not easy to do because individuals are often reluctant to give up media that they control, especially if they are uncertain how to use a new medium well. This is where a manager's leadership and power come into play. He or she could promote a new medium, mandate it or use peer pressure to gain its acceptance. In the early days of word processing, newspaper reporters rejected computer terminals and retained their typewriters. One newspaper solved the problem by taking every typewriter out of the newsroom except one, which reporters had to use in full view of fellow journalists.

When marketplaces do not allow a reduction in media, a form of simplicity is possible through developing communication structures aligned with the message receivers' states of persuasion. Especially in the case of large-scale brands that account for millions of economic transactions a year, consumer diversity demands large communication campaigns. For example, one brand manager traditionally marketed soap to every type of soap user, from loyalists to price-conscious buyers through common messages and advertising, couponing, promotions and publicity campaigns. This kind of all-encompassing media approach ignored fundamental differences among the customer groups. In recent years, marketers have begun to communicate to individuals by major segments, such as loyal users, competitive users and swing users.[13] Managers are placed in charge of each segment within a brand, and they deploy media based on specific economic outcomes that are planned for each segment. This is a simpler, more focused approach. For example, a manager in charge of the loyal user segment will build specific appeals to get loyalists to extend their use of the product. This manager may employ direct marketing, advertising, sales promotion, public relations and event marketing to get a message across, employing frequencies and times that are different from those used for price-point buyers. When individuals are well defined, the manager of the loyal user segment will not have to fear confusing message overlap with price-point buyers because the habits of both are tracked directly.

Measurement is more difficult in a corporate communication structure that cannot reduce the number of media in use. One can build feedback devices into each medium to show whether the messages have reached the target individuals, but the accuracy of such devices in large-scale campaigns may be suspect. In other cases, the measurement of any one medium's effectiveness may not be practical. However, the combined effect of media may be measured against a subsequent state of persuasion and action among target individuals. One can determine whether a loyal user has increased his or her purchase frequency or whether a swing user has become a loyal user through scanner data. Information can also come through rewards that accrue to frequent users, such as free airline miles.

Influentials add another complication to a simple corporate communication structure. They may add layers of media, messages and structure that the company might otherwise dispense with. If a company is the focus of protest by special interest groups—such as a mining company besieged by environmentalists—a simple corporate communication structure might require messages and media beyond what competing mining companies use.

Ultimately, corporate communication structure is developed by ranking the key audiences with direct power over a company's ability to complete economic transactions and survive. Once messages and media have been developed and deployed for these audiences, a manager can examine other media for usefulness.

Media grow like weeds. Reports, memos, newsletters and E-mail messages spring up without need for water or sunlight. Managers must audit messages and media continuously and prune communication to keep the structure simple. Some executives let employees write them by E-mail, and they receive hundreds of messages daily. A few executives doggedly answer them all, but others have realized that it is impossible to respond to everyone's concerns and also keep a company running. While complaints about cafeteria food are a morale problem, it may be more important for a CEO to focus on a lagging project that is eating cash. However, if a CEO stops responding to E-mail after having promised to do so, subordinates are likely to feel that the company has become distant and bureaucratic. It would have been better had the CEO never made the promise or opened his or her mailbox to general use.

A manager constantly simplifies communication to key external audiences as well. Directness and simplicity are not easy to achieve or maintain. They usually require infusions of machinery to capture and put messages to work. For example, a computer company may assemble machines on demand for delivery in five days. To get this done, the company routes telephone orders from a customer department to parts specification and then assembly, thus testing the parts and shipping them in a synchronized flow. The flow only looks easy to achieve. Below the surface is an enormous database connected to a sophisticated telecommunication system that links every part of the company.

With so many choices for corporate communication structure, the best a manager can do is to follow guidelines while making decisions. Guidelines include:

- Simplicity and directness: a communication structure should have the least possible number of steps between a key individual and message sender.
- Timeliness: messages must reach individuals in time for them to act on the content to the economic benefit of the company.
- Openness: any individual with direct power over a company's success or failure must be included in the communication structure.
- Definition: a company identifies and documents communication links between the individuals who directly affect its survival and success and the company functions.

- Flexibility: a communication structure allows for rapid change in the business environment.
- Individuality: communication structure is built on individuals, and not on groups or segments.
- Meaningfulness: communication structure concentrates on effective messages and media that are directly linked to economic transactions and survival.
- Measurability: communication structure builds in measurements that tell whether messages, media and actions support economic transactions and survival.

A final guideline involves history. History may indicate what a company should do or it may be a straitjacket from which a company should escape. Most managers belong to established enterprises with defined communication structures. They have no choice: they are forced to optimize the messages and media within dated structures.

A pragmatic manager will not destroy an existing communication structure unless there is evidence that it is not working because the change may be disruptive. Target individuals and message senders may have adjusted to the existing media and messages and be reluctant to give them up. Adopting another approach without responding to the unique needs of individuals can create opposition and noncompliance.

Every organization has formal and informal communication structures. Formal structures are clear and unambiguous, while informal structures are the opposite. Formal structure is imposed, while informal structure evolves naturally from social interaction. Organizations need a formal communication structure for expected everyday action and an informal communication structure for out-of-bounds events and some normal activity. For example, a manufacturing manager may find the formal purchasing system too slow. To keep from being blindsided by missing material, he or she will establish personal relations with the head of purchasing, whom he or she will call for updates. The purchasing paperwork, in this case, confirms a message that has already been sent through the informal communication structure. Bypassing the formal communication structure is a time-honored tradition in some organizations.

The challenge that managers face with informal communciation is that its structure might bypass key steps or controls. To keep a factory running, supervisors sometimes swap tools and parts with other supervisors and neglect to fill out the paperwork. When it comes time to take inventory, shortages and overages show up everywhere. In the U.S. Army, supply sergeants swapped material from unit to unit to keep operations running because the inventory system was difficult to use. The result was that the army never knew what supplies it had. Managers who deal with this kind of difficulty must balance the needs of the organization against the needs of individuals performing essential tasks. Generally, communication structure should favor the individuals who are involved in direct economic trans-actions.

Finally, pragmatic managers bypass communication structure regularly to find out how it distorts messages. Structure is itself a message, which calls for expected behaviors and actions. Sometimes, however, the expected behaviors and actions are inappropriate. Managers who are unaware of the incongruence can miscommunicate through formal structure without ever knowing that they are doing so, as when a malfunctioning computer duns customers for bills paid months before. The company can lose customers and never know that the communication structure caused the break.

STAFFING CORPORATE COMMUNICATION

Corporate communication staffing starts with individuals who do a company's business and ensure its success. This does not mean that every employee is, or should be, trained in persuasion, writing and speech. Individuals communicate successfully in specialized languages within the functions and tasks for which they are responsible. They learn their languages through formal education and experience. As long as message receivers understand the messages and perform effectively without a need for translation, there is no need for formal communication training. However, when a manager must send universally clear and consistent messages, there is a need for a common language. This is where formal training in communication is desirable. Managers are so often co-opted by their specialized language that they cannot communicate to anyone who does not speak it.

Communication staffing begins with the CEO, who can be both a conductor and a player in the corporate communication structure. The CEO understands the architecture of the organization and interprets its strategic message in terms of action designed to support present and future economic transactions. The CEO may observe the business environment, customers, owners, employees and other key influentials and communicate their concerns to points where actions can be taken to satisfy their needs and wants. However, the CEO may also turn over day-to-day communication responsibilities to others as long as the organization is successful.

The CEO also influences communication style. A CEO may unify the style or leave it diversified. A manager's manner may be blunt and brutal or friendly and indirect within the same corporate communication structure. Some CEOs demand a uniform way of communicating to everyone, while others allow managers to communicate as they wish, as long as the end result is achieved. Both approaches are legitimate, and they depend on the leader's preference. Those who report to a CEO translate the core message into functional activities. Translation damages communication links and divides cultures through what is called "trained information incapacity."[14]

A CEO can handle communication in a number of ways. He or she can be the principal message sender and be involved in every part of an operation. Alternately, he or she can assign daily operational activities to subordinates and limit personal communication to key individuals, such as owners and customers. Finally, the CEO can restrict personal communication to certain issues, such as the future of the company. One CEO in charge of a major U.S. corporation nearly disappeared. He let his subordinates speak in his name and rarely gave interviews. His views of the future of the company were largely unknown and his working style was mysterious. Nonetheless, the CEO served his term successfully.

One might argue that a CEO should not give up a focus on key messages and media because an organization's economic life depends on personal attention and authority. However, in complex organizations, this may not be the case. The "invisible" CEO described in the previous paragraph headed a company where the divisions ran themselves as separate businesses. His disappearance did not affect the primary message of each division because each general manager set strategy for their own division.

Few CEOs are qualified to handle all communication chores. Some are "inside" persons, who are oriented to process, and others are "outside" individuals, who focus on the marketplace. A perfect balance is difficult to achieve. Business environments, individuals and organizations oscillate constantly and unpredictably. At any time, the success of a company may depend on either internal or external communication or both. If a CEO needs help from a chief operating officer, the only requirement is mutual communication and understanding between them. Without it, a company will stall. For the most part, however, CEOs are icons who personify the reasons for an organization's existence.

CEOs are selective in communicating to key audiences because they lack the time to be all things to all people. This is why CEOs often surround themselves with individuals with whom they work easily. Pragmatic CEOs, however, know that some subordinates test their forbearance but are useful, so suffer their presence. General Dwight Eisenhower faced this situation with General George Patton and British Field Marshal Bernard Montgomery during World War II. Eisenhower was under intense pressure to fire Patton and demote Montgomery, but he knew that Patton would perform and that the political fallout from benching Montgomery would damage the Allied cause.

Normally, a CEO should keep communication staffing simple. The fewer the layers, the closer a CEO stays to customers, influentials and others with economic power over a company's life. Even when the job is overwhelming, a CEO needs to understand the business environment. However, few companies are normal, and a CEO assigns staffing that works for the company at a given moment in time. If a CEO needs to be shielded, a larger staff is in order. Every organization has traps that can hurt a person's credibility and render the individual ineffective. A CEO may use substitute spokes-persons as a shield against potentially threatening circumstances. On the other hand, if a CEO needs to lead a company into aggressive participation in the marketplace, a reduced staff will project a lean, action-oriented environment.

The essence of simplicity in corporate communication lies in directness and timely response. The fewer the layers of managers, the more open an organization is. However, a lean structure can have two outcomes:

- The positive outcome is that it forces managers to define messages and media more accurately. They will learn to stick to the essentials because they have little time for anything else.
- The negative outcome is that lean structures often block communication because the employees are overextended and are unable to send or receive messages in a timely manner.

Managers balance over- and understaffing in communication while recognizing that changes in the marketplace and technology will shift the balance over time. Information technology has taken over many routine tasks, allowing managers to get out of their offices and closer to where money is made. The downsizing of the ranks of middle managers in the late 1980s and 1990s was a partial result of the advent of productive information technology. Downsizing moved customers many steps closer to the CEOs. On the other hand, it also caused burnout as employees tried to shoulder the burdens of their departed colleagues. For the most part, organizations made little effort to show those who remained how to use information technology efficiently to stay in touch with customers and influentials and get their jobs done.

A CEO has four communication staffing options: one-on-one, hierarchical, oligarchical and team. In a one-on-one structure, every subordinate reports and communicates directly to the CEO. Small companies often use this approach. In a hierarchical model, heads of functions report separately to the CEO, and a chain of individuals reports to them. Oligarchical communication staffing involves a committee or council of executives (with or without the CEO) who communicate to each other in order to integrate a message. They may represent major disciplines or operating divisions. Team staffing in corporate communication is either permanent or temporary.

In a pure hierarchy, the CEO serves as the medium and message among functions because he or she alone sees and understands the entire business. This works well in cases where a CEO's span of control is feasible and where key executives have a mutual understanding of the direction. For example, one autocratic beer baron is passionate about the quality and perfection of the beverage that his family company has made for more than 100 years. The CEO's devotion to the family's beer has proven to be customer-centric because the product has grown under his leadership to become the most successful of all beer brands in the United States. Key executives reporting to the CEO know that they must have the same passion about the beer, and they know that those who fail will be dismissed and targeted by the company. The executives remember when fraud surfaced in the company's promotion department. The CEO launched a campaign of vilification and lawsuits against the culprits that was so aggressive it shocked even the CEO's friends. The ferocious assault was as much a message for those who remained as it was for those who were thrown out. In this case, a hierarchical communication structure worked well. Everyone understood his or her task in the organization, along with the outcome for failing to act honorably in accomplishing it.

Hierarchies can respond quickly to business environmental changes when communication lines lead directly to the center of power and the center of power is ready to respond. Hierarchies also work well in businesses where there is little process relationship among departments or in large organizations in a stable business environment. Hierarchical communication staffing breaks down when the center of power is unresponsive or misdirected, when there are businesses with multiple product lines that respond differently to marketplace influences and when the primary message fails to convey the reason for customers to buy from a firm.

Internally focused messages and media, such as profits, do not provide a sufficient information base for economic transactions and survival. For example, the beer company mentioned previously won back its market share from a competitor when the latter changed its beer formula (and taste) in order to produce better profits. The competitor's profits were temporary as its market share plunged, and the company eventually returned to the original formula.

An oligarchical communication structure may represent functions or lines of business. When it represents functions, messages and media are thrashed out for departments such as manufacturing, distribution, human relations, marketing and accounting. Functions fit their messages to company goals and communicate laterally to other functions. They attempt to get other functions to speak with one voice about their speciality. Human relations will attempt to establish one personnel system, and manufacturing will try to establish standards for material and production flow. Controllers will try to set uniform overhead cost structures and purchasing, involving rules for procurement. Each group then communicates its proposed structure to line managers. Line managers often protest the system because they believe that local variation makes their units different, they do not want to be held to rules made by others and they believe that they can perform the same tasks more efficiently and effectively under local systems. The CEO often mediates between the oligarchical function and line managers to achieve a consistent message and corporate communication structure.

Establishing an oligarchical communication structure by function requires integrated communication within a discipline but not necessarily within a company. Each function struggles to make itself heard, sometimes to the harm of a company's customers and influentials. Oligarchy members also can become more concerned about communicating the value of their discipline than the message of the company. They tie the "proper" use of a discipline to company survival, sometimes without sufficient evidence. This shows in attempts to become better professionals but not necessarily more effective managers. Calls for greater professionalism might win admiration from peers but not from the company or its customers.

When an oligarchical communication structure consists of line executives who are directly involved in economic transactions, functional specialists remain one step away in communication structure. Line executives of divisions interpret messages and strategy for the specialists who report to them and are part of the specific economic transactions attached to the particular business unit. Specialists, in turn, reinterpret messages into tasks within each division. This maintains a unified approach within the economic entity, but it also disintegrates into multiple media with overlaps among divisions. A major U.S. corporation discovered that it had dozens of payroll systems and employee compensation plans. The firm moved to unify both—a lengthy task that generated anxiety among employees, who felt their benefits were being adversely affected by standardization.

Teams are relatively small, cohesive units. Permanent teams design, test and build products and services to the point of final assembly under tight deadlines and budgets. Ideally, in a permanent team, a manager can know every worker by name and know something about how the worker functions as well. Permanent teams gather individuals from various functions to communicate and work on a single issue. Auto manufacturers use permanent teams and team leaders to develop new platforms. Permanent teams have a life of their own, with their own media and messages. They stand apart from an organization, while working in and for it. Their benefit is that the whole picture of a product or service is represented on the team and conflicts are resolved more quickly. Permanent teams duplicate labor and effort, but they communicate more easily within their small structures than within large, functional groups. In traditional manufacturing, each function negotiated and completed the requirements for a product and then communicated these requirements to the next function in the chain. The next function also negotiated internally and completed its requirements. Function managers negotiated conflicts between sets of requirements and raised serious issues to the executive level for decision. This slowed communication, consensus and action. Function-driven development often takes more than twice as long as team-driven development.

Teams may be sited locally to enhance communication, as in Chrysler

Corporation's development center, or tied by videoconferencing and multimedia to enhance relationships in distant locales, as Ford Motor is doing
worldwide. Teams break down if communication is infrequent and contacts
are too formal. Teams also can steer a company off-course if they are not
well managed: A team leader has to be an effective communicator to bring
projects in successfully.

Ad hoc teams communicate to solve problems and then dissolve. They
focus information, messages and media on a single issue for a short period.
Ad hoc teams are not intended to produce continuous media or messages
in corporate communication structure, and they are not helpful for supporting daily communication. Messages and media from ad hoc teams are
incorporated into existing communication structure.

Ad hoc teams get rid of bureaucracy and cut across organizational lines,
but they do not necessarily effect change. That is, a team may communicate
recommendations and depart without action being taken. As a result, organizations that attempt to run primarily on ad hoc teams can foul communication lines and organization activity. In one major attempt to run an
airline without a formal organizational structure, the chaos became so serious that the airline went bankrupt.

There is no perfect way to staff communication structure. Managers
should not put faith in any structure as ideal because each one has both
good and bad points. They must understand the positives and negatives in
structural choices and anticipate how to handle them. They are also aware
of, and accept, both serendipitous and unfortunate outcomes.

For example, a manager may want to decentralize communications and
"empower" supervisors to take over quality control from a central inspection department. However, the manager knows that two of six supervisors
are not ready to handle statistical quality control, while the other four feel
they are being held back. If the manager lets the four proceed, the two
supervisors will demand the same privileges. If the manager holds back all
six, the manager may lose a frustrated supervisor to another department.
If the manager sets conditions for the lagging supervisors, the other four
may "gang up" on them or the grapevine may hurt their authority with
their subordinates. The manager knows that any decision will have unwanted and, perhaps, unexpected outcomes.

A manager also learns to change communication staffing as the business
environment changes. For example, a hierarchical communication structure
with specific task messages works well with workforces performing simple
tasks, such as in *maquiladora* factories on the U.S.-Mexico border. As
workers become proficient at multiple tasks, however, a manager should
be prepared to change the communication structure to fit new skills. Sweeping rules about how companies should communicate and structure themselves ignore local variations that may prevent a communication structure
from taking root. On the other hand, individuals also are self-interested

and resistant to change, and it sometimes requires a sweeping declaration to force movement. A manager must judge each case on its merits and regularly evaluate communication staffing for effectiveness.

A manager can also outsource communication staffing and structure, especially if the business is an investment in which the manager has no operational responsibility. An owner may give full communication responsibility to company managers as long as they perform well on the investor's behalf. This was how the *Wall Street Journal* grew. It was owned by two daughters of the founder, but operational authority was vested in a group of managers.

On the other hand, a manager can outsource key media, but not key messages, in enterprises where he or she has direct responsibility for the completion of economic transactions and the exchange of wealth. The manager can turn media over to a company that creates presentations, distributes them, gets feedback, completes the economic transaction and collects the wealth. Professional telemarketing companies handle accounts for hundreds of manufacturers, and computer service companies take over the mainframes, databases and networks of major corporations because they can run them more efficiently.

Outsourcing media has good and bad points. The good side is that in this way, a company can use a medium more efficiently or only when needed. Buying an outside service is usually more expensive than performing a task in-house, but embedded overhead is hard to remove and its long-term cost can be greater than the expense of buying the service. The bad side of outsourcing is that a manager may not recognize when a new or different medium is needed internally, both for efficiency and to complete economic transactions more effectively. For example, a company may contract with a local exchange carrier to operate an internal phone system. The company saves money by dismissing its telecommunications staff, but it harms its ability to implement new telephone features. This happens because the employees who paid attention to the media were fired; remaining employees, who are preoccupied with their own jobs, do not learn about new features in the system; and employees cannot experiment with advanced systems easily enough to find ways to improve economic transactions.

Outside specialists have two liabilities. They can be committed to one medium that they know and overconfident about what it can do, and they need start-up time. For example, in the early days of automatic teller machines and point-of-sale devices, specialists failed to understand how conservative users are about money and financial communication. It took nearly ten years for consumers to become comfortable with communicating to ATMs rather than human tellers. Second, an outsider can rarely understand the nuances of an audience and message in relation to a company or culture. In advertising, sensitivity to cultural differences is essential. A television commercial in Japan might not mention the product. A magazine advertisement from Holland has a look that Dutch identify with but Americans do not. A wall poster in the United Kingdom may show a sly wit that is uniquely British and foreign to anyone else.

Deciding to outsource media is a manager's judgment call. There are times when it is economically obvious to do so and times when it is not. Most of the time the decision is not obvious, and a manager must depend on judgment, preferences and persuasion to make and enforce a decision.

The principal challenge to corporate communication staffing and structure comes from message receivers. Some are the same for all messages and media, some are different and some are the same but communicated to differently. Both human relations and manufacturing send messages to assemblers. The messages from human relations are about benefits, and those from manufacturing, about line speed. Both functions work for the same company and have the same goals, but an employee may not see it that way. The employee may curse the company for boosting line speed while he or she picks through the options in a health care package to get the best deal. Similarly, a maker of consumer goods may sell two different products to the same customer under different names and from different parts of a store, and the customer will make no association between laundry soap and cosmetics.

Managers face a choice in communicating to customers and influentials—whether to dedicate staff to messages and media or make them generic message carriers. Does one use a dedicated sales force for each product or produce a catalog of products? Companies in the same industries and selling the same products use both methods. For complex products requiring an in-depth understanding of a customer's challenge and the product, a dedicated sales force is a natural choice for communication staffing and structure. For well-understood products, a catalog also is a natural choice. Between these extremes, staffing and structure can go either way and can move from complex to commodity as customers and influentials come to better understand the products and services. In the early days of personal computer sales, a salesperson often walked a customer through a sale. As PCs became better understood, however, direct marketing companies like Dell Computer began to successfully sell their products through catalogue and 800-numbers.

To communicate generically, a manager teaches employees either an overriding message or multiple messages, along with how to deliver them to customers and influentials. This is not easy to do. It is often difficult to learn the subtleties of different message sets. A salesperson may not be skilled enough to sell more than one type of computer, and a client's challenge may not dovetail with either an overriding message or a specific product message. A buyer also must agree to a catalogue approach, and a salesperson must assume that the buyer understands the distinctions among the products being sold.

Some businesses provide salespersons with a full range of products but let them concentrate on a few as long as they can communicate effectively and sell. This has been the practice in the financial services industry. Most brokers concentrate on a fraction of the financial products that are available from their firms. Moreover, even within that fraction, brokers target defined products, such as a specific stock, through "learning the story" of the stock and preparing a "story book."[15]

Internally, the process is the same. In some companies, each function contacts an employee with a dedicated message. In others, functions contact supervisors, who catalogue and deliver messages to subordinates, and still other companies use both approaches. The choice of medium is sometimes less dependent on a message receiver's preference than on a message carrier's ability. It is just as hard for supervisors to master the different messages flooding their desks as it is for salespersons.

OTHER ISSUES AFFECTING COMMUNICATION STRUCTURE

Simple communication structure hides complexity but does not get rid of it. For example, a company might communicate to a million customers. If each customer is identified by basic information, such as name, address, city, state, zip code, phone and previous order, the company will have seven million pieces of basic information. If information is outdated at a rate of 2 percent a month, the company will change nearly 25 percent of its database each year.

Every business, no matter how simple, keeps an information database that is integral to the communication structure. The database may be in a manager's head, in a filing cabinet or in a machine.

Whether a database is animate or inanimate and centralized or decentralized, its structure affects how an organization communicates and is affected by the business environment. Theoretically, an organization can adapt any type of data storage. Practically, however, the marketplace forces the choice. For example, a distributor may have had ten computerized warehouses with self-contained inventory systems, but as margins in distribution plunged, the distributor may have moved to a centralized database to increase inventory turns from all ten warehouses. With the introduction of bar codes and automated inventory picking to reduce labor, the distributor distributed the database back into the ten warehouses, with local control to speed processing. Finally, the distributor extended the database into the store itself to help the retailer reduce inventory and increase turns by keeping stock at the ten warehouses until it was needed.

Drawing from one database ensures consistency in message content, but centralized control over databases and messages can involve greater bureaucracy and a loss of speed and flexibility. Suppose a computer maker with huge investments and profits from mainframes successfully launches a personal computer made up of standard components. The PC takes on a life of its own, and over ten years, the PC's rapid growth in power and price/value erodes the economics of mainframes. However, the integrated voice of the company continues to stand solidly behind the mainframe until the company can no longer hold out in the marketplace.

This scenario which IBM suffered, might have played out differently had the centralized data allowed for decentralized message creation. The PC division might have pitted itself against the minicomputer division, and the minicomputer division against the mainframes. Ultimately, minicomputers and PCs would have cannibalized IBM's investment in mainframes and forced an internal restructuring before the marketplace required it.

The decentralization of message creation provides freedom of choice to customers and influentials, but it can also allow a company to lose focus. This is harmful when economic transactions depend on the clarity of the company and good when the product or service carries its own economic and benefit message. Decentralized message creation is wasteful, but integration may be out of the question in fast-moving markets. IBM structured messages so that each computer class covered a specific segment, but the marketplace and technology outstripped the company. The assets and overhead that IBM had built up to support mainframe profit margins depreciated at a frightening rate. Even with a "year of the customer" promotion, the company could not turn back change sweeping over it.

Decentralized information databases with decentralized messages work well when products and services are in self-contained units. A consumer products company may establish each product line as a brand, with its own marketing, information collection, communication and administration services. The brand line may even have its own factories and distribution.[16] The core of the organization provides personnel, accounting, marketing, training, R&D and other services on which all units can draw if they wish.

In at least one company, secrecy among competing brands is so great that communication about plans and activities outside a given unit is cause for dismissal. Each product builds its own economic existence. Similar segmentation exists in industrial organizations supplying materials and products with little relationship among lines. In these instances, the core of the company might be accounting consolidation more than anything else. The firm also might let subsidiaries keep separate communication structures and resources for research and development, accounting, human relations, compensation, training, marketing and distribution.

The common storage of facts can unite an organization more quickly around a mission, but it can also pull an organization apart when information does not provide clear direction. "Data wars" have existed for years among managers and will get worse as the amount of data on which to draw continues to grow. A data war occurs when opposing sides present "unassailable" facts and arguments for their views of what a company should do. In such instances, common data becomes an enemy of economic action rather than support for it. It is little wonder that CEOs taking over paralyzed companies will ban lengthy discussions and presentations in favor of action whether or not a direction is optimal.

The overall advantage of common data storage is that it can link individuals to every part of a business. A customer's buying habits can be known immediately in any department from human relations to purchasing. Human relations decisions can be known immediately anywhere from manufacturing to sales. Sales decisions can be known immediately anywhere from accounting to the shop floor. This can be important because:

- the human relations department needs to know the kind of sales personnel it should be recruiting and training;
- purchasing needs to know what is being bought in order to adjust inventories;
- human relations decisions on benefits affect factory workers as well as sales staff;
- sales decisions affect accounting numbers and products produced on the shop floor.

Within this commonality, however, there is much information that a department does not need, from operating processes to staffing schedules and memos of departmental meetings. The key to simple corporate communication structure is to filter out what is not needed and keep what is. That is never easy to do. Information technology is still a long way from perfection. "Perhaps the biggest problem facing Information Systems (IS) developers is how to provide users with the data they require to run the business in a timely manner."[17]

Databases age like everything else. Their structures become dated by comparison to competitive solutions and they require constant upkeep and maintenance. At the time of this writing there existed an estimated 50 to 70 billion lines of the old COBOL computer language code in mainframes throughout the world. Some of this code dates to the beginning of computerized corporate information technology. Millions of business rules and communication decisions are buried in code, much of which is unstructured and undocumented. A part of the information technologist's task is to phase out code or learn to work with it in the context of modern solutions.[18] The task is enormously difficult, and communication structure is directly affected by the solutions. The information technologist's task is not made easier by the lack of integrated communication in the past, when "software products [were] acquired on a one-off basis, not as the result of a strategic business plan."[19]

Most organizations have little patience and less money to model business processes and communication in detail, and besides, too many real-world changes occur during modeling. That is why some companies continue to automate their structure on a piecemeal basis.

Comprehensive data models must provide information editing, linking, presentation and filtering to prevent noise from overcoming messages and media. This cannot be done entirely by machines. Particularly with soft data, such as rumors or sales intelligence, a manager must evaluate both the source and the information.

Companies have built integrated data warehouses—centralized or decentralized on-line libraries of key hard and soft information—from which individuals may draw. These warehouses are also linked to commercial services and merge data from published sources with proprietary intelligence to let businesses refine their messages and media more accurately. The availability of so much information opens a legitimate question of its usefulness in communication, especially when managers still make wrong decisions. Proponents of deep information resources argue that organizations run better if all information is available to all individuals all the time. The contrary argument is that organizations will be buried in the spoil of undifferentiated data, through which no one can easily pick. Success depends on building a clear set of core messages around which information is arrayed. The messages must model the working enterprise.

Information technologists cannot build a successful and expandable model of an enterprise in a vacuum: they must have help from managers and employees. Some parts of communication structure remain the same because rules remain the same, such as in bookkeeping. Other parts are inherently unstable, such as customer service and sales, which respond to environmental changes. The information technologist is challenged to build two kinds of communication structure at the same time—a stable core and a flexible edge structure that responds rapidly to business conditions.

In an ideal communications structure, there are consistent interpretation, analysis, messages and media at both the core and edge. Everyone has simultaneous access to key hard and soft data and can adjust their actions without waiting, but actual organizations never reach the ideal. Individuals do not use the information available to them: there is too much. Even if there is a proper volume of information, individuals disagree over its meaning. Even if the information is fully known and the goals are clear, people fail in the execution of tasks. Further, organizations often cannot respond to information. The fastest an auto company can design and build a new auto is in two to three years. The requirements for the new car platform are set well before a car reaches a showroom. Should new information become available during tooling, it is too late to do anything. Similarly, commercial airframe manufacturers place what amounts to multibillion dollar bets on marketplace conditions when a new plane is to be completed years later. Even a computer-designed plane like a Boeing 777 faces an uncertain future by the time it rolls out of the hangar for the first time. The reality is that instant response to environmental changes occurs only in narrow, well-understood activities, such as package delivery.

Ideally, managers and information technologists organize facts in ways that anyone in a company can take advantage of at will in order to understand the marketplace and the directions a company should take. In actuality, there is no single method of presenting data that is suitable for everyone. The most that an information technologist can do is to provide tools that let managers view information as they need at the moment.

Data can be examined for meaning on several axes, including columns, rows and in-depth. Within axes, the techniques of presentation are many. Messages can be constructed from any of the axes and modes of presentation. Moreover, soft information can be joined in logical or intuitive ways to build messages or discover concepts. Such creative leaps require new tools to shape concepts in ways that numerical thinking might never allow. In addition, a technologist should provide views of the organization that let a manager see both the total process and the individual segments. The total view provides a broad sweep, like an aerial photograph of a forest, while a segmented view looks at one tree in the forest. Both approaches are essential to balancing communication structure, but such a synthesis takes time. The image of business as a video game in which one reacts to bends in an electronic road is not what happens.

Media also affect communication structure. For example, when there were no telecommunication networks or computer-imaging systems, media included hundreds of secretaries and clerks who typed and moved files from office to office. Since the advent of networks and imaging databases, the same task is done in the mail room where incoming letters are scanned at high speed into a networked imaging system. All materials can appear on a terminal within minutes.

Media change by type and within types. Media that were used 30 years ago were different than media used today. Media 30 years from today will be different, too. The paper file, which is the medium for printed information, is rapidly evolving into a digital file on CD-ROM. The typewriter, a medium for printing information, has given way to the personal computer. The telephone is moving from sound transmission to sound and visual transmission. The workstation has replaced the drafting boaid and the video camera, the motion picture film camera. Each change affects how an organization does business. First, fewer people are needed to tend the mechanical tasks of media today. Second, changes in media correlate with changes in data speed. Ten years ago, organizations were still communicating at 1,200 to 2,400 bits per second on standard analog telephone lines, while at the time of this writing, modem communications on analog telephone lines have surpassed 28,000 bits per second and, with compression, 56,000 bits per second. Digital communications start at 56,000 bits per second and are rapidly moving toward billions of bits per second. In ten years, data pipelines have moved from the diameter of a straw to that of a tunnel.

The organization that fails to take advantage of new media endangers itself when competitors do so successfully. However, as often is the case, employing new media is not a question of instant application. Behaviors and processes must change and new skills must be learned. This may take months or years and be accompanied by the rise of barriers and serendipitous opportunities. For example, in the early 1980s, while using a crude word processor, an employee discovered that she could make elegant boxes around typefaces and produce "tombstone" advertisements. Tombstone ads are announcements of completed financial transactions which are published daily in the financial sections of newspapers or magazines. Before the employee's discovery, the company had used a designer and typesetter to make the same ad in twice the time and at more than twice the cost.

Implementing and managing the media of an organization is always a troubled experience, which is made more difficult by the human users. Even media with the same functions work differently with different tools. Data capture at the source immediately permits high granularity (i.e., specificity). This correspondingly reduces variance in the estimation of revenue flows and allows for greater cost savings. For example, high speed in changing price and revenue estimations was put to enormous advantage by American Airlines in its Sabre reservation system. Sabre accurately estimates plane loads, quickly varies ticket prices and provides an immediacy in reporting passenger revenue miles that reshaped the airline industry.

However, fine-grained detail and rapid processing cannot give a company total control. Sabre could not stop the fare wars or wild swings in fuel prices. Variation also increases with a closer focus on individuals. For example, it is common for business persons flying home on Friday night to book two or more flights in advance under different names to be sure to get a seat. The airlines know this and try to prevent it, but they cannot control it.

As media are so finite, one should ask if there is any limit left to measurement and communication structure. Should every management activity be priced and allocated to the cost of economic transactions? Lawyers and other service businesses do this because they sell their time. However, many management activities involve more than directly productive work. Managers often set up circumstances to aid work being completed by fending off distractions or providing needed materials, resources and concepts. On the other hand, this activity is a necessary part of production that has been lost in communication structure.

In an ideal world, every activity is measured against its value and contribution to the economic transaction and is communicated to the organization. There is no break in the communication chain from the economic activity to the company core. In reality, however, the measurement of managerial activity has been onerous until recently. Thomas Edison might have clocked himself in and out of his research labs in West Orange, but what Edison did each day was not recorded. With little change, this is how managers have labored to the present.

However, measurement cannot communicate everything that a manager experiences, such as the pressures a person is under, the hitches in processes and the labor of hard thinking. Measurement cannot depict the reasons for variance, either, but only the variance itself. Finally, measurement may not keep a customer happy. Just because something is measured, it may not be what a buyer wants. One pays a doctor for his or her best efforts but not necessarily for success. Again, a manager uses judgment about measurement in corporate communication structure as much as with other media and messages.

A manager's corporate communication task is never-ending and is essential to the well-being of the enterprise. Machines can shoulder the burden of rote communication, but they cannot account for variation or make judgments about what to communicate next. Corporate communication calls on every skill that a manager has. Irrational factors constantly erupt in the workplace, and effective corporate communication still depends on individuals who send messages to other individuals that lead to economic action and corporate survival.

NOTES

1. JoAnne Yates, *Control through Communication: The Rise of System in American Management* (Baltimore: The Johns Hopkins University Press), p. 230.

2. David H. Freedman, "Culture of Urgency," *Forbes ASAP: A Technology Supplement to Forbes Magazine,* September 13, 1993, pp. 25–28.

3. John O'Shaughnessy, *Business Organization* (London: George Allen & Unwin, 1969), p. 14.

4. Ibid., p. 14.

5. Bruce Brocka and M. Suzanne Brocka, *Quality Management: Implementing the Best Ideas of the Masters* (Burr Ridge, IL: Irwin Professional Publishing, 1992), p. 175.

6. Montieth M. Illingworth, "Virtual Managers," *InformationWeek,* June 13, 1994, p. 42.

7. Andy Reinhardt, "Video Conquers the Desktop," *Byte* 18, no. 10 (September 1993): p. 64.

8. Cary Lu, "Publish It Electronically," *Byte* 18, no. 10 (September 1993), p. 95.

9. Michael Garry, "Efficient Replenishment: The Key to ECR," *Progressive Grocer: Special Report, Technology,* December 1993, p. 5. See also Jerry Morton, "EST: Up and Running," *Progressive Grocer: Special Report, Technology,* December 1993, p. 23.

10. Alan Deutschman, "Odd Man Out," *Fortune* 128, no. 2 (July 26, 1993): p. 42.

11. Robert Mylls. *Information Engineering: Case Practices and Techniques* (New York: John Wiley & Sons, 1994), p. 103.

12. Laurie Hays, "Using Computers to Divine Who Might Buy a Gas Grill," *Wall Street Journal,* August 16, 1994, p. B1.

13. Don E. Schultz, Stanley I. Tannenbaum, and Robert F. Lauterborn, *Integrated Marketing Communications* (Lincolnwood, IL: NTC Business Books, 1993), p. 161.

14. Charles Conrad, *Strategic Organizational Communication: An Integrated Perspective* (New York: Harcourt Brace Jovanovich College Publishers, 1989), p. 129.

15. LeRoy Gross, *The Art of Selling Intangibles* (New York: New York Institute of Finance, 1982), p. 98.

16. Kathleen Deveny and Gabriella Stern, "Lever Brothers Regroups, Plans Job Cuts," *Wall Street Journal,* April 5, 1994, p. B11.

17. Fred Schuff, "Simple Satisfaction," *Database Programming and Design* 7, no. 9 (September 1994): 31.

18. *CA90s: Computing Architecture for the 90s* (Islandia, NY: Computer Associates, 1993).

19. Ibid., p. 4.

11

Moving Toward Cost-Effective Corporate Communication

The hard part of the business is the soft part of the business.
—Dennis Pawley, Vice President of manufacturing, Chrysler
Corporation; quoted in Paul Ingrassia and Joseph B. White, *Comeback:
The Fall and Rise of the American Automobile Industry*[1]

We have covered many concepts to show how communication permeates a corporation. This last chapter addresses the challenge of starting to implement cost-effective corporate communication. There are several guidelines, but none is absolute.

The first rule of thumb is that success is incremental. Establishing effective corporate communication takes time. Managers who succeed stay focused. Depending on the size of an organization, it may take years to effect major change. Effective corporate communication needs consistency in direction, methods and execution. Managers should use methods they are comfortable with and stick with them as long as they work because otherwise there is too much for individuals to absorb at one time, and too many changes are forced onto the process by environmental change. Moreover, effective corporate communication is never perfected: it either improves or deteriorates.

The second guideline is that one can start at any time to move toward effective corporate communication because there is rarely a good time to begin. When companies are successful, it is harder to change behavior than at other times. However, during good times a manager can sometimes maintain a sense of urgency, whereas during crises, a manager has people's attention but not the resources or time.

The third guideline is to accept the facts. This requires introspection from action-oriented managers and objectivity from ambitious managers.

The fourth rule of thumb is the need for action. Managers must avoid getting bogged down or having their efforts dissipated. They should set achievable goals and build on them. Managers and employees can easily become lost in defining messages, media and measurements and forget that corporate communication is a necessary aspect of business, and not simply of itself.

Finally, it safer to pilot-test before implementing changes. According to Ben Rich, the former head of Lockheed Aircraft's Skunk Works:

My years inside the Skunk Works . . . convinced me of the tremendous value of building prototypes. I am a true believer. The beauty of a prototype is that it can be evaluated and its uses clarified before costly investment for large numbers are made.[2]

Rich was responsible for the development of the Stealth fighter plane, arguably the most important breakthrough in aviation since radar. Rich and his predecessor, Kelly Johnson (the founder of the Skunk Works), also were skilled at using existing tooling and parts to develop new ideas cheaply. Effective messages and media are often developed in the same way.

THE MAP OF EFFECTIVE CORPORATE COMMUNICATION

The map of effective corporate communication can assist a manager in getting started (Figure 11.1). Begin by understanding the environment, and then proceed clockwise around the map to "structure" and "budget," where the process starts over. Use the eight guidelines to help define effective messages and media.

Grounding oneself in the environment is not just a manager's task. Grounding distills facts and perceptions into a consistent, company-wide view of what is happening in the marketplace and the company. Whenever possible, one should use summaries for grounding rather than studies in order to speed the process. If possible, list facts on one side of a standard sheet of paper. This forces a focus on important issues. Colleagues, employees, customers, influentials and others should review and revise these summaries to enhance their accuracy. Choose some reviewers randomly to avoid bias. Review and revision should be done under deadline to prevent grounding from taking on a life of its own.

It is usually fastest for one person to write grounding documents and then to ask others to critique them. Composition by committee rarely works well, and humans are generally better at amplifying existing work. Authorship should be kept confidential as well in order to get honest opinions. Throughout the process, collect conclusions, diagrams, analyses, ac-

Figure 11.1
A Map of Effective Corporate Communication

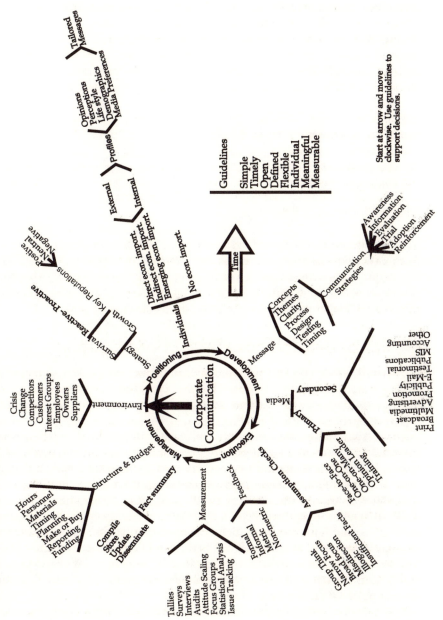

tion proposals and deadlines in one place in order to build a fact summary. There are readily available software tools that can speed this process and save the labor of correlating and collating.

Among environmental topics needing to be summarized are:

- the industry and the marketplace;
- ways in which customers perceive products and services;
- means by which customer thinking is reflected in messages and media;
- influentials' perceptions of the company;
- views of key constituents, such as owners, interest groups, communities and regulators;
- the company's internal communication structure;
- the company's communication style.

To aid in understanding, diagram the path of major messages and media from raw material to sale. This is the chain of messages and media that can result in economic transactions and increases in wealth. Diagramming can be done by hand, but software tool kits make the job easier. Diagramming often suggests actions to help improve communication.

Summaries and diagrams usually spark debates that result in deeper understanding and more effective messages and media. Debate should result in action items and deadlines, even if the action is to engage in further research. It is often better to act and later improve than to delay. Of course, there are exceptions to this rule of thumb. For example, Japanese managers are known for lengthy discussions that dissect issues in ways that few American managers could tolerate.

Once a company-wide diagram has been completed, the departments should diagram their communication structures. An example is included in Figure 11.2. The communication structure of the market research department shows inputs, the department communication process and targets. It also defines key messages, desired results and measures of success.

Departmental diagrams should fit together in an expanded chain of communication linking every part of the company to its core internal and external audiences. The expanded chain should be an explosion of the company-wide diagram. If it is not, it should be revised. When managers and employees first review an expanded corporate communication diagram, they may be dismayed to see how complicated corporate communication is, but they also will see shortcuts and improvements. Using the example of the market research department in Figure 11.2, note that the department creates both monthly written reports and an on-line Lotus Notes database report. In this case, it might be more cost-effective and timely to get rid of written reports. Further, one might bypass market research altogether with

Figure 11.2
Communication Structure of a Market Research Department

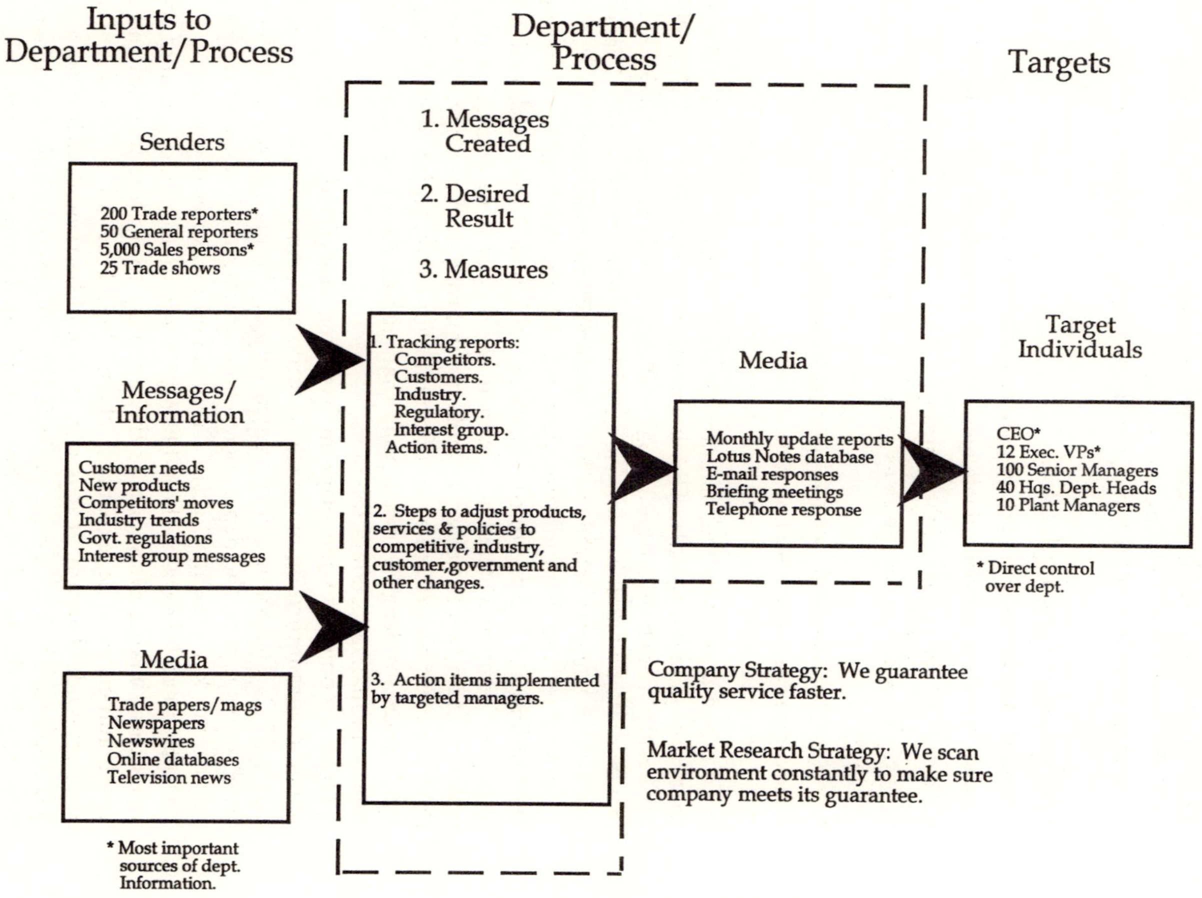

Inputs to Department/Process

Department/Process

Targets

Senders

200 Trade reporters*
50 General reporters
5,000 Sales persons*
25 Trade shows

Messages/Information

Customer needs
New products
Competitors' moves
Industry trends
Govt. regulations
Interest group messages

Media

Trade papers/mags
Newspapers
Newswires
Online databases
Television news

*Most important sources of dept. information.

1. Messages Created
2. Desired Result
3. Measures

1. Tracking reports:
   Competitors.
   Customers.
   Industry.
   Regulatory.
   Interest group.
   Action items.

2. Steps to adjust products, services & policies to competitive, industry, customer, government and other changes.

3. Action items implemented by targeted managers.

Media

Monthly update reports
Lotus Notes database
E-mail responses
Briefing meetings
Telephone response

Company Strategy: We guarantee quality service faster.

Market Research Strategy: We scan environment constantly to make sure company meets its guarantee.

Target Individuals

CEO*
12 Exec. VPs*
100 Senior Managers
40 Hqs. Dept. Heads
10 Plant Managers

* Direct control over dept.

certain information and send it directly to users if they can interpret it easily and use it quickly.

A key step is to require managers and employees to explain how messages or media might be either cut back by 50 percent or deleted. They should define the measurable impact on individuals upstream and downstream from the department and on the department itself. This forces a justification of messages and media and helps get rid of ineffective communication. Explanations will spark debate, deeper understanding, revision and action items. Some media will be unique to each department because they are essential to its strategic mission. The question that managers should ask is how to extract as much economic utility from these media as possible.

Upon understanding the environment, managers should test their understanding of strategy. One way to do this is for senior managers to write their versions of the company's strategic message without looking it up and then to ask a random selection of employees to write their versions, again without looking it up. By comparing responses, managers can learn quickly how well the strategy is understood. This exercise can also be used to track the effectiveness of internal communication over time. The strategic message should be linked directly to departmental communication diagrams. In the market research example (Figure 11.2), company and departmental strategies are printed next to each other. The diagram shows how strategy is communicated through departmental processes.

Defining core individuals is not easy. To speed the process, one person should compose an initial master list of individuals with direct economic importance, including:

• customers representing 80 percent of the business;

• owners holding majority control;

• employees on whose skills the company's welfare rests;

• influentials who could shut the business down;

• competitors who could overwhelm the business;

• regulators who could stop work;

• interest groups who could stop sales;

• others who could help or harm the company today.

The list should define both the verbal and nonverbal messages and media going to each group and the measurable results expected from communicating to each.

Departments also should identify the internal and external individuals with direct economic power over the department's mission and the company's survival and success. Moreover, they should list the verbal and nonverbal messages and media going to each and the measurable results expected from communicating. Many core individuals on these lists will be on the master list; some will not. This may mean that the master list is incomplete or that a department needs better focus. Managers and employees should review and revise all the lists into a master document. If there is disagreement—and there will be—progressive budget reduction (described earlier in Chapter 6) can be helpful to break through logjams.

A company should then build profiles of core individuals including their relationships to the company. Managers and employees should examine how they would communicate to these persons if media and messages were cut by 50 percent or deleted and then should recommend action items.

If the company's strategic message needs to be stated or replaced, one person should write a strategic message, which should be a simple sentence that is easily reduced to a headline. This sentence should be reviewed and revised by executives, peers and subordinates (they are the ones who must carry it out). Departments should then each write their own one-sentence adaptation of the new message and department members should list the information they need to get their jobs done. Information requirements then become action items.

If a company does not need a new strategic message, you should review how the existing strategic message works throughout the organization. Revise information inputs, processes, messages and media on diagrams, if appropriate. Have departments explain how they might work with 50 percent fewer media to get the same information and the action items required.

One person also should compile a master list of major verbal and nonverbal media as derived from the diagrams and summaries. (One medium should be compensation.) Major media comprise 20 percent of media, on which managers depend 80 percent of the time. Departments also should rank the major media. After comparing lists, a revised master list of major media should be added to the fact summary and highlighted on communication diagrams. Departments should then explain how to merge 50 percent of the media they use into major media and still operate effectively. From this should come action plans for media integration.

Communication measurements are part of communication diagrams, but they should be examined for consistency. One person should compile a master list of major measurements, that is, of the 20 percent of all measurements on which 80 percent of managers depend. Departments should compile their own master lists of major measurements and then compare them to the master list. From this exercise should come common measures and benchmarks. Managers should explain how the company might operate effectively with fewer measures as well as how it might automate feedback and measurement.

A fact summary is an orderly compilation of discussions. It should record the environment, strategy, key internal and external individuals, messages, media, benchmarks of success and measures. It should have a one-sentence summary/conclusion, a summary of key facts and appendices with supporting data. The fact summary will change as the company evolves and should be updated regularly. As a result, it should be kept in an easily accessible location where managers and employees can refer to it, such as on-line storage. Open issues should be part of a fact summary, as well as action plans, deadlines, measures and budgets. Project management software is often useful for summarizing data into visual diagrams that are easier to follow than text.

Assumption checking may sound redundant, but the smart manager will undertake a final check. This might be done through having impartial outsiders review the fact summary, such as consultants and the board of directors, or through debating the fact summary's contents. In a debate, one team presents arguments supporting the accuracy of the summary and the other team presents arguments against it. If appropriate, the fact summary should be revised. Assumption checking need not be continuous, but it should happen periodically, with the intervals depending on the rate of environmental change. Some industries might continue for several years with the same messages and media and others, only a few weeks or months.

Structure and budgeting will fall naturally from the analysis done so far. Still, the company should summarize both company-wide and departmental communication structure. These summaries may imitate the process flow diagrams outlined earlier in this chapter, with names of individuals attached to aspects of the process. Managers and subordinates should be required to examine and explain how departments might work to communicate to customers and other key audiences more effectively if their structures changed. Comparing company-wide communication structure with department structures will make apparent variances needing review and revision. It will also raise questions about staffing, and especially the compatibility and skill of staff with the existing and desired structures.

Budgeting is dealt with last but it has really occurred throughout the exercise, which requires managers to find more efficient and effective ways to communicate. If the exercises have been done properly, the final budget requests should reflect the action items already identified. The cost and timing of implementation will be an issue because it is unlikely that a company can do everything it wants to do in one budget.

It takes strong managers to lead an organization through continuous improvements in corporate communication without becoming sidetracked. However, by keeping it tied to the heart of the business, the rationale for cost-effective corporate communication will remain clear.

NOTES

1. Paul Ingrassia and Joseph B. White, *Comeback: The Fall and Rise of the American Automobile Industry* (New York: Simon & Schuster, 1994), p. 442.

2. Ben Rich and Leo Janos, *Skunk Works: A Personal Memoir of My Years at Lockheed* (Boston: Little, Brown and Company, 1994), p. 331.

Index

About the Author

JAMES L. HORTON has extensive management and other experience in investor relations, corporate communications, marketing, and communications consulting. Among his clients are financial services firms, computer and high-tech companies, a German auto manufacturer, oil, chemical, and environmental treatment firms, consumer packaged goods manufacturers, basic manufacturers and utilities. Horton writes and lecturers frequently on business management practices and quality in corporate communications.